SAMUEL TAYLOR COLERIDGE

SAMUEL TAYLOR COLERIDGE

by

HUGH I'ANSON FAUSSET

Stop, Christian passer-by! — Stop, child of God,
And read with gentle breast. Beneath this sod
A poet lies, or that which once seem'd he. —
O, lift one thought in prayer for S.T.C.;
That he who many a year with toil of breath
Found death in life, may here find life in death!
Mercy for praise — to be forgiven for fame
He ask'd, and hoped, through Christ.
    Do thou the same!

NEW YORK / RUSSELL & RUSSELL

FIRST PUBLISHED IN 1926
REISSUED, 1967, BY RUSSELL & RUSSELL
A DIVISION OF ATHENEUM HOUSE, INC.
BY ARRANGEMENT WITH ESTATE OF HUGH I'ANSON FAUSSET
L. C. CATALOG CARD NO: 66−15429

PRINTED IN THE UNITED STATES OF AMERICA

to

JENNIFER

CONTENTS

PORTRAITS

FOREWORD

As in other studies I have tried here to explain a poet's
achievement in terms of his personality and against
a background of his life, and my main concern has been
neither to justify nor condemn, but to understand. In so
far as either a moral or medical interpretation has insinu-
ated itself, it is because both aspects presented themselves
to Coleridge himself, and because they do, I think, contribute to an understanding of the man and of his frustrated genius.

Wherever possible I have drawn on original and contemporary sources, and particularly on Coleridge's own
letters and note-books. But I am also greatly and gratefully indebted to Mr. Dykes Campbell's edition of the
Poems and Biographical Memoir, and to Mrs. Sandford's
Thomas Poole and His Friends.

H. I'A. F.

Woe to the man with projecting unfathomable discords in his being. Parts of his nature outstrip others, and there is war within himself.

ADRIAN STOKES

THE CHILD OF ILLUSION

§ I

IT was a matter of singular importance to the small boy who loitered in the parlour of the Vicarage of Ottery St. Mary in Devonshire that its windows failed to catch the early rays of the morning sun. The reason was curiously connected with a much-thumbed copy of the *Arabian Nights' Entertainments*, which lay in a corner of the window-sill and seemed, judging by the frequency with which he turned his large eyes in its direction, to exercise over him a fascination not unmixed with dread. The fact was that those loose Arabian tales, which, as a poet of our day has written, 'were but profane ninnery and doting fantasy to the Nomad's stern natural judgment,' had affected very differently this child of six whose sensibility even the unobservant would have marked as peculiar: so differently that after reading them in the evening, as he regularly did seated on his stool by his mother's side, he was haunted by spectres whenever he was in the dark. And yet his appetite equalled his terror and only needed the cheerful confirmation of the sun to triumph over it. No sooner had the moment arrived for which he waited, when the morning sun reached and nearly covered the book, than he seized and hurried off with it to a retired corner of the playground.

For his home was not only a vicarage but a school. His father, the Reverend John Coleridge, whose ninth son and youngest child he was, combined the duties of a parish priest with the mastership of a Free Grammar School. He combined, too, considerable learning as a linguist, mathematician, and antiquarian, with a native eccentricity as lovable for the simple unworldliness to which it testified as it was laughable in some of its manifestations. Among other ingenious works he was the

13

author of a *Critical Latin Grammar* in which he proposed for students' better understanding and easier recollection of the cases to re-name them 'prior, possessive, attributive, posterior, interjective, and quale-quare-quidditive' – a proposal which, if never adopted, has at least passed into humorous history, as has the story of his being tricked by short-sightedness at a dinner party into stuffing a considerable portion of a lady's white gown into his waistcoat's orifice under the delusion that it was his own errant shirt front.

To the child of his middle-age, born on the 21st of October, 1772, and christened Samuel Taylor, he had transmitted in no slight measure his dominant characteristics, chief among them his generosity of heart, his unpractical *naïveté*, his guileless piety, and a more than physical short-sightedness. Nor would it be altogether fanciful to see in the long and sententious school prospectus, which the amiable Vicar appended to his *Miscellaneous Dissertations*, the original of many similar announcements which were eventually to issue from the fertile imagination of his son.

The most noticeable quality in the child, however, as the rite already described will suggest, was an excessive sensibility, a quality at once fascinating and exasperating in its consequences, which doubtless his practical mother regarded with the same mixed feelings as the friends and benefactors of a later day. Unfortunately, as the mother of a large family, she was in no position to give her youngest child careful attention, and no circumstance could have been more calculated to render morbid an imagination born precocious than to be in turn the pet and the butt of a crowded household.

Genius is a stranger in every household, but it is seldom made conscious at so early an age of its abnormality. Among his handsome elder brothers and sisters the young

Coleridge soon became a diminutive Joseph, with his brother George acting the part of the tolerant Reuben. Neither physically nor mentally could he share in their concerns, and his inability to do so intensified his sense of difference and his absorption in himself. To them he was either an annoying oddity or a nuisance, sufficiently spoilt by their father, who cherished for a son so true to type an especial fondness, and sufficiently egotistic in himself to discourage any very sympathetic attention. We hear for example of his brother Frank's violent love of beating him, tempered by an affectionate curiosity at his quaint ways.

To expose the weak, particularly if they are possessed of genius, to the kindly meant barbarities of the strong, is generally to distort and always to exaggerate their tendencies. For if genius is often weak where the normal are strong, it is yet, even in childhood, dimly and rebelliously aware of a strength transcending theirs.

Being therefore 'huffed away from the enjoyments of muscular activity,' the child took refuge in books and the talk of his elders. The dame's school to which he was sent at the age of three only increased the number of tormentors from whom such a refuge was necessary, while his precocity in reading at once fed the isolation which it provoked.

'As I could not play at anything,' he wrote in later life, 'and was slothful, I was despised and hated by the boys; and because I could read and spell, and had, I may truly say, a memory and understanding *forced into almost unnatural ripeness*, I was flattered and wondered at by all the old women. And so I became very vain, and despised most of the boys that were at all near my own age, and before I was eight years old I was a *character*. Sensibility, imagination, vanity, sloth, and understanding, were even then prominent and manifest.' All of which were but symptoms of a sensibility over-indulged, of a self-cultivation uncorrected by positive activity. And while the priggishness could be outgrown, the habit of escaping from the actual into the imaginary was to prove the one absolutely consistent, if pathological impulse in a vacillating career. He was driven, to quote his own words again, from life in motion to life in thought and sensation. He never played except by himself, and then only acted over what he had been reading or fancying, or half one and half the other.

Into this twilight playground of the mind and memory all his childish energies were turned. He read incessantly, and quickly outgrowing the innocent curiosity which fed on nursery tales, he drank deep of the *Arabian Nights*. The effect on his mind was comparable to that which a narcotic or alcohol would have had upon his body. He would lie and mope, his brain crowded with alluring or sinister phantoms, his body tingling with sensations which cried out for physical expression, and then as the fantastic fever burned too fiercely for him to bear, his spirits would come upon him suddenly and in a flood and he would run up and down, cutting at weeds and nettles in a desperate striving after self-escape.

His senses thus being constantly exposed to literary rather than to natural stimuli ceased to react normally to the external world. He lived in a sort of vacancy peopled by spectres, and lost at six years his ability to distinguish between the miraculous and the normal, and with it his capacity for surprise or incredulity. Even the contrasts between night and day, sleeping and waking, ceased to be clearly defined. Already the present was like a somnambulist's dream, and a dream equally at noon and midnight, although it was doubtless in the dark hours when the heated fancy could not be relieved by sudden bodily activity that he suffered the worst terrors, and yet continued with a morbid appetite to indulge in the reading which begot them.

Later in life he attributed with some complacence to his early reading of fairy tales and about genii and the like the fact that his mind was 'habituated to the vast,' and that he never regarded his senses in any way as the *criteria* of his belief, but regulated all his creeds by his conceptions, not by sight, even at that age. And he proceeded to argue that children ought to be permitted to read romances and stories of giants, magicians and genii, on the ground that only so does the mind learn a love of the Great and the Whole.

Under normal circumstances his view is defensible. A purely rational education must tend to produce men who cannot see the wood for the trees. But Coleridge was never in danger of losing that sense of the Universal, which he rightly claims himself to have possessed to an unique degree. And though 'Infancy,' as he wrote elsewhere, 'presents body and spirit in unity: the body is all animated,' his own organic unity must have been from the beginning precariously balanced; so precariously that a prolonged course of giants and genii permanently upset its equilibrium. And since, on his own confession, 'in poetry as well as metaphysics that which we first meet with in the dawn of our mind becomes ever after *fetish*,' we may reasonably attribute to his early absorption in the fantastic both his habit in later life of pursuing and arguing about a Whole which had little reality, a phantom meshed in logic, and that failure to relate his imagination to actuality which was his tragedy as a poet and a man.

And now, as then, 'the soothing things' he dreamt, not only 'lulled him to sleep' but kept him feverishly awake. He paid in the subtler agonies of hallucination for the material crudities from which he fled, and 'the dangerous putrid fever' which he had in his fifth year and in which he would see 'half-awake and half-asleep . . . armies of ugly things bursting upon him' and the Four Good Angels of his evening prayer 'keeping them off' was doubtless only the crisis of a continuous distemper. For pitifully enough it was the very innocence and credulity of childhood which made him the victim of the miraculous. 'Alas!' to quote his own words, he 'had all the simplicity, all the docility of the little child, but none of the child's habits.'

And circumstances drove him to extravagant courses in the world of fact as well as of fancy. Once, in his eighth year, tormented by his brother Frank, he ran away to a little hill that sloped down to the River Otter. And here, fortified by obstinacy, a prayer-book, and the glowing satisfaction of thinking how miserable his mother must be, he stayed until it grew dark and he fell asleep. The autumn night was stormy: he 'felt the cold in his sleep and dreamed that he was pulling the blanket over him,' but in attempting to do so rolled from the top of the hill to within three yards of the unfenced river. Half-awake and half-asleep he knew that he was wet and stiff; a calf was lowing across the river; the sound impressed itself on his memory so vividly that he remembered it half a century afterwards. Waking about four in the morning he found himself unable to rise and walk. Meanwhile his distracted parents had organized search parties and the Ottery crier had announced a reward. Eventually his faint crying attracted a searcher, who carried him home, to the 'outrageous joy' of his mother and the confounding of the young lady, who hoped that she would whip him.

The physical consequences of this exposure, as of a similar event in his later boyhood, are necessarily quite uncertain. There may of course have been no connection between it and the mysterious form of rheumatism from which he was later to seek relief in laudanum.

But from brain-storms, as well as from exasperating brothers, Nature could and did provide a salutary refuge. As he grew older he could escape to her as well as to books from the barbed trivialities of domestic life. The happiest, the most vivid moments in his life were born of this communion.

The broken Devonshire countryside, so rich in vegetation, so indolent and various, proved a narcotic for the dreamy boy which exacted no toll in nightmares. Its lush meadows and deep hedgerows, the 'scattered cots' that sank into the landscape, the flickering sunlight on the cool foliage, the warm winds that waved the reeds – all soothed, like an opiate, his troubled nerves; while the church bells, 'the poor man's only music,' added an element of mournful sanctity, peculiarly in harmony with his spirit.

But it was from the element of water that this child, so fluid in himself, so little attached to solid earth and so overheated, derived his purest pleasure, whether it was the River Otter, that 'wild streamlet of the West,' along which he 'skimmed the smooth thin stone,' with its marge of 'willows grey' and bedded sand that

'Vein'd with various dyes,
Gleam'd through thy bright transparence,'

or the pebbled village spring with 'milky waters cold and clear,' upon which, like Shelley, he launched his paper navies or was soothed by its murmur like 'the sad woodnymph, Solitude.' Water that is so wild and whimsical, so transitory, gay and mysterious, reflected intimately a temperament in which

'Life's current then ran sparkling to the noon,
Or, silvery, stole beneath the pensive Moon.'

For his trembling sensibility brought him excess of rapture as of pain, and while in his reading he had sought the mysterious with as much terror as delight, in the hush of Nature the phantasmal was kindly. There was nothing malignant in her soft liquescence, only a delicious, tantalizing intangibility, which led him already obscurely to apprehend

'The lovely shapes and sounds intelligible
Of that eternal language'

which he was later to read into the universe.

To him Nature was never, as she is to the normal boy, a country into which a young pioneer adventured intent on practical discoveries. She was a feast of colour and sound and movement upon which he fed with a voluptuousness half-spiritual – a picture that continually dissolved as he tried to fix it in abiding forms.

Yet necessarily he became more active as he advanced from childhood to boyhood, and consequently more expansive in his abandonment to sensation. And this process was perhaps accelerated by events which without warning hurried him from the Ottery backwater into an active world.

In October 1781 his father died suddenly, and in the following spring he was sent to London to await admission into Christ's Hospital, to which a presentation had been secured. After spending ten weeks with an uncle who took him to his favourite taverns, and allowed him to earn applause as a prodigy and 'completely spoilt and pampered both mind and body,' he entered the Junior School at Hertford in July 1782. From there, after six happy weeks of ample feeding, with 'pudding and vegetables almost every day,' he was transferred to the sterner environment of the great London School.

§ 2

Any stranger who, attracted by the sound of a harsh and cantankerous voice, had been bold enough to peep into the Grammar School of Christ's Hospital at this time would have seen presiding at its far end a 'short, stout, round little man.' He sat 'under a deal-board canopy, behind a lofty wooden desk, his wooden chair raised upon a dais of wooden steps, and two large wooden shutters or slides projecting from the wall on either side to screen him from the wind.' Upon his head, according as his mood was at its best or its worst, he wore either a large, white, fresh-powdered wig, or an old, discoloured and unkempt one, but neither succeeded in softening the sardonic vigour of his features, his 'aquiline nose, long convex upper lip, sharp mouth and little cruel eyes that darted ferocious glances right and left.' His very hands, as a sensitive pupil confessed, were 'enough to make your cheeks tingle to look at them,' and his 'short thick legs covered with worsted stockings and shoes adorned with large silver buckles' tapped the magisterial dais like the warnings of fate. His favourite exclamation or rather explosion was 'God's-my-life!' and whenever he said this, turning upon some trembling pupil and opening his eyes like a fish, the victim in question might expect 'to find one of his hands taking him with a pinch of the flesh under the chin, while with the other he treated his cheek as if it had been no better than a piece of deal.'

His character, like his appearance, was 'tight and succinct,' so tight that peevish Nature was driven to find relief in violent outbursts of temper. As the same pupil wrote, he 'restrained his passions by giving vent to them' in volcanic changes of mood, cynical pinchings and ferocious floggings larded with moral discourse. Even his humour was saturnine, his jests an omen of wrath to come.

But the 'rages and tempest storms which blew up, terrible to witness, let alone endure' were the defects of undeniable qualities. The driving power of this harsh pedagogue was not confined to his cane, and while his rabid pedantry effectually closed the 'healthier and cheerfuller roads to knowledge,' it propelled the young mind along the rougher roads with a grim efficiency.

As a teacher he suffered from an eighteenth-century cramp, tending to treat all the humanities like so many propositions of Euclid. Yet there was always sense in his severity, and if he discouraged enthusiasm and the milder graces, he pruned the extravagances of sentiment. Blind towards all that transcended the logical, he disdained alike the imaginative and the effusive, the sublime and the affected. No phrase, metaphor, or image, 'unsupported by a sound sense, or where the same sense might have been conveyed with equal force and dignity in plainer words' could survive the thrust of his realism. 'Harp? Harp? Lyre?' he would sneer: 'Pen and ink, boy, you mean! Muse, boy, Muse? Your nurse's daughter, you mean! Pierian Spring? Oh aye! The cloister-pump, I suppose!'

In short he was as formidable an opponent of artificial diction as of romantic sensibility, and his clericism was no more than moral, muscular and official.

Yet the Institution over which the Reverend James Boyer ruled was a 'religious' as well as a 'royal and ancient' foundation, and in its buildings, its customs, and its ceremonies the atmosphere of an old monastic establishment lingered. The Christ's Hospital boy, whether he wished it or not, was considered 'a religious character.' His school had 'its peculiar prayers, its services at set times, its graces, hymns and anthems, following each other in an almost monastic closeness of succession.'

The mediævalism, if not the religiosity, of such a

school could not fail to affect the sensitive. The Bible-reading in the wards on Sunday morning and evening might not incline them to piety, but the 'hymns, anthems and well-tuned organ' must have tended to foster a religious mood, such a mood as haunted one who was far too human ever to be orthodox, but who recalled in later life with fondness 'the carol sung by night at Christmas, which, when a young boy, I have so often lain awake to hear from seven . . . till ten, when it was sung by the older boys and monitors, and have listened to it, in their rude chanting, till I have been transported in fancy to the fields of Bethlehem, and the song which was sung at that season by angels' voices to the shepherds.'

A historian of the time has gone even further and claimed that the atmosphere of the place not only made the boys' 'sense of right and wrong peculiarly tender and apprehensive,' but also rendered them prone to superstition through 'the thousand tales and traditions which must circulate with undisturbed credulity,' and that 'with this leaning towards an over-belief in matters of religion . . . may be classed a turn for romance above most other boys' – suppositions which, if applied to the boys in general, suggest a turn for romance in the worthy historian himself, but if applied to the particular boy whose sojourn at this School is our concern, are certainly in key with the character of one who was to be the poet of the miraculous, the philosopher of Anglicanism, and who was to confess that moral obligation was to him so very strong a stimulant, that in nine cases out of ten it acted as a narcotic.

§ 3

The young Coleridge, however, needed no religious foundation to develop in him the 'self-concentration of a monk' or a sense of his schoolfellows as 'a sort of laity.' It was this laity of seven hundred boys and not the grotesque Boyer, still for some years a distant terror, who made him feel the waif in the world that in truth he always was. If he could have retired alone to the 'old and awful cloister' or even to the stately dining-room hung round with vast pictures by Verrio, Lely and others, he would have been less forlorn. But there was no physical escape possible in so peopled a universe. He was too far gone as 'a playless day-dreamer' for any rough routine to recall him to the normal. The clash and clamour of a school, the claim of objective things bidding him come out from himself, only served to drive him further in, to emphasize his essential solitude.

Actually, too, he was more lonely than his fellows, set down without warning in what seemed a great friendless city amid strange faces, with a home so far away. And although his brother George, who was a master at a Hackney school, and a number of acquaintances to whom he had been commended, offered him many kindnesses, still their attentions struck the sensitive boy as being rather forced and formal, and they failed him by degrees.

On leave-days, a wistful, unregarded figure, he would watch 'the swarm of "bee-clad youth," with voices of perpetual spring, issuing pell-mell from the lodge in Newgate Street,' homeward or friendward bound, while for him there was no home and no friend outside himself. Nor did holidays bring change and renewal; for it was seven years before he saw Ottery again. The silence of the deserted playgrounds as the long, warm days of summer dragged to their end was more oppressive than their term-time uproar. No wonder that all his homeless life he was to hunger after a home.

It was not long, however, before he ceased to shed tears over his memories of Ottery, with its 'church and trees and faces.' His yearnings for 'those unfledged years' became less tragic, and he contemplated 'making or finding his way of life a detached individual, a *terræ filius*, who was to ask love or service of no one on any more specific relation than that of being a man, and as such to take my chance for the free charities of humanity.'

Yet no boy, as no man, was less a *terræ filius* than Coleridge, or less capable of such a masculine detachment as this to which he aspired. His detachment was at once more and less complete than that of the ordinary boy, who emerging from the chrysalis has to find his own wings. It involved for him a hypochondriac self-absorption, very different from independence. So far from being self-reliant or even self-sufficient, he craved the sympathy of others with a feminine excess. All his life a sense of isolation, of the barriers set between himself and others, which only a mutual and unqualified sympathy so seldom found and seldom retained, could dissolve, lay like a dead weight upon his heart. To give himself wholly to others and so lose himself in a wider harmony was but one aspect of the same impulse which hurried him away from the threat of discord into solitary abstractions. He dreaded loneliness, but he dreaded conflict or even callousness more.

It was doubtless in consequence of this that he suffered less from the paltry tyranny of monitors and 'markers' or from the barbarities of his equals than such a boy as Shelley. Persecution is not for the amiable eccentric with a yielding disposition, but for him whose strangeness challenges the mob. And Coleridge had no need or impulse to rebel, because he could sink at will into himself and taste there experiences which rendered realism insignificant. This power of fugitive abstraction, which rather awoke in others a tolerant protectiveness than excited any aggressive instincts, preserved him all his life from the worst tortures, to which genius in its positive denial of conventional values is usually exposed. From first to last it qualified also the sincerity of his genius.

Nature, too, where there was nought lovely to see 'but the sky and stars,' no longer competed with books. Before a singular accident made it possible for him to continue his incessant indulgence in random reading, he had to content himself with a rapid survey of the books which he fetched from circulating libraries for subscribers. But later a stranger with whose coat-tail pocket he had become absent-mindedly involved in the street, possibly on one of those whole-day leaves 'when he would go prowling about objectless and shivering at cold windows of print shops, to extract a little amusement,' and who at first took him for a thief, was so charmed by his subsequent conversation that he made him free of a library in Cheapside. Henceforth he would run all risks in skulking out to get the two volumes to which he was entitled daily.

Thus to over-feed the mind, while starving the body not only of activity but even of the food necessary to its growth, was not likely to better his condition. Excepting on Wednesdays, in his own words, he never had a full belly. 'Our appetites were damped, never satisfied; and we had no vegetables.' And so he could write of himself at fourteen: 'I was in a continual low fever. My whole being was, with eyes closed to every object of present sense, to crumple myself up in a sunny corner, and read, read, read – fancy myself on Robinson Crusoe's island, finding a mountain of plum-cake, and eating a room for myself, and then eating it into the shapes of tables and chairs – hunger and fancy!'

Against such influences even the Reverend James Boyer could make little essential headway, when Coleridge passing from the Lower Grammar School, that 'Castle of Indolence' presided over by the mildest of masters, Mathew Fielde, came into direct contact with his bullying superior. Deserve though he might Boyer's half-pitying, half-derisive label of 'sensitive fool,' he was beyond the reach of aggressive tactics, and the more common sense was commanded of him, the more, beneath an outward conformity, did he luxuriate in the fantastic.

There were indeed two occasions on which he drifted into a quaint opposition to his terrifying master. When about fifteen, he made friends with a shoemaker and his wife, who lived near the school and whose homely establishment seemed such an oasis in the desert of school life that he persuaded the man to apply to the headmaster for leave to take him as an apprentice. It was the first of those many efforts which Coleridge was to make, each as fantastic as the last, to escape from the abstract to the concrete, and it failed as decisively as them all. The example of Jacob Böhme might commend itself to Coleridge, already dabbling in mystical literature, but it was unlikely to soften the temper of the Reverend James Boyer, who ejected the credulous cobbler with assault and battery.

It was Coleridge himself, however, who suffered physically for his other venture in proclaimed originality.

The Reverend James Boyer was but a poor expositor of Christian values, but he had no doubts of Christian dogma, and when a pupil had the effrontery to proclaim himself an infidel on the strength of a study of Voltaire's *Philosophical Dictionary*, it was no time for expostulation or for argument, in which he might well have come off worst. He cured him by the severest flogging which he ever received at his hands. And since all his life Coleridge was to be torn between the appeal of Christianity to his heart and of dialectic to his mind, it may be that this soundly physical argument had more to do with the unsatisfactory compromise which caution was to dictate than has generally been supposed.

Upon his budding literary sense too his master's narrow but thorough classicism did undoubtedly leave a lasting impression. Far from the eighteenth century as his imagination was to roam, his style as a poet was always to preserve something of the clarity and polish of the age of good sense, a verbal neatness and cunning upon which he was to fall back when inspiration failed, and an epigrammatic talent in default of lyrical impulse.

But the boy, like the man, was even more absorbed in ideas than in images, and Boyer's attempt to enforce a clear logical system of thought, although it may have strengthened and organized his precocious reasoning powers, merely aggravated by suppression his transcendental enthusiasm. The intellectual dogma which Boyer preached simply failed to correspond with his experience. It took no account in its barren propriety of the ideas which to him were an immanent reality. The intelligence, to adopt the distinction which he was later to borrow from Germany, might be content with a system which expounded common sense by syllogisms, but the creative reason worked on far other premises and dealt not only with the logical but the real.

And so when his talents had elevated him mechanically to the ranks of the 'Græcians' – the small intellectual aristocracy of the school chosen to prepare for University exhibitions – although, as he admitted, he was without a spark of conventional ambition, and as for emulation, it had no meaning for him, his real life was passed, not in the class-room in subjection to Boyer, but in 'the wide, wide wilderness' of his own conjecture, littered as it was with 'unarranged book knowledge and book thoughts' of which Boyer had no knowledge and as little understanding. Religious infidelity can be attacked with a cane, but metaphysical enthusiasm is a condition for which human ingenuity has not yet discovered a cure.

§ 4

Indeed the cloisters knew a different Coleridge from the class-room. Here the passing stranger might have been arrested by a spectacle more appropriate to the porches of Athens than the precincts of a London school. A boy noticeable for a slightly exotic cast of feature, his grey eyes large and beaming, his hair glossy black, his complexion unusually fair, and full, animal lips, was the centre of an admiring group of schoolfellows. Like his companions he was clothed in a long coat of blue cloth, belted with a red leather girdle, in yellow stockings and black shoes. His manner expressed at once animation and abstraction, a generous expansiveness, and a state of trance. He seemed to hypnotize his audience without directly addressing them.

Possibly it was the quality of his voice, which had a sort of caressing unction, possibly it was the flow of his words that took the attention captive and bound it in the labyrinth of a sustained soliloquy. Certainly the young scholar was an actor, though he assumed the part of a philosopher. His conversation soared far beyond the schoolboy's ordinary horizon. It glided imperceptibly through the mazes of metaphysics or quickened by recitation the Greek of Homer or of Pindar.

But the material of his utterance was of secondary importance. Oblivious of his words as of his audience, the boy seemed to worship expression for its own sake, as if upon the mere tide of fluent speech he was swept out from some low marsh within himself, where feeling grew stagnant and thought congested, into a world of life and motion. In such monologue he realized himself best because he reconciled his self-absorption with the need of sympathetic contact with others, and he preferred monologue to discussion because he was engaged not in solving an inner doubt, but in escaping an inner friction.

This was the Coleridge whose existence, if Boyer suspected, he thought to clamp under the cast iron of classical propriety. But no dam can stay the water that overbrims it. And while Boyer had been commanding correctness, Coleridge had been drinking to intoxication. He had discovered a new kind of *Arabian Nights*, and just as in childhood he had been driven to relieve his overcharged nerves by acting his fairy-stories, so now he acted his metaphysics, and acted so well that for the rest of his life he was never to lack an audience.

§ 5

The normal development of consciousness is from a perception of images to one of ideas. Youth sees objectively and experiences actively. Only later, for certain minds at least, are images dissolved into their elements as ideas, and thought seeks behind the fleeting moments of the actual, as sensation records them, for a resting place in the real.

But Coleridge had never from childhood seen objectively, with a clear, hard sense of outline. Always to his tender abstracted gaze the world was fluctuent, always the object expressed more than itself. The consequence in childhood was a natural preference for the fantastic, in adolescence a hunger for the ideal. To the extreme materialist there doubtless seems little difference between the two, since to him all interpretation of fact as other than fact is fantastic. Yet such an interpretation is in itself an indisputable fact. It is at least a psychical reality to which thousands can testify. To many sensibilities facts are, like words, the media of meaning. For them most objects have a dual aspect. They exist for their senses materially, but for another kind of perception, or rather for a completer perception, in which instinct and intelligence, being and knowing, are creatively combined and heightened, they seem fraught with an inner significance, a reality underlying their appearance. To the mystic this perception is spiritual, to the poet it is imaginative, to the philosopher it is an act of intuition.

These experiences which transcend equally the mental and the physical, which claim to be timeless apprehensions in a world of time and to abstract the real from the actual, are the central concern of all philosophy engaged in examining the nature of reality. How to distinguish the true illusion from the idle dream, in a sphere in which the ordinary criterion of fact is irrelevant, has always been the problem.

And yet few can doubt that such a distinction exists. The mystical insight of a great poet or seer convinces us of a reality profounder than either the logical or the sentimental. It is something different from hallucination or from any whimsical and purely arbitrary indulgence in the fantastic. It does not transgress the actual which it transcends. Yet obviously the imaginative man is always in danger of surrendering his inner judgment to the unreal if he lacks a bedrock of sensuous experience. Instead then of spiritualizing the material by filtering it through his senses, his emotions, and his mind, disengaging in the process its real from its accidental elements, he will merely impose a fanciful description upon something which for him never had an actual existence.

The reality therefore of an idealist's vision depends essentially on the balance of his faculties and particularly on the relation of his instinct to his thought. If these two faculties are perfectly co-ordinated in an act of creative apprehension, his experience will be true and he will translate fact into purer terms of consciousness: it will be false and fanciful so far as one faculty is developed at the expense of the other and their fusion is incomplete. For in harmonizing the physical and metaphysical elements in his own nature, he will also harmonize subjective desire with objective actuality.

Every poet is an idealist and every creative philosopher. The one translates experiences into images, the other into terms of thought: the one desires to make it coherent by embodying it in an artistic form, the other in a logical system. And the poet who cultivates imagery for its own sake instead of translating vital experience into imaginative terms, reveals the same detachment from reality as the philosopher who spins between himself and fact a web of abstract ratiocination.

It has been necessary to emphasize this distinction between the ideal and the fantastic, because it lies at the root of Coleridge's genius, character and career. Much of his life may be explained by reference to his lack of will power. Yet the will is only the co-ordinating faculty: it unifies body and mind in an effective act of expression. Coleridge's temperament was too unbalanced to allow it to function healthily. He was always in flight from a weight of inorganic matter which he could not assimilate into a realm of ideas which lacked a material foundation.

The qualities and defects of his writing originated in this deranged sensibility, in emotional and intellectual energies which never had a sure foundation in sensuous experience. His lifelong hunger for the infinite, his

'yearning to touch, to feel
The dark Impalpable sure'

never grew naturally out of the soil of realism. The tree of his experience was planted in shallow earth, and so although it shot up with precocious speed and laced heaven with its branches, the live sap of reality ran but thinly through them.

His metaphysical instinct, through trespassing too early

upon physical experience, deprived itself of that substance from which later it might have extracted significance, and at fifteen, through exhaustive reading of transcendental philosophy, he became as bewildered by ideas as the normal imaginative boy is excited by images and metaphors.

The motive behind this strange metaphysical debauch was, like that which earlier plunged him into the miraculous, a desire for escape from an actuality which jarred; from

'the keen insult of the unfeeling heart,
The dread dependence on the low-born mind,'

and in 'the sunny mist, the luminous gloom' of Plato he found a kindred spirit.

Plato too wrote at a time when the concrete world had begun to pain men by its oppression and difficulty and ugliness, when the tremors of a coming disintegration shook faintly the pillars of Paganism. And turning from the discord which troubled him he bade the individual relate himself to a whole which transient material things could not touch, to live in the idea of a Divine harmony, of certain intelligible, changeless realities, which transcended sense-perception and united in a sovereign Beauty, eternal, self-sufficient, unproduced and indestructible. Plato made little attempt to relate this self-conceived harmony to the facts of life. His philosophy was the interpretation of a subjective mood: he was more occupied in explaining his own intuitions than in reconciling them with an objective necessity, and often, as in his famous account of the reincarnation of souls, he was merely fabulous.

The value and originality of his philosophy lay in its explanation of that theory of intuition, in which he combined sense and thought, and upon which he based his distinction between particular sensible beauty and universal intellectual beauty. It is a theory which has been expounded in different terms from his day to ours, and on Coleridge it dawned like a personal revelation.

For he too was haunted by a sense of beauty which transcended the particular objects which it mystically and rather uncertainly embraced. He too was troubled by an incapacity to reconcile his subjective vision and sublunary longings with the objective world about him. And just as in his human relations he hungered to resolve the conflict between self-absorption and a sympathetic communion with his fellows, so in his consciousness he wished to escape from solitary fantasy by combining a visionary with a natural perception of things. Plato seemed to supply him with a key to that escape, to explain and justify the visionary moods which troubled him, and to prove that only by such vague ecstasy as he experienced, in which it was nice to believe that the thinking subject and the object contemplated became in some strange way one, could the truth be really known.

Chance, however, soon introduced Coleridge to a philosopher even more comforting to his self-esteem. Newton and Locke, by grounding all ideas in sensation, had for some time discredited intuitional philosophy as a form of amiable dreaming. The first round of the duel between analytical science and synthetic apprehension had gone altogether in favour of the former. One of the few Englishmen, however, who resisted this reaction was Thomas Taylor, and as a counterblast to the superficial philosophy which reduced all thought to physical terms he had published in 1787 a paraphrase of Plotinus' essay ' Concerning the Beautiful,' which Coleridge was happy to discover at the age of fifteen.

Plotinus carried Plato's ideas still further in a mystical direction and submitted them less to logical thought. Neo-Platonism, as his system was called, was the last utterance of Greek philosophy, already tinged with Christian yearning and aspiration, and at the same time very akin to the Vedantic system of Indian philosophy and to those various forms of Eastern 'Mysteries' which promised redemption through sacramental ritual. Like Plato, Plotinus sought to acquire a knowledge of the Unity, the essence and first principle of all things by direct intuition, and he traced the emanation of life or being from the Nous or Absolute Mind to the world-soul and the souls of men.

Since therefore there was an essential identity between the Divine in man and the Divine in the Universe, that intelligence was only of value which, like its prototype in the Absolute, was creative. He differed from Plato in reducing the conscious mind to a quite secondary faculty, and he divided man's faculties into spirit, soul and body, a prism in which the rays of primal unity were deflected. The aim of the seeker after truth, he declared, should be to combine this trinity into a unity. And this was to be done by merging himself in a supra-rational ecstasy with the Absolute One and so apprehending a Reality which eluded any partial approach.

Such a system, by denying beforehand the credentials of the conscious mind, armed itself against criticism. On the strength of its argument that all true consciousness was a state of the soul, an inner illumination, it could advance such fanciful theories as that souls which have only lived a life of sensation pass into animal bodies, or even, if entirely vegetative, into plants, while its disciples were enjoined to pass from the outer world of sense into an eternal world of dreams.

To Coleridge, haunted by the inexpressible, troubled by a trance-like confusion in which he hardly knew whether he was asleep or awake, and hungering for an ecstatic sensation of well-being, such a system made an overwhelming appeal, an appeal even stronger than Plato's because in its kinship with Christian mysticism it was more consolingly human. Alike his readiness to experience Beauty as some pure essence but faintly associated with things, his natural piety and benevolence, and his precocious system-spinning mind were satisfied by a philosophy which treated the Good, the True and the Beautiful as experiences of one originating harmony; which tended to shirk the problem of matter, which is also the problem of evil, on the rather unwarranted assumption that bodies only 'rested on a substratum of matter,' and brought none of its convictions to the test of fact. (Did, for example, the Beautiful always exist in conjunction with the Good and the True?)

It was enough for him to seek an immediate communion with Beauty (and the rest would be added to him), to embrace, sentimentally, an ascetic ideal, to dismiss all earthly considerations, and 'to mount aloft in pure intellect and in perfection of goodness and in intuition of Godhead.'

Coleridge, who was now becoming conscious of his love of the absolute and of the abstract, a tendency which before had been implicit in his melting perception of Nature and thirst for the miraculous in novels and romances, was inevitably drawn to this philosophy which scorned the relative spirit that was even then beginning in philosophy, as it was later in inductive science, to dominate the thought of the Western world.

Yet partial as any purely materialistic philosophy must, in our opinion, be, there was a sickliness in Coleridge's passion for first principles and abstract entities common to much idealistic thinking. He was constitutionally incapable of interpreting things truly in idealistic terms because he could not experience them vividly in physical terms. Caught in the flux, surrendering himself to life as to some tidal music, he sought despairingly to fix it in certain eternal outlines, and in this ancient philosophy – at once poetic, religious and, if its premises were granted, logically presented, he found something which exactly conformed with the needs of his own nature, even at such a tender age.

He could not of course grasp any of its ideas clearly: that was the charm of it; for he could grasp enough to be consoled. But they set the tone of his thought for life because they accorded with his temperament and seemed to justify its abnormality. Meanwhile – 'nothing else pleased me. History and particular facts lost all interest in my mind. Poetry itself . . . yea, novels and romances, became insipid to me. In my friendless wanderings on our leave-days . . . highly was I delighted if any passenger . . . would enter into conversation with me. For I soon found a means of directing it to my favourite subjects

'Of providence, fore-knowledge, will, and fate,
Fixed fate, free will, fore-knowledge absolute,
And found no end in wandering mazes lost.'

§ 6

From this 'preposterous pursuit' he was happily deflected in 1788 by two events: his accidental introduction to an amiable family, and to an amiable style of poetry. Among the younger boys at Christ's Hospital was one named Evans. Coleridge had shown him kindness, and this led to an introduction to his family. His mother, a widow and 'such a nice lady,' had three daughters, and in this household Coleridge met with the kindness and affection to which he always naïvely responded. He delighted in being addressed as 'Brother Coly,' acclaimed Mrs. Evans as his foster-mother, and in the course of two years fell vaguely and discreetly in love with the eldest daughter.

It was an event which had ultimately unhappy consequences, but its immediate effect was to reclaim him, to
some extent, from the abstract. Even he could not reduce
Miss Evans, in the first realization of adolescent rapture,
to first principles, nor consider 'how often the loving heart
and imaginative spirit of a young man will mistake the
projected creature of his moral yearning, seen in the
reflecting surface of the first not repulsive or vulgar
female who treats him affectionately, for the realization
of his idea.'

The allurement of metaphysics gave way on Saturdays
at least before the duty of escorting the Misses Evans
home from the millinery establishment where they were
employed, or before the pleasure of pillaging on summer
mornings the flower-gardens within six miles of London
for nosegays and presenting them with sonnet or love-
rhyme attached. Possibly too it was a desire to sustain
more gallantly these 'hours of paradise' which led him
to plead with his brother George that a new pair of
breeches would be 'no inconsiderable accession to his
appearance'; for, as he wrote long afterwards in a note
which surprisingly illuminates the amiable softness of his
character — 'to be feminine, kind, and genteely (what I
should now call neatly) dressed, these were the only
things to which my head, heart, or imagination had any
polarity.'

Thus the last years of his school life brought him the
congenial happiness of vaguely luxuriating in tender feelings which he did not bring himself to admit more
exactly, far less to communicate, until six years later their
object engaged the attentions of another.

By this time too he had surrounded himself with a
circle of friends, captivated by his affectionate and expansive nature, among them Thomas Middleton, like himself,
a scholar in his teens, he who, as first bishop of Calcutta,

'is to be seen to-day in St. Paul's in all the pomp of marble wig and lawn, where he stands blessing two nude and tiny Indians, male and female, and by the unlearned is frequently mistaken for the Almighty creating Adam and Eve': Charles Valentine le Grice too, sanguine and nimble-witted; Favell, who was to die young on the plains of Salamanca; Meyer, the future portrait painter and engraver; little Horne, whose voluminous authorship in later days was perhaps traceable to his initiation by Coleridge into the mysteries of the Greek alphabet; Robert Allen, with his 'cordial smile and still more cordial laugh,' and the 'gentle-hearted' Charles Lamb, the only friend at once human and freakish enough to love him all his days.

Warmed by the admiring attachment of such friends Coleridge was another being from the lost spirit, self-pitying and self-absorbed, who consoled himself with Neo-Platonic phantasies. Never was there a boy or man who reflected so sensitively the atmosphere which he breathed. Just as in later days he could announce an approaching depression with the exactitude of a barometer, just as his features in repose, at best lethargic, at worst a 'fat vacancy of face,' beamed genius when some responsive fellow-being kindled them to expression, so in the stimulation of these school-friendships, he grew buoyant, enthusiastic and even jocose.

The dignity of a 'Græcian' did not allow him to indulge in the common amusements of leap-frog and baiting the bear, but he could divert himself in ways more suitable to his temperament. He could set off with his friends 'without map, card, or compass' on a serious expedition to find out 'Philip Quarll's Island,' or at night, a chosen tale-teller, he could quicken his inventive powers in stories concerning genii, fairies and witches, enchanted castles, tender females held captive by tyrants, subterranean passages and solitary cells. Even when through swimming across the New River in his clothes and letting them dry on his back he was confined to the sick ward for nearly half a year with jaundice and rheumatic fever – an indiscretion to which his subsequent ill-health has been attributed – his feelings were in such a state of pleasurable, if drooping, animation, that he could, it seems probable, reward the daughter of the school nurse for her sympathetic attention with some lines, which are so typical in their sickly sentiment and soothing cadence, that six of them must be quoted:

> 'When sinking low the sufferer wan
> Beholds no hand outstretched to save,
> Fair, as the bosom of the swan
> That rises graceful o'er the wave,
> I've seen your breast with pity heave,
> And *therefore* love I you, sweet Genevieve.'

The italicized 'therefore' is significant; for it was always rather as a convalescent, grateful for sympathy, with emotions relaxed and swimming senses that Coleridge loved. Love was never a passion to him. It was at once a melting mood and a sigh of gratitude. It was a narcotic blessed with dreams.

Yet faint as was his physical sense of things there were moments of almost animal delight, as when on holiday mornings he would sally forth into the fields with a party, 'strip under the first warmth of the sun, and wanton like young dace in the stream, getting appetites for noon . . . the very beauty of the day, and the exercise of the pastime, and the sense of liberty, setting a keener edge upon them,' until, 'faint and languid,' they would return towards nightfall. It is Lamb's description, but doubtless it was Coleridge's experience too, and doubtless too it was in one such twilight as this that he saw the evening star,

'newly bathed as well as I,' and suffused with a delicious
lassitude, associated its 'pensive serene brightness' with
his ideal of love and with Mary Evans in particular, em-
balming his fancy in one of the best of his early sonnets:

'O meek attendant of Sol's setting blaze,
   I hail, sweet star, thy chaste effulgent glow;
On thee full oft with fixed eye I gaze,
   Till I, methinks, all spirit seem to grow.
O first and fairest of the starry choir,
   O loveliest 'mid the daughters of the night,
Must not the maid I love like thee inspire
   Pure joy and *calm* delight?
Must she not be, as is thy placid sphere,
   Serenely brilliant? whilst to gaze awhile
Be all my wish 'mid Fancy's high career
   E'en till she quit this scene of earthly toil,
Then Hope perchance might fondly sigh to join
   Her image in thy kindred orb, O star benign!'

The young milliner, as events were to show, had more
material ambitions than a constellated union of 'pure joy
and calm delight' with the benign spirit of 'Brother Coly.'
But for the time being she served gracefully to preside
over what her dreamy admirer called 'the era of poetry
and love,' though in the matter of poetry there were other
influences at work.

§ 7

Boyer's strict classicism did not exclude an interest in
English literature. He made his pupils read Shakespeare
and Milton, while they were studying the Greek tragic
poets, and both with a disciplinary purpose. If Plato persuaded Coleridge of the essential madness of the poet,
Boyer emphasized his sanity, showing by analysis how the

loftiest and seemingly wildest odes had a logic of their own, 'as severe as that of science; and more difficult, because more subtle, more complex, and dependent on more and more fugitive causes.' Into these fugitive causes Boyer was perhaps not very competent to inquire closely, but his assertion that 'in the truly great poets there is a reason assignable, not only for every word, but for the position of every word' was to live in his pupil's later definition of poetry as 'the best words in the best order.'

Yet no one would have accused Boyer of being a poet, and excellent as he might be in enforcing the rules of taste, he was more likely to deride than to inspire originality. It was natural therefore that Coleridge's earliest compositions should express their author as little in English as in Latin or Greek. Nevertheless so early as 1788 verses, not directly designed to win Boyer's approval, reflect rather the wistful and metaphysical temper of the seventeenth century than the good sense and conventional idiom of the eighteenth. The 'Sonnet to the Autumnal Moon,' for example, which he wrote in this year, is mildly Miltonic. So also in places is the 'Anthem for the Children of Christ's Hospital,' written in the following year to gratify the Authorities; but it is also, like the mock heroics entitled 'Julia,' which gained a place in Boyer's collection, predominantly Augustan, and doubtless won his approval by such couplets as:

'The young uncultur'd mind imbibes the ray,
And Vice reluctant quits th' expected prey.'

or the more obvious echo of Pope:

'From future Almanacks the day be crost!
At once her Lover and her Lap-dog lost.'

Coleridge was naturally imitative because he was hypersensitive, but always he was sincerely and obliviously to reflect only that with which his own temperament was in harmony; and had no particular circumstances encouraged him to be plaintive and maudlin, not even a Boyer could have for long kept him loyal to the school of Pope. 'I was not blind,' he wrote, 'to the merits of this school, yet . . . they gave me little pleasure . . . and I saw that the excellence of this kind consisted in just and acute observations on men and manners in an artificial state of society, as its matter and substance; and in the logic of wit, conveyed in strong epigrammatic couplets, as its form . . . the matter and diction seemed to me characterized not so much by poetic thoughts, as by thoughts translated into the language of poetry.'

Already he had turned instinctively for refreshment to the luxuriant classicism of Milton and Spenser; already in the style of Cowper he had defined his domestic aspirations by naming 'Hymeneal bliss' 'that more than friendship, friendship mixed with love,' when on his seventeenth birthday his friend Middleton presented him with a volume of sonnets by the Reverend William Lisle Bowles.

There can never have been clerical characters more antithetical than Bowles and Boyer, and if ever the round little pedagogue scanned the verse of 'the maudlin prince of mournful sonneteers' we can imagine with what a snort of derision the 'first great oracle of tender souls' was capped as another 'sensitive fool.'

But Coleridge was enraptured with the discovery of a twin spirit. As Plotinus had justified his mystical cerebration, so Bowles consecrated his sentiment. His blandly soothing sonnets 'written amidst various interesting scenes during a tour under youthful dejection' caused by 'the death of a deserving young woman,' seemed to him at once tender and manly, natural and real, dignified and harmonious. They floated like the soft airs of summer into a world frozen by Boyer's wintry discipline, melting his inhibitions and inducing now a fervid, now a languid glow.

For just as later he was to rebut the charge of plagiarism brought against his metaphysical theories by claiming that all the main and fundamental ideas in which he resembled Schelling were born in his mind before he had read a page of the German philosopher, so his obligations to Bowles were rather those of affinity than of plagiarism. Throughout his life, feeling himself an alien among his associates, with cravings which they lacked, and a sense of life which they could not understand, he gave himself with an excess of gratitude and surprise to any writer who seemed to reflect a temperament similar to his own.

It is this which explains the conflagration which so small a flame as Bowles kindled. Here was a man who in his weakness as in his strength was such a one as Coleridge might have been, without his genius and without his wildness. His resort to poetry as a consoler of mild melancholy, his limp simplicity, and the often cloying sweetness of his mood, the amiable moralizing which he interwove with his descriptions of Nature, his hypochondriac sentiment and the dissolving cadence of his verse — were all tendencies latent in Coleridge which it was Bowles' distinction to touch to poetic life by such lines as:

> 'O Time! who know'st a lenient hand to lay
> Softest on sorrow's wound, and slowly thence
> (Lulling to sad repose the weary sense)
> The faint pang stealest unperceived away;'

or

> 'Languid, and sad, and slow, from day to day
> I journey on, yet pensive turn to view
> (Where the rich landscape gleams with softer hue),
> The streams, and vales, and hills that steal away.'

or

> 'The waving branches that romantick bend
>   O'er thy tall banks, a soothing charm bestow;
>   The murmurs of thy wand'ring wave below
> Seem to his ear the pity of a friend.'

Bowles, to quote his own words, presented

> 'fairy vales, where the tir'd mind
> Might rest, beyond the murmurs of mankind,'

but at the same time they were drawn from nature and suffused with feeling, which, if languishing and lachrymose, was fresh with life in contrast with Augustan proprieties.

Had Bowles' feeling not been as genuine as sentimentality can be, and had he not possessed a real vein of poetic talent, even the assurance that he had

> 'droop'd beneath life's early showers'

or known

> 'the fragrant breeze
> Breathe on the trembling sense of wan disease,'

would not have captivated Coleridge as it did. Particularly in his descriptive evocations of Nature he did communicate a joy as well as 'wake the Tear, yet steal away the pang.' He records the 'grasshopper's faint pipe . . . the bleat of the lone lamb . . . the bird's last twitter from the hedgerow scene,' the glitter of pebbled streams, with a faint but dewy freshness, and even woos

> 'The ideal spirit that abides unseen
> 'Mid rocks, and woods, and solitudes,'

in tones sufficiently unfabricated to lisp the great organ

music that was to be devoted to that theme. But it was above all his continual yearning for a humble dwelling folded in the peace of a summer evening, for an enchanted retirement where he could luxuriate over his emotions, that led Coleridge to call him 'the exquisite Bowles,' and to accord him the sincerest form of flattery in such lines as

> 'Thy native cot she flash'd upon thy view,
> Thy native cot, where still, at close of day,
> Peace smiling sat and listen'd to thy lay.'

Among poets who sacrificed 'both heart and head to point and drapery' Bowles appealed like a kind face and a natural manner in a room full of glassy elegants; and the effeminacy of the appeal was less noticeable because it was spiced with pastoral classicism. The 'oaten reed,' 'sylvan muse' and 'Sicilian pipe' were discreetly mingled with the village bells and the 'melancholy musick' of the sea, and

> 'Instruction bland
> With young-ey'd Sympathy, went hand in hand
> O'er classick fields:'

Within less than a year Coleridge's proselytizing zeal had produced more than forty transcriptions of Bowles' poems for the edification of his friends, but the best evidence of his devotion to the god of his idolatry, was his imitation, an imitation which on occasions extended to the choice of subject and word, but which in general went no further than mood.

The relaxed insinuating note henceforth to be so typical of his yielding sensibility begins to be heard, curiously mixed with the self-conscious phraseology learnt in Boyer's school of taste, and still to be transmuted by genius into impalpable music, although such lines as

'Slumbrous god of half-shut eye!
Who lovest with limbs supine to lie;
Soother sweet of toil and care
Listen, listen to my prayer;
And to thy votary dispense
Thy soporific influence!'

clearly anticipate it. With Bowles too he communed with
Anna's 'pensive ghost,' loving 'to sit upon her tomb's
dank grass,' and with Bowles he hymned hypochondriac
Youth viewing 'the crowd whom Youth and Health
inspire' with a sigh and a thought that

'I too could laugh and play
And gaily sport it on the Muse's lyre,
Ere Tyrant Pain had chas'd away delight,
Ere the wild pulse throbb'd anguish thro' the night.'

Yet pleasant as these sickly sallies, these 'musings in
torpid woe' were, charming as it was to pictorialize

'The hideous offspring of Disease,
Swoln Dropsy ignorant of Rest,
And fever garb'd in scarlet vest,
Consumption driving the quick hearse,
And Gout that howls the frequent curse,'

there were moments of rapture, unknown to Bowles, in
which he felt them to be

'vain Phantasies, the fleeting brood
Of woe self-solac'd in her dreamy mood,'

moments when life beckoned like a 'glorious prospect,'
when wisdom and knowledge hailed him from afar and
he cried, personifying his faculties with typical metaphysical fervour:

'My eye shall dart thro' infinite expanse
And Thought suspended lie in Rapture's blissful trance.'

And not only in his personification of mental and moral attributes did he model himself upon earlier poets than Bowles. In such verses as 'Music' and 'Devonshire Roads' he both imitated and parodied Milton, and in such different monodies as that 'On the Death of Chatterton' and that 'On a Tea Kettle' he studied the versification of Spenser.

When too in 1789 the Western world was thrilled by the fall of the Bastille he devoted a bombastic ode to the theme in a style which would have jarred the domestic and elegiac soul of Bowles. It was his first experiment in political rhetoric, and although he was later to communicate his enthusiasm for Freedom in verse less artificial than

'Yes! Liberty the soul of Life shall reign,
Shall throb in every pulse, shall flow thro' every vein,'

yet his attachment to this romantic abstraction was to prove like that of others among his contemporaries, too sentimental to survive the trial of experience.

But there was one quality in his early verse which he owed neither to Bowles nor to Milton nor to Gray. Doubtless it had been fostered by his consumption of second-rate romances, but it originated in the wild recesses of his own nature. Beneath the surface of domestic and moral platitude, beneath the florid effusiveness and the childish humour in which he at times indulged, there was a gulf of childish credulity and fear, a place of dark mysteries and 'dank horrors,' a place too of wild enchantment where

'The wizard Passions weave a holy spell.'

It was still a conventional and melodramatic mystery-chamber, a hall where

'hog and devil mingling grunt and yell,'

a haunt of 'Grim phantoms,' 'Scorpion Kings,' and 'A hideous hag, th' Enchantress Pleasure,' but its malign and tormented ghosts were those which he was later so exquisitely to refine and individualize; it was in this crude alembic that he was to distil his purest and most ghostly music.

§ 8

To one learned in the retrospective style of Bowles the occasion of leaving school was a heaven-sent opportunity. Forgotten were the restraints, the harsh routine and the sense of desolation. Already agreeably posed as a care-worn youth Coleridge longed for those happy days to return when he 'heard of guilt and wonder'd at the tale,' while even the grim face of Boyer assumed a winning expression fitting to parental scenes to which a 'grateful heart still fondly clings.' And having done full justice to such sentiments in a sonnet and an ode, in the summer of 1791 he bade what was to be his last farewell to the 'much-loved cloisters pale' of the London Charity School.

CHAPTER TWO

THE PANTISOCRATIC DREAM

§ I

IN October 1791, after a few months of renewed acquaintance with his family at Ottery, Coleridge travelled to Cambridge by a night coach. He was met by Middleton, who had preceded him by two years to Pembroke, and by him was conducted to Jesus College, at which he had been awarded a school exhibition and a Rustat Scholarship. The school authorities had sent him to Jesus as the college most likely to offer favourable preferment to the Church, and the scholarship entailed an informal obligation to take Orders. It was a prospect in which a young Romantic was not likely to acquiesce, despite his inherited piety, and although he could still sign himself six months later in a letter to Mrs. Evans as 'Reverend in the future tense.' Essentially, perhaps, the signature was a true one, but it was never to be formally ratified.

At first, however, he was too conscious of the new delights of freedom to abuse them. After the enclosed town life the lyrical landscape of Cambridge was in itself a rapture. Walking with Middleton through the country, discoursing with his usual fertility,

> 'Obedient now to Hope's command,
> I bid each humble wish expand,
> And fair and bright Life's prospects seem,
> While Hope displays her cheering beam,
> And Fancy's vivid colourings stream,
> While Emulation stands me nigh,
> The goddess of the eager eye.'

There was even a pleasure in writing that

> 'Pale Disappointment hangs her head
> O'er darling Expectation dead!'

So remote did the possibility seem. For the present was a harmony and the future a dream, and it was perhaps of this time, when spring came round, that he wrote: 'The first sight of green fields with the numberless nodding gold cups and the winding river with alders on its banks, affected me, coming out of a city confinement, with the sweetness and power of a sudden strain of music.'

And he could share it all with Mary Evans, that invaluable conductor of emotions that, without an object upon which to direct them, were apt in their delicious vagueness to excite without fully satisfying; writing to her in his best Bowlesian manner: 'what a lovely anticipation of spring the last three or four days have afforded! Nature has been very profuse of her ornaments to the country about Cambridge; yet the clear rivulet that runs through the Grove adjacent to our College, and the numberless little birds (particularly robins) that are singing away, and above all, the little lambs, each by the side of its mother, recall the most pleasing ideas of pastoral simplicity, and almost soothe one's soul into congenial innocence.' It was only to her sister Anne that he could write of the Cam as 'a handsome stream of a muddy complexion.'

And with these 'dear silent pleasures of the Heart' went an 'uncommon flow of health,' a state which it was agreeable to impute to the care of Mrs. Evans with whom he spent a fortnight at Christmas, but which was in truth the physical reflection of his emotional well-being, as later his ill-health was attributable far more to psychical discord than to obscure rheumatics. The intimate connection of the two is a fact of primary importance in its bearing on his career.

And in the Master of his college, the Reverend Doctor Pearce, he found a personality almost as remote from Boyer as Bowles himself, a mild and well-intentioned scholar, who reduced the chains of discipline to silken bands. Under these conditions it was easy at first to be a reasonably industrious student, the more so that Middleton, with whom he read in the evenings, unlike the genial Le Grice, who followed him up a year later, was a model of studiousness, and the prizes which the University offered still allured. He gained the Browne Gold Medal for a Sapphic Ode on the Slave Trade, and came so near winning the Craven Scholarship as to be one of the last four selected candidates. At the same time he developed a passion for Simpson's Euclid, to the charms of which he tried to convert his friends, and even found leisure to send his brother George some sermons. For, as he confessed elsewhere, he was still a politic conformer. 'Though I am not an *Alderman*, I have yet *prudence* enough to respect that *gluttony of faith* waggishly yclept orthodoxy' – a position to which he was finally to return after life had had its way with him.

For more than a year then he could justly claim not to have relaxed in his exertions or to have indulged unduly in the wanderings of his 'castle-building Imagination,' although at times he confessed to being 'most villainously vapoured.' But possibly this was due to 'the wild Bacchanalian sympathy' with which he joined in undergraduate supper-parties or to the 'fiddle-scraping' and 'flute-tooting' against which in self-defence he began to take lessons on the violin.

When, however, in 1792 his 'patron and protector' Middleton left Pembroke, having sacrificed his chances of a fellowship to his republican ardours, the essential fluidity of Coleridge's nature could no longer contain itself, and it flowed as was inevitable at the time into the political channel. Mr. Fox was at the moment the hero of young Cambridge Radicals, and his recently published 'Letter to the Westminster electors' was 'quite the political go.' It fired Coleridge's enthusiasm and led him to a Radical debauch as vague and Gargantuan as his metaphysical had been.

One of the most interesting characteristics of the Romantic temperament is that its excessive individualism induces a longing, equally excessive and uncritical, for self-escape. Suffocated by his own sensations, the Romantic seeks to project them into a system or a fiction or a creed. From childhood Coleridge had felt this need to an imperative degree, and had sought to satisfy it in the vicious circle of miraculous tales, sentimental poetry and sublunary philosophy. He now threw himself into political and religious Radicalism, and since politics was the least abstract of all his refuges, it was the one which involved him in the direst consequences and upon which disillusionment descended most quickly.

His Radicalism was of the fantastic sort to be expected of one who was temperamentally incapable of relating theory to fact. Just as his metaphysical ideal of perfection was purely subjective, so his notion of human perfectibility was not that of the gradual fulfilment of creative tendencies latent in man, but, like his master Rousseau's, a miraculous jump back into a state of natural innocence. It was another fairy story, and how essentially for him it was a fairy story, is proved by his inability later to graft the ideal truth, which like an allegory it did present, on to the facts that experience had forced upon his notice.

But for the time Jacobinism was as satisfying a conduit for enthusiasm as Mary Evans was for tender emotions. Æschylus and Plato and Thucydides were pushed aside in favour of countless political pamphlets. They served, as metaphysics had done, his passion for effusive self-expression, and his fame as a talker spreading through the college, his room on the ground floor became the constant rendezvous of friends hypnotized by his animated and interminable monologue.

Taking 'little exercise for the sake of exercise' he spent his mornings in reading pamphlet after pamphlet, and his evenings, oblivious of the practical jokes played on him by the more flippant of his audience, in paraphrasing their substance, spinning them into new shapes, or in repeating whole pages of them word for word.

For one of the symptoms of his abnormally passive sensibility was a memory almost mechanical in its retentiveness. Often in time to come he was unconsciously to reduplicate whole passages in letters to different friends, and the prolixity of his utterance throughout life was due to the fact that, unlike the ordinary reader, he could not absorb the essentials of his vast reading without at the same time retaining it verbally, and that his remarkable mind, in its effort after self-expression, was for ever struggling to rid itself of the mass of mere material which Memory had accumulated. His mind in short was like a sponge which must be continually wrung out if it is to preserve its condition.

But to the listener, ignorant of the extent to which he was drawing on his reading, the brilliance of his apparent extemporization was undeniable. And if his appearance did not at first attract, the pale brow and benevolent eyes bulking less upon the attention than the loose mouth, bad teeth, and short, formless nose, he had only to sail out on the stream of his eloquence for even his bad features to be forgotten as such, so brimming with expressiveness they were. And so he sat, like some beautiful exotic – an impression strengthened by the long hair parted in the middle which framed his face – transporting his friends to Arcadian regions where Nature's morals were unquestionable and man was no longer vile.

No tiresome economic analysis, no laborious statistics

shackled his feet as they wandered over the enchanted
meadows of Freedom. 'Feeling was all'; it solved all
problems by dissolving them in its genial glow. Expediency, duty, the great dualism of life, so hard to reconcile, between faith and reason, matter and spirit, desire
and necessity, all the pedestrian motives of prudence, and
legality, every jealous distinction, vanished before the
miraculous summons, 'Rise, God of Nature, rise!' France
had already sounded the summons with phenomenal
effect. She had proclaimed her faith in the Absolute
ideas of Liberty, Equality and Fraternity, and doubtless
all else would be speedily added to her. For these were
not catchwords but mystic symbols, spells which had only
to be uttered to regenerate mankind. As for the fate of
Louis XVI, surely 'no Englishman need be alarmed at
the execution of an individual at Paris?' He refused to see
any more significance in it than in a street accident. The
unfortunate monarch had been run over by the traffic of
progress, a traffic which would now proceed at such a
speed that in an incredibly short period it would deposit
humanity in the promised land of a perfect domestic
concord.

Some of his enthusiasms might indeed have struck his
audience as a trifle contradictory, had not his whole
purpose been to affirm the identity of all things. It was
strange, for example, that so fervid a worshipper of
Nature should espouse the cause of William Godwin, who
was so blind to the power of natural instincts, that he
reduced man to a lay figure of reason like himself, and
even more peculiar was the equal applause which he offered
to the philosophers Berkeley and Hartley, although the one
explained all physical things as mental phenomena, and
the other related all mental phenomena to physical conditions. But it was by enforcing such distinctions, he
would have argued, that the individual grew mean and

separated himself from the generous flow of indiscriminate benevolence of which Nature was the fount and origin.

In religion too, as in politics, he preached the gospel of Nature. To a devout disciple of Plotinus, to whom the Deity was an abstract of the first principles of the Good, the True and the Beautiful, of which Nature was the exposition, anthropomorphism was a childish superstition, while such orthodox dogmas as Original Sin, the Atonement, and the Divinity of Christ must either be rejected outright or accepted in a purely symbolical sense. If Fox was his political hero for denouncing Pitt's declaration of war against the Apostles of Nature in France, Priestley, the famous chemist, was his religious hero, for opposing Reason and Personal Revelation to crusted theology, and paying for it in the destruction of his books and instruments and a necessitous flight to America.

But Cambridge itself was to offer him the opportunity of testifying publicly to his admiration for the heroes of free thought. Among the fellows of Jesus was a Unitarian disciple of Priestley's named William Frend, who early in 1793 alarmed the University authorities by attacking the Established Church and its Thirty-nine Articles in a pamphlet euphemistically entitled 'Peace and Union.' In May he was brought to trial before the Vice-Chancellor and required to recant his heresies and also certain Radical opinions in politics, which had shocked the Academic mind, on pain of losing his fellowship. This, in a vigorous speech in his own defence, he declined to do, to the delight of Coleridge and his circle, who, seated in court, could hardly refrain from a public demonstration on behalf of the victim of oppression.

His speech however did not appeal so winningly to the authorities; Coleridge realized that the trial was going against him; the spell of first principles had strangely failed to work, and when some tentative observations

were made in Frend's favour which seemed to him 'a
dying hope thrown out,' he sought with guileless im-
petuosity to strengthen their appeal by a sudden burst of
violent clapping. Fortunately the young man sitting near
him, whom the Proctor accused of committing this inde-
corum, could prove his innocence by holding out the stump
of his right arm, and when Coleridge confessed his responsibility later he was dismissed with a severe warning.

But if he avoided suffering himself as a victim of
oppression, two years of University life had been enough
to deflect him far from the sober road which led to
Ordination. He was possessed by the Genius of enthusiasm and had drunk to intoxication of self-expression.
Freed from discipline, but without private judgment, he
was henceforth to stake all, generously and uncritically,
on his sensibility, to feel the joy and wonder of life as only
those can who make such an unqualified surrender to
direct emotion, but to stand also naked and defenceless
against the stabs of circumstance.

Revolutionary aspirations, however, diverted him from
poetry as well as from his reading for the Schools. His
was an eloquent, but not a rhetorical nature, and happiest
therefore when letting his political idealism flow along the
unassuming channels of extempore conversation. And it
was only when, with the long vacation of 1793, his
audience dispersed and he himself retired to Ottery, that
in an atmosphere unconducive to the expression of
political or religious heresies he began to luxuriate again
in those softer emotions for which verse was a pleasant
outlet, primarily associated with Mary Evans, but attach-
able to any sympathetic female form.

To the influence of Bowles had now been added that of
Ossian, whose dreamy extravagance inevitably fascinated
one who, so far as he loved a woman, loved her less for
herself than as an excuse for melting sentimentalism or

even for 'complimentary effusions in the poetic way.' It was poetry of this order which he addressed to Miss Fanny Nesbitt, who travelled with him in the Tiverton diligence from Exeter, and whom he thought 'a very pretty girl,' a poetry as artificial in its echoes of Spenser, Fletcher, Thomson, or Bowles, as it was in its faint eroticism.

She, like the young ladies whom he conducted 'half-way up a wood-covered hill' to 'an excavation called the Pixies' Parlour, one of whom, of stature elegantly small, and of complexion colourless yet clear, was proclaimed the Faery Queen' in an ode, redolent of Milton, like too the 'lonely Otter's sleep-persuading stream' to which he dedicated a sonnet closely modelled upon Bowles' 'Sonnet to the River Itchin,' existed for him no more than a perfume that induced a languid mood, a mood so sickly and evanescent that without pseudo-classical formulas and personifications it could never have achieved expression at all.

Yet there were moments of personal feeling amid the derived decoration, if indeed such a description can be used of a voluptuousness half-emotional, half-sensuous, that indulged itself in 'soothing witcheries.' They are to be found particularly in the 'Lines on an Autumnal Evening,' in which he invoked with mock ceremony the phantom presence of Mary Evans. It was, as he confessed, a 'dear Deceit'; the maid in whose 'bright blue eyes' he saw 'Chaste Joyance dancing' never attended a millinery establishment. She was 'formed by the wondrous Alchemy of Heaven'; in the best eighteenth-century manner

'A thousand Loves around her forehead fly;
A thousand Loves sit melting in her eye;'

and she looked like a landscape deliciously dissolved in moonlight:

'When the bent flower beneath the night-dew weeps
And on the lake the silver lustre sleeps,
Amid the paly radiance soft and sad,
She meets my lonely path in moonbeams clad.
With her along the streamlet's brink I rove;
With her I list the warblings of the Grove;
And seems in each low wind her voice to float
Love whispering Pity in each soothing note!'

That a young man enjoying his vacation should invoke the
lady of his fancy in these valetudinarian tones is sufficient
evidence of his proneness to sickly sensationalism, a
sensationalism which conditioned also his raptures, as
when he wrote of a kiss:

'O'er all my frame shot rapid my thrilled heart,
And every nerve confessed the electric dart'

or in a more decorative mood,

'When twilight stole across the fading vale,
To fan my Love I'd be the Evening Gale;
Mourn in the soft folds of her swelling vest,
And flutter my faint pinions on her breast!
On Seraph wing I'd float a Dream by night,
To soothe my Love with shadows of delight:
Or soar aloft to be the Spangled Skies,
And gaze upon her with a thousand eyes!'

The poet who wrote in this style was at best a verbal
sensualist. He knew no healthy physical reaction to life.
Desire might fret his nerves for a moment, but seductive
fancy was enough to soothe them. Well might he write

'Ah why refuse the blameless bliss?
Can Danger lurk within a *kiss*?'

since for him a kiss was an imaginary sensation and its

refusal an abstract concern which a little literary cunning
could turn into the most endearing consent:

> 'Well-pleased to hear the whisper'd "No!"
> The whisper'd "No" – how little meant!
> Sweet Falsehood that endears Consent!
> For on those lovely lips the while
> Dawns the soft relenting smile,
> And tempts, with feigned dissuasion coy,
> The gentle violence of Joy.'

Just, therefore, as in his Utopianism he allowed his aspirations to masquerade as convictions, because he derived
such pleasurable sensations from their expression, so, as
a lover, he projected his emotions into dreams of desire,
and through excess of sensibility recoiled from the world
of fact outside himself, by contact with which both his
desire and his idealism might have discovered reality.

§ 2

But fact was preparing to take its revenge. During the
two years which he had spent at Cambridge he had not
ceased to correspond regularly with the Evans family,
sunning himself in Mrs. Evans' 'tenderness scarcely
inferior to the solicitude of maternal affection,' and
assuring her that she had 'the very first row in the front
box of my heart's little theatre.' Amid all variations of
mood his 'love and gratitude' remained 'unalterably
fixed,' and when the lady was embarking on a journey to
Wales she was to have himself as an unseen companion,
one 'whose heart will melt with unutterable tenderness at
your maternal transports.' 'I write to others,' he confessed, 'but my pen talks to you,' while to impress on her
the sincerity of his piety he sent her 'a little work of that
great and good man, Archdeacon Paley.'

The cynical reader who should attribute these effusions

to an astute design on Coleridge's part to reconcile Mrs. Evans to the idea of accepting him as a son-in-law, would be entirely mistaken. No one enjoyed maternal transports so much as he. 'Surely,' as he wrote in praise of her unselfishness, 'the pleasures that arise from whispering peace to those who are in trouble, and healing the broken in heart, are far superior to all the unfeeling can enjoy.' And it was indeed almost worth while breaking his own heart to qualify for so tender a treatment. Like a child he loved to be petted, and his attachment to the lady who showed him motherly attention was in truth far more real than the sentiment he associated with her daughter.

Possibly Mary Evans was dimly conscious of this, since we find him complaining of the formal conclusions to her letters and signing himself with a 'God bless you,' 'your affectionate and grateful S. T. Coleridge.' But the tone of his letters to her was not calculated to inspire a more intimate signature. His own description of them as 'a heap of nothingness . . . a river of words and a spoonful of sense' could not be bettered. They were as artificial as the poetry which he occasionally included, and though his 'dear sister,' as he called her, might appreciate the gift of his 'softest affections' and 'the ardour of his eternal friendship,' they were not likely to kindle a passionate devotion in her heart. Again, while it was honest, it was scarcely complimentary to inform her that 'really, I have written so long that I had forgot to whom I was writing.'

Nevertheless it was very pleasant to have a sympathetic correspondent into whose ear one could whisper an innocent vanity concerning the new 'swanskin waistcoat, a most attractive external,' or communicate a melancholy, sententious or aspiring mood, or even a jest at one's own sentimentalism by comparing oneself to the old Greek philosopher 'who once harangued so movingly on the miseries of life that his audience went home and hanged themselves, but he lived many years afterwards in very sleek condition.' He could hear them all laughing over dear 'Brother Coly's' facetiousness as he wrote, and the thought of it was like a breath of warm air in a cold world.

Yet it was from this very hothouse of sentiment that the stab of realism came. Mary Evans, he learnt, had an admirer to whom she was affectionately inclined, and one who doubtless, unlike himself, had other aims than to feel everything and do nothing. No longer could he listen to Hope's bland whisper 'soothing with many a dream the hour of rest.' It would be too much to say that 'Jealousy with feverish fancies pale . . . jarred' his heart's 'fine fibres with a maniac's hand': for jealousy requires physical passion for its basis. But for such a nature as Coleridge's the loss of a romantic illusion was even more desolating than hatred of a realistic rival. He never felt a woman as a fact until she became an unpleasant one or ceased to be his to associate with a swooning tenderness. The distraction was all the greater because he was as uncertain of his own feelings towards Mary Evans as he was of the rumoured rival.

Certainly he admired her 'sensibility regulated by Judgment, her gaiety proceeding from a cheerful heart, acting on the stores of a strong understanding.' He derived exquisite enjoyment too from 'voluntarily inviting the recollection of these qualities into his mind . . . making them the perpetual object of his reveries, and yet entertaining no sentiment beyond that of the immediate Pleasure annexed to the thinking of her.' But did this justify him in passing beyond brotherly benediction and avowing a passion with all the material consequences which that would involve?

Irresolute as he was, he lacked the conviction to take such a step. To fancy Mary Evans twining a laurel wreath around his brow was well enough; to approach her as a prospective husband was another matter; and it was only during the year which followed that in brooding on his loss, clinging 'with desperate fondness to this Phantom of Love, its mysterious Attractions and hopeless Prospects,' he deluded himself that he really did harbour an unsubduable passion and despairingly confessed it. Meanwhile he broke off without explanation all correspondence with the family and luxuriated in a melancholy as sentimental as his previous rapture. Once again he was a waif in the world, expelled from the 'arbours' of his Eden, and doomed to nurse in his bosom his indulgent and unpractical day-dreams 'with an agony of Affection, even as a Mother her sickly infant.'

But realism attacked him in the form of a 'polite upholsterer' too. This gentleman, taking advantage of his simplicity, had furnished his rooms at his own figure, and when the bill was presented Coleridge was staggered by a sum far beyond his means. Unfortunately the tradesman of a University town was not as ready as himself to dismiss as worthless the paltry motives of self-interest, and the double humiliation was too much to bear. To plead his own difference from normal men, his innate sense of genius, was for him but poor comfort. No doubt it was true that 'mine is no common case,' but if the abnormal sensibility of genius is not balanced by an abnormal aggressiveness, it is at the mercy of circumstance.

Coleridge's invariable impulse, when hurt by life, was to run away and hide like a child, anywhere, in the hope that he might dream undisturbed. On the present occasion he fled to London, where the lottery was to be drawn, in which he had taken a ticket in the hope of retrieving some at least of his fortunes. And while awaiting his fate he addressed the fickle goddess in a set of verses at once frivolous and pathetic, speaking of the 'One

Flower of Hope' – a flower mystically composed of Mary
Evans and the lottery ticket – and how

'At Love's behest
Trembling, I plac'd it in my secret breast:'

a flower

'Oft moistened with the tear's ambrosial dew!
Poor wither'd floweret! on its head
Has dark despair his sickly mildew shed!
But thou, O Fortune! can'st relume
Its deaden'd tints. . . .'

Fortune however refused to be seduced by his languishing verses, and a recruiting poster advertising for 'a few
smart lads for the 15th Elliot's Light Dragoons' having
caught his eye, he presented himself for enlistment. It
did not matter that he was preposterously unsuited to
play the part of a 'smart lad' or that he was to be trained
for what he had called 'systematic murder' against the
very French Republic which was still in his eyes the
Champion of Liberty and the hope of the world. It did
not matter that he had always cherished 'a violent antipathy to soldiers and horses.' The unpleasantness of an
actuality was to him inconceivable save in the immediate
moment of experiencing it. Wise men have been known
to enter the Army because they wanted time to think, but
Coleridge entered it rather to forget – to forget dunning
upholsterers and tantalizing young ladies, to lose himself
in a strange, insensitive world, a world which in prospect
seemed rather attractively concrete and in which, if he
wished to dream, his dreams would be heightened by
contrast.

And so, half-crazed and quite irresponsible, turning a
deaf ear to the enlisting corporal's kindly dissuasions, one
of the most incompetent recruits who ever accepted the

King's service enlisted on December 2, 1793, and two days later was attested at Reading, under a name which surely ought to have figured in humorous fiction rather than on the shop-front from which he is said to have borrowed it – that of Silas Tomkyn Comberbacke.

§ 3

Nearly thirty years later Coleridge was to say in a lecture that 'Magic and War – itself a magic – are the day-dreams of childhood; love is the day-dream of youth and early manhood.' And possibly his enlistment was an unconscious recoil from one day-dream to another, a testing too of his theory that 'some sudden revolution, some unexpected change of place' was required to combat the *vis inertiæ* of the human mind.

The earlier day-dream was even more rudely shattered than the later. His inability either to sit or groom his horse cannot have eased his relations with his sergeant-major, although his obvious good-nature and smiling incompetence, and still more his readiness to indite love-letters or entertain with romantic stories, soon endeared him to his fellow dragoons. But quaintly unreal as the life seemed at first, its romance did not survive a confinement in Henley Workhouse, due to some 'dreadfully troublesome eruptions,' nor the duty of nursing there a comrade stricken with confluent small-pox. Even the sympathy of a 'beautiful girl' in the Institution did not compensate him for 'the almost total want of sleep, the putrid smell, and fatiguing struggles with his delirious comrade-in-arms.'

Already he could write, 'mine is a sensibility gangrened with inward corruption and the keen searching of the air from without,' and it was small comfort to be told by an expansive Swedenborgian, whom he met in a tavern a month later, that 'from the intellectual atmosphere that emanated from him and enveloped him' he found him to be in 'a state of recipiency.'

It was only too tragically true. He was so recipient that he suffered acutely from anything which time or distance had not softened. Even his rooms at Jesus, with their furniture unpaid for, possessed now the charm of unreal things, and within six weeks he confided his situation to some friends at Christ's Hospital. Although he affected displeasure that the confidence was abused, he was unaffectedly relieved that his family were informed of his whereabouts and through them his commanding officer, who must already have detected some mystery about the very indocile equestrian of the cultured speech, whose abilities were better employed in nursing sick dragoons than in parading with sound ones.

His relief was certainly mixed with humiliation. He was thankful, but he shrunk and shivered too. What a spectacle he had made of himself! How could conventional relations understand the complexities of his panic and irresolution? He felt for them too, as well as for himself. Their embarrassment even planted his 'pillow with thorns' and made his 'dreams full of terrors,' and when he received a letter from kind brother George, he lacked the courage either to burn or open it, and luxuriated instead in the wildest self-recrimination. 'Alas! my poor Mother! What an intolerable weight of guilt is suspended over my head by a hair on one hand; and if I endure to live – the look ever downward – insult, pity, and hell! God or Chaos preserve me! What but infinite Wisdom or infinite Confusion can do it?'

And when he did bring himself to open the letter, what a delirium it excited. His iniquity was enormous and yet his 'feeble and exhausted heart' lacked the energy to abhor it.

'O my wayward soul!' he wrote, 'I have been a fool

even to madness. What shall I dare to promise? My
mind is illegible to myself. I am lost in the labyrinth,
the trackless wilderness of my own bosom. Truly may I
say, "I am wearied of being saved." My frame is chill
and torpid. The ebb and flow of my hopes and fears
has stagnated into recklessness. One wish only can I
read distinctly in my heart, that it were possible for me
to be forgotten as though I had never been!' . . . and so
on through a crescendo of 'anguish,' 'intolerable images
of horror' that 'haunt my sleep and enfever my dreams,'
theatrical intercessions for annihilation to the climax –
'my brother! my brother! pray for me, comfort me, my
brother! I am very wretched, and, though my complaint
be bitter, my stroke is heavier than my groaning!'

And there was the same hysterical excess in his expression of gratitude – 'I am indeed oppressed, oppressed,' he
wrote in a later letter, 'with the greatness of your love.'
'Mine eyes gush out with tears, my heart is sick and
languid with the weight of unmerited kindness.'

Such were the fruits of the gospel that 'feeling is all.'
Throughout his life Coleridge was to be reduced to such
a state as this by every material crisis and to relieve and
indulge himself in similar effusions. He was as incapable
of seeing things in proportion as a child stung by a
nettle. He was no more conscious of self-deception than
Rousseau was. He really believed that his 'soul sickened
at its own guilt' even while he proved the opposite by the
manner of his confession. His very prayers for self-annihi-
lation reeked with the emotional sophistry of egotism.

It required however neither 'infinite Wisdom' nor
'infinite Confusion' to procure him his discharge after a
letter couched in terms of Biblical fervour had been
addressed to his eldest brother, Captain James Coleridge,
– a letter which must have afforded him considerable
pleasure to write. To prostrate himself before the matter-

of-fact, to accuse himself with all the devices of romantic rhetoric, to invoke the forgiveness of his Creator and the softer consolations of religion – how superbly and pathetically incongruous it was in the person of a misplaced dragoon!

'In a mind,' he wrote, 'which vice has not utterly divested of sensibility, few occurrences can inflict a more acute pang than the receiving proof of tenderness and love where only resentment and reproach were expected and deserved. The gentle voice of conscience which had incessantly murmured within the soul then raises its tone and speaks with a tongue of thunder. My conduct towards you, and towards my other brothers, has displayed a strange combination of madness, ingratitude, and dishonesty. But you forgive me. May my Maker forgive me! May the time arrive when I shall have forgiven myself!'

Whether Captain James Coleridge was favourably impressed by this letter or not we do not know, but it must have at least convinced him that its writer was more suited for the pulpit than the saddle. And on April 10, 1794, Silas Tomkyn Comberbacke, after enduring a fortnight of daily tumbles off a horse as young and undisciplined as himself, and with his 'shirts worn to rags,' procured his discharge and returned to Cambridge.

§ 4

The immediate result however of the 'shocks of adversity' which had 'electrified his frame' was to make him feel 'a convalescence of soul' and become 'like a being recently formed from the hands of Nature.' His faculties too were greatly refreshed by four months' forced abstention from reading, and since he escaped with no more than an admonishment by Dr. Pearce in the presence of the Fellows, a month's confinement to College, and the task of translating the works of Demetrius Phalareus into

English, his sense of remorse was not unduly prolonged, nor for that matter his newly aroused intention of orderly endeavour.

Certainly he made a beginning. He dropped his acquaintances 'solemnly and for ever,' and in competing once more for the Greek Ode prize, announced his aim to be at 'correctness and perspicuity, not *genius*,' and an avoidance of the sublime and unintelligible. But try as he would, it was the sublime and unintelligible which haunted him and the sentimental which allured. And though he was to exclude genius from his Greek ode, it was to quicken with a sudden momentary inspiration his expression in English poetry.

A dragoonship had not erased from his mind the fugitive image of Mary Evans, but had rather served to idealize it more vividly. And now in the refreshment of his release the dreams of despair which had flattered the pride and soothed the sickness of his nature, excited too his imagination. Suddenly without warning his hunger for the unrealizable melted into music, such music as makes us ask with Ferdinand, 'Where should this music be? I' the air or the earth?' – the music which was to justify Coleridge's life, so long as English poetry is read. Like an incantation it transcends the physical and the intellectual and yet captivates the senses. It hovers in the air like wind and lulls like stealing waters. It is at once transparent and iridescent, unearthly and yet in-woven with rich, dissolving images. No poet could con-trol such enchantment. Like some magic potion it was distilled of strange contrarieties. Coleridge discovered it when circumstances favoured an involuntary surrender to emotion powerful enough to harmonize temporarily all his peculiar faculties and tendencies, his faint physical and far-reaching metaphysical instinct, his langour and his effusiveness, his dreamy mysticism and his pining sensuousness, his hope and his despair. These moments when his nostalgia became creative, his sense of the real just vivid enough to communicate in its elusive motion his prevailing sense of the unreal, were gifts of Fortune, conditioned by a mood more precarious than any healthy creative impulse is, as it was more strange and unanalysable in its issue. His spirits, to use his own description of this state in childhood, came upon him now suddenly and in a flood that swept him into the stream of expressive life and changed the unsatisfied longing over which he had so long impotently brooded into a music as universal in its inspiration as it was personal in its tone. Such was the love-chaunt, the tender appeal and reproach named 'Lewti,' of which he wrote the first draft at this time:

'At midnight by the stream I roved,
To forget the form I loved,
Image of Lewti! from my mind
Depart; for Lewti is not kind.

'The Moon was high, the moonlight gleam
    And the shadow of a star
Heaved upon Tamaha's stream;
    But the rock shone brighter far,
The rock half sheltered from my view
By pendent boughs of tressy yew —
So shines my Lewti's forehead fair,
Gleaming through her sable hair,
Image of Lewti! from my mind
Depart; for Lewti is not kind.

'I saw a cloud of palest hue,
    Onward to the moon it passed;
Still brighter and more bright it grew,
With floating colours not a few,
    Till it reach'd the moon at last;

Then the cloud was wholly bright,
With a rich and amber light!
And so with many a hope I seek
  And with such joy I find my Lewti;
And even so my pale wan cheek
  Drinks in as deep a flush of beauty!
Nay, treacherous image! leave my mind,
If Lewti never will be kind.

'The little cloud – it floats away,
  Away it goes; away so soon?
Alas! it has no power to stay:
Its hues are dim, its hues are grey –
  Away it passes from the moon!
How mournfully it seems to fly,
  Ever fading more and more,
To joyless regions of the sky –
  And now 'tis whiter than before!
As white as my poor cheek will be,
  When, Lewti, on my couch I lie,
A dying man for love of thee.
Nay, treacherous image! leave my mind –
And yet, thou didst not look unkind.

'I saw a vapour in the sky,
  Thin, and white, and very high;
I ne'er beheld so thin a cloud:
  Perhaps the breezes that can fly
  Now below and now above,
Have snatched aloft the lawny shroud
  Of Lady fair – that died for love.
For maids, as well as youths, have perished
From fruitless love too fondly cherished.
Nay, treacherous image! leave my mind –
For Lewti never will be kind.

.   .   .   .

'I know the place where Lewti lies,
When silent night has closed her eyes:
   It is a breezy jasmine-bower,
The nightingale sings o'er her head:
   Voice of the Night! had I the power
That leafy labyrinth to tread,
And creep, like thee, with soundless tread,
I then might view her bosom white
Heaving lovely to my sight,
As these two swans together heave
On the gently-swelling wave.

'Oh! that she saw me in a dream,
   And dreamt that I had died for care;
All pale and wasted I would seem,
   Yet fair withal, as spirits are!
I'd die indeed, if I might see
Her bosom heave, and heave for me!
Soothe, gentle image! soothe my mind!
To-morrow Lewti may be kind.'

In substance this poem, particularly in the last two
stanzas where the inspiration is failing, is as sickly as
many which preceded it, but its sickliness is for the most
part immaterial in both senses of the word. Those 'sounds
and sweet airs that give delight and hurt not,' that buoyant and impalpable rhythm, that sensuous charm refined
as it were by fever, that childlike, yet inevitable simplicity
in which Coleridge was unique as a poet, were heard here
for the first time. Hints of these qualities his earlier verse
had given, but only now were they fully realized.

Yet the realization was fugitive. A month later he
sought relief from the same heart-sickness in a poem
entitled 'The Sigh,' but the miracle was not to be repeated. The *vis inertiæ* had supervened and he could
only write such lines as:

'I fain would soothe the sense of care,
And lull to sleep the Joys that were!
Thy Image may not banished be —
Still, Mary! still I sigh for thee.'

It was not until three years later that through a quick-
ening influence more potent than Mary Evans the power
of poetical enchantment was to return for a brief and
brilliant season, and then fade from a world too hard and
a temperament too stricken to harbour it.

§ 5

Early in June, however, Coleridge took the best
possible measure against introspection by setting out on
a walking tour with his friend Hucks, a cultivated but
not too exciting companion. Instead of going direct to
Ottery, their plan was to reach it by way of Wales, stopping first at Oxford to visit Coleridge's old school-fellow
Allen. The consequences of this chance visit to Oxford
were considerable: for there he met a Balliol undergraduate named Robert Southey, a tall self-possessed
youth two years his junior, with a shrewd face, black
bushy hair, lips almost as full as his own, but decisive in
their lines, and eyes as piercing as his own were softly
luminous. To complete the determination of his aspect,
his nose was high and prominent.

A shrewd observer of the features of these two under-
graduates might have guessed that their temperaments
were complementary. In those of the one was a suave
and judicious self-assurance, the assurance of the man
whose energies are effective because their direction is
limited. In the other's there were no strong lines. His
face like his character was fundamentally formless. By
the way in which it trembled and glowed with feeling,
it proclaimed a nature void of self-considering motives,

a mind incapable of self-limiting aims. Yet both possessed the animation of the poet, and it was doubtless
Coleridge's realization of their inverted correspondence
which led him to write later: 'I think that an admirable
poet might be made by *amalgamating* him and me. I
think too much for a poet, he too little for a great
poèt.'

Both too at this time were in revolt: Southey, with a
dour and definite self-conceit, against every power which
sought to impose its authority on youth; Coleridge, with
an amiable vagueness, against the principle of the finite
in everything. It was as inevitable that two such beings
should immediately coalesce as it was that they should
eventually draw apart.

Their boyhood too showed points of similarity. Robert
Southey was the son of a superior Bristol linen-draper.
Like Coleridge he had as a child no propensity for boyish
sports, although this may have been due to the aunt
who encouraged him rather to stay indoors pricking play-
bills with a needle. The same aunt, who was an amateur
patroness of the Stage, introduced him at an early age to
the theatres of Bath and Bristol, and so quickened his
interest in poetry and drama that he was experimenting
in both before his teens. 'It is the easiest thing in the
world to write a play,' he is reported to have said at the
age of eight, and the remark is typical. Like Coleridge
too he read voraciously, procuring his material from a
circulating library, the Arabian tales amongst it. But
unlike Coleridge he had a passion for historical information and was keenly interested in botany and entomology,
while his earliest compositions took the severe form of
epic dramas. At Westminster School he edited a periodical entitled *The Flagellant*, and was expelled by a humour-
less headmaster for contributing to it an article attacking
corporal punishment. This aét of petty tyranny had

strengthened both his rebellious instinct and his inclination for authorship. He went up to Oxford determined
to discover 'pedantry, prejudice, and aristocracy' if only
as an appropriate background to the attitude that he had
adopted of a 'rebellious spirit, which neither authority
nor oppression could ever bow.' Like Coleridge he had
lost his father, and although supposed to be reading for
Orders, proclaimed his devotion to 'heathen philosophy
and Grecian republicanism.' But his philosophy was
Epicurean rather than Platonic, and his democratic sentiments were practical. He had caught the 'Wilkes and
Liberty Epidemic' as a boy from old periodicals, but it
appealed to him only as a general statement of his own
strong desire not to sacrifice his independence to making
a livelihood. Like Coleridge he had 'pleasing visions of
domestic life,' but they were leavened with the common
sense to be expected of a young man who wrote truly
enough in his twentieth year, 'Don't think me drunk, for
if I am, 'tis with sobriety,' and who was justly described
as possessing 'health, strength of mind, and confirmed
habits of strict morality.'

In his letters he could certainly conceal his 'very strong
predilection for life' under a pose of pompous moralizing
and reflective melancholy, and since his humanitarian
ideals were not, like Coleridge's, a purely subjective
dream, he was not quite so blind to the implications of
the Terror in France. At least it was pleasant to indulge
the sentiment of disillusionment between bouts of defiance, to 'look round the world, and everywhere find the
same mournful spectacle – the strong tyrannizing over
the weak, man and beast; the same depravity pervading
the whole creation; oppression triumphant everywhere':
to write of his hopes as 'extinguished' and of himself as
having 'no object of pursuit in life but to fill the passing
hour and to fit himself for death.'

But while it was agreeable to repeat the prevailing romantic gesture that

'Weary of love, of life, devour'd with spleen,
I rest, a perfect Timon, not nineteen,'

he was far too practical merely to indulge in such sentiments. His was not a nature to find refuge from the depravity of man and beast in conceptions of primeval innocence. At the age of six he had 'formed a delectable plan with two school-mates for going to an island and living by ourselves,' and six months before Coleridge met him he had commended Cowley's intention 'to retire with books to a cottage in America, and seek that happiness in solitude which he could not find in society,' adding that he would 'be pleased to reside in a country where men's abilities would ensure respect . . . and man was considered as more valuable than money; and where I could till the earth, and provide by honest industry the meat which my wife would dress with pleasing care.'

The idea was not visionary. America for him was not a lost Eden to be recovered, but an undeveloped country which offered real opportunities to the pioneer, and he pictured himself as wielding the axe, grubbing up roots, building a snug little dairy, sleeping on rushes, and sharing his labour with an emancipated negro, until the wife presented herself to dress the meat with pleasing care. Rhyming and philosophizing were to occupy his mythical leisure.

The project became more attractive as his prospects of a professional career in medicine or the Civil Service, both of which he contemplated, grew more remote, and his pronounced Unitarianism, confirmed by the intolerance and subservience to 'useless forms' which he found in Oxford, prevented him from considering the Church. And it was at this moment when his plans had failed to mature and his horizon was uncomfortably objectless, that Coleridge descended upon him like a fertilizing sun, bringing to his material project the breath and inspiration of a creative idea.

Coleridge, the most dependent person in the world, had a passion for abstract independence; Southey, most sturdily independent as a man, was too prudent and practical to leap before he looked. The conjunction of the two was exactly calculated to invest with probability a scheme upon which neither alone would have seriously acted. The responsibility belonged to them both, although Southey, the cautious family man of later years, was of course convinced that it was Coleridge and Hucks who introduced the scheme of pantisocracy to him. Doubtless Coleridge christened it, doubtless too he enfolded it in his amazing eloquence, converting a mere suggestion into a cloud-capped vista of fraternal enterprise, but it is difficult to believe that Southey did not originate it. And certainly he materialized it. When the tourists left Oxford the project was still quite fantastic. There was vague talk of collecting as many brother adventurers as possible, of purchasing land with their contributions and cultivating it by their common labour. But like the countless other projects entertained by Coleridge, it would have remained a pleasant subject for a poem, possibly for a prospectus, and assuredly for effusive conversation, had not Southey and his friend Burnett, with conscientious thoroughness, agreed to sit on it like a committee, talk it into shape, and present their report in a few weeks' time. The combination of Rousseauism and Benthamism was irresistible.

§ 6

Meanwhile with a parting toast to 'Health and Republicanism to be!' Coleridge pushed on to Wales, 'now

philosophizing with Hucks, now melancholizing by himself, or else indulging those day-dreams of fancy that
make realities more gloomy . . . ever and anon plucking
the wild flowers of poesy and consigning them to a little
book.' But the philosophizing was commendably rural,
the melancholy was transient, and the wild flowers of
poesy, at any rate in such lines as

> 'And o'er the dowried maiden's glowing cheek
> Bade bridal love suffuse its blushes meek'

would seem to have been plucked before starting in the
Garden of the Reverend William Bowles.

Roads so dazzling in the heat that they seemed to
undulate as they ran across a country bare and unhedged
to the wild heights beyond did not invite gloomy abstraction, still less, when they reached the mountains, the
'sun-glittering water' dashing down rugged clefts which
'soothed without disturbing the ear.' And the towns and
villages they passed offered plenty of diverting incidents,
whether it was the 'two great huge fellows of butcher-like
appearance at Llanfyllin' who, excited by a sermon on
'pantisocracy' or 'asphetism' – the other title which Coleridge had coined for his dream of ideal communism –
'danced about a room in enthusiastic agitation'; the Welsh
democrat at Bala from whom he feared that he had caught
the itch but who was 'charmed by his sentiments, and
bruised his hand with a grasp of ardour'; or the local
worthies in a tavern who were inclined to resent his drinking the health of Dr. Priestley but ended by acclaiming
him 'an open-speaking, honest-hearted fellow.'

At Wrexham, however, his holiday mood was rather
seriously disturbed. He had forgotten that here Miss
Eliza Evans, sister of Mary, lived with her grandmother,
and as chance would have it, Mary Evans herself was on
a visit. While standing at the inn's window he was

amazed to see the two sisters pass. So agitated was he that he 'sickened and well nigh fainted' but managed to conceal his identity. It may be that this fragmentary incident revived his languishing sentiments by recalling, as he put it, ' "thoughts full of bitterness and images" too dearly loved! now past and but "remembered like sweet sounds of yesterday!" ' But for the moment he was too healthily occupied to prolong his reminiscences. 'Love,' as he could write, 'is a local anguish. I am fifty miles distant, and am not half so miserable.' Mary Evans was reserved as a subject for self-wounding soliloquy until a later and more forlorn occasion.

Meanwhile she was superseded by 'the terrible graces of the wild wood scenery,' by a romantic flute player and a mounting moon near a ruined castle at Denbigh, by the spectacle of promiscuous bathing by the naked of both sexes at Abergeley, and by the 'very handsome young lady who put her head out of a coach-window' and paid for a compliment by a charming blush.

And then, when he reached Bristol, Southey and 'Pantisocracy' awaited him; a combination which was so satisfying because it promised to put poetry into practice. To materialize his aspirations he felt more and more to be the essential need of his nature, a need which by himself he could never satisfy. But Southey was a practical man: he had already worked out in detail, with the industry which he brought to everything he undertook, the scheme of colonial communism so vaguely sketched at Oxford. Even the architecture of the literary backwoodsmen's cottages had been planned, and the date of embarkation was to be the following March. The number of gentlemen involved was to be twelve, and they were to be of good education and liberal principles, and were to embark with twelve ladies (qualities unspecified) for 'somewhere in a *delightful part* of the new back settle-

ments.' It is true that 'the *minutiæ* of topographical
information' had yet to be acquired, but a convenient
distance from Cooper's Town, on the banks of the Susquehanna was a picturesque, if scarcely precise, suggestion.
Surely only a 'grand river' could boast so imposing a
name, a name which seemed by some inherent virtue in
it to attract pleasurable associations, and invite such
incantations as:

> 'Yet I will love to follow the sweet dream,
> Where Susquehanna pours his untamed stream,
> And on some hill, whose forest-frowning side
> Waves o'er the murmurs of his calmer tide.'

A communistic colony, it was calculated by reference
to Adam Smith, would only require two or three hours'
manual work a day from each man, provided that the
ensuing winter was spent by those 'whose bodies, from
habits of sedentary study or academic indolence, have
not acquired their full tone and strength' in learning 'the
theory and practice of agriculture and carpentry.' The
rest of their time was to be devoted to study, discussion,
and the enlightened education of the children.

'The regulations relating to the females' caused them
the most difficulty. Did liberal principles, for example,
allow of the marriage contract being dissolved if agreeable to one or both parties? But of the women's employ-
ments there was less doubt. They were 'the care of infant
children and other occupations suited to their strength.'
At the same time the greatest attention was to be paid
to the cultivation of their minds. Apart from this every
one was to enjoy his own religious and political opinions,
and every individual was at liberty to withdraw from the
society whenever he pleased – a concession of somewhat
doubtful value to a forlorn dissenter in the backwoods
of America.

Such a scheme, however, presupposed two things: money and marriage. Not even Coleridge, in the highly edifying and sententious prospectus which he drew up, could altogether avoid reference to these necessities. Certainly the most important point was that all the pioneers, despite the fact that their total was as yet incomplete, were 'highly charged with that enthusiasm which results from strong perceptions of moral rectitude, called into life and action by ardent feelings.' But the fact remained that wives had to be found graced with similar perceptions, and that although each man's *quota* was not 'to be settled with the littleness of arithmetical accuracy,' £2,000 should be the aggregate of their contributions.

He himself had advertised in the *Cambridge Intelligencer* a forthcoming volume of 'Imitations from the Modern Latin, with a Critical and Biographical Essay on the Restoration of Literature' – a work in two volumes in which he was going to introduce, too, 'a copious selection from the Lyrics of Casimir, and a New Translation of the Basia of Secundus.' So far it had not advanced beyond an advertisement, but doubtless with a little effort it would supply the £125 required from himself, while Southey's poem on Joan of Arc would do the same for him. The prospects, however, of the other members of the brotherhood so far enrolled were less encouraging. Neither Robert Lovell (a young Quaker friend of Southey's), George Burnett (the son of a Somersetshire farmer), nor Robert Allen, had private means; while Edmund Seward, who had, was curiously uncertain in his allegiance.

The problem of marriage was, however, more soluble. Lovell had recently married a Miss Mary Fricker, the daughter of an unsuccessful Bristol manufacturer of sugar pans or moulds, who had lately died, leaving his widow and six children wholly unprovided for. Southey had already contracted an informal engagement with her sister Edith, and there remained another daughter, Sarah, whom it was almost uncharitable to exclude from the 'transatlantic pursuit of happiness.' To one at least so susceptible to local atmosphere as Coleridge the suggestion was difficult to resist. 'Pantisocracy' had taken the place of Mary Evans as the elusive image to be caressed, and surely in this case delightfully captured. Sarah Fricker, a comely and sensible young person, fitted excellently into a design so benevolently domestic. His confidence had only to rise for him to declare his affections engaged. And the additional confidence was supplied by a walk with Southey into Somerset to see Burnett and enrol some more recruits and converts.

On the 18th of August they reached the little county town of Nether Stowey, where it nestled at the foot of the Quantock Hills, those 'ferny' hills broken up by steep coombs and wooded glens, over which Coleridge was to wander in the days of his glory and to which he was to return so often in memory in the days of his dejection. And there he met with Thomas Poole.

§ 7

Tom Poole, as he was known to his relations and friends, was a partner in his father's tannery at Stowey. Like the young men who descended upon him, brimming with enthusiastic projects and generous sentiments, he was a man of sufficiently rooted liberal sympathies to preserve his faith in republican and democratic ideas even in the face of the French guillotine. He was convinced that all the powers on earth could not destroy 'the glowing spirit of liberty,' which, he thanked God, pervaded the earth, ceased to powder his hair, read and appreciated Paine's *Rights of Man*, and, practical in everything, arranged to find employment as an ordinary workman in a London tanyard.

Naturally his views exposed him to suspicion and obloquy, the more so because his goodness of heart, capacity and integrity could not be denied. That such a man should sympathize with a movement, which to the conventional-minded stood for nothing but vileness and anarchy, was peculiarly exasperating. Even his cousins, sharing in just such an ignorant and interested panic as has been witnessed in recent years, were pained and shocked. 'To be humane and honest now,' he wrote with justice, 'is to be a traitor to the Constitution, a lover of sedition and licentiousness.'

Yet he was not blinded by his enthusiasms. He trembled 'lest the present excesses may not give a greater stab to liberty than the Tyrants of the world who are combined against it,' and while he hated to see England 'guiltily leagued with despots' by her declaration of war against France, he realized how ambiguous the issue was. 'If the French conquer,' he wrote, 'will licentiousness instead of liberty prevail? If the French are conquered Europe is enslaved.'

And this lover of the 'French Philosophers and friends to mankind' laboured also in the Sunday school. He had not enough imagination to be either a poet or a fanatic, but he had 'a good head and an honest, feeling heart,'and the combination of the two not only enabled him to fulfil a life of usefulness, but also to appreciate genius, the one quality which for him 'covered everything but gross vices' and made him 'tolerant of great errors.' He had entered trade at his father's wish, but he clung quietly and tenaciously in the face of every discouragement to his love of literature and by persistent self-education was well-read.

This was the man, seven years his senior, to whom Coleridge unfolded his pantisocratic scheme. One who

had described the French Constitution as 'the most beautiful fabrick that was ever erected by the human mind' could
not fail to be appreciative. And only a year before he had
confessed: 'I am weary of thinking of European politicks.
America seems the only asylum of peace and liberty – the
only place where the dearest feelings of men are not
insulted; in short, the only spot where a man the least
humane and philosophical can live happily.' But although
Poole really felt this, really agonized over the inhumanity
of European civilization with a sincerity unknown to
Coleridge's sentimental egotism, and although he had
himself practised the ideal of a contemplative life based
on manual industry, he was too sane to accept more than
the abstract beauty of the airy pinnacles which he saw
rise before his eyes. He was not the man to damp
enthusiasm. But his face, at once shrewd and sensitive,
assumed, we fancy, a quizzical expression. The eyes
were all kindness, the mouth was too practical to agree.
'Could they realize their plan,' he confided to a friend,
'they would, indeed, realize the age of reason; but however
perfectible human nature may be, I fear it is not yet perfect
enough to exist long under the regulations of such a system'; and he added the obvious criticism that 'a man
would do well first to see the country and his future hopes,
before he removes his connections or any large portion of
his property there.'

But his whole heart, so tender and tolerant, sweet, wholesome and staunch, went out to Coleridge himself. Whatever his projects or ideas they reflected a sincerely humanitarian personality, and it was a genius who expressed them.
Southey, he seems to have felt instinctively, was just the
clever young man who proclaimed his essential orthodoxy
by the very violence of his heresies, the sort of theatrical
young man who on hearing of Robespierre's death in his
presence, laid his head down upon his arms and exclaimed,

'I had rather have heard of the death of my own father.' It was safe to prophesy that in middle age he would lecture young poets for their Jacobinical extravagance.

But Coleridge was of another order. He satisfied his expectations of a poet, he beamed benevolence, he made his hearer almost ashamed of common sense when he pronounced that 'men anxious for this world are like owls that wake all night to catch mice.' And plainly, from his own account, Coleridge talked to him not only 'with much elegance and energy, and with uncommon facility' but, as occasion arose, in that tone of moral self-disapprobation, very affecting to a Sunday-school teacher, which he had adopted towards Captain James Coleridge a year before, confessing with earnest regret to feeling 'the justice of Providence in the want of those interior abilities which are necessary to the rational discharge of the duties of life,' admitting that 'his aberrations from prudence had been great,' but promising now 'to be as sober and rational as his most sober friends could wish' – a promise all the more endearing because it could so obviously not be kept.

Poole's own habit too of philosophizing in things, though on a far less ambitious plane, would draw him to one who would philosophize even the gnat which bit him; while Coleridge on his part derived great satisfaction from intercourse with a man who actually produced an article of primary necessity, who did succeed in reconciling abstract concerns with concrete activity, like the cobbler which he had wanted to be.

The best proof of the feasibility of 'pantisocracy' was that such a man did not deny it. The real reason of course was that Poole had not the heart to do so, although even he may have been dazzled by Coleridge's eloquent confusion of fact and conjecture. For such a scheme was not unfeasible in itself if it had had an adequate practical basis. But unfortunately the generous spirits who could make a private experiment in communism a success usually lack the initial, and, in a still predatory world, essential means, while those who possess the means are too comfortable to be fired by an ideal. Many an undergraduate since has sketched just such an Utopia in the fraternal atmosphere of a college room and drawn back from attempting to put it into practice through cowardice and convention rather than prudence and reason.

But science had not sanctified caution and verification in 1794. The recklessness natural to two young poets was enhanced by the reckless forces of the age into which they were born. The way in which even moderate men turned their eyes to America was in itself significant. Life seemed to be smothered in Europe, and the effort of emancipation there was so difficult. It was so much easier to escape and start afresh, just as in literature it was so much easier to cast off the logic which had degenerated into a barren correctness, and consecrate feeling, whatever its quality, as the only value. It was so much easier to pour faith into words, to oppose nature to civilization, without examining the facts of either, liberty to authority, sentiment to social abuse. It flattered an undisciplined egotism to be intoxicated with feeling rather than first saddened and then braced by the truth. For the facile romantic is not content to state his ideal in unqualified terms and then work for it. He deludes himself that he has realized it by professing it.

Thus 'pantisocracy' was symbolical of the strength and weakness of the Romantic Movement which had already begun. Essentially right as were the fraternal ideals which animated it, they were prejudiced by the motive of escape. The motive which inspired the Pilgrim Fathers in their transatlantic venture was one of stern refusal. But Coleridge was only capable of refusing to see the actuality which balked his visionary delight, the actuality of his own nature and of non-existent funds. Many other projects in his life were feasible, but he lacked the will to carry them through: in this case he had the will, but the project was quite unpractical.

Unfortunately, however, for him the matter did not end there. Whatever Southey's temporary convictions were, they did not entangle him in mistakes which he could never rectify. But the scheme meant far more to Coleridge, it meant, as he felt, no less than a solution of a crying inner need, the reconciliation of the theoretical enthusiast in him and the real man, an escape from that solitary slavery to the abstract which was both his luxury and his torture. To achieve this contact between himself and a physical, social existence, he was willing to sacrifice every other need; to achieve it at once it was necessary to banish all doubts of the project's realization.

And so, on his return to Bristol, to fortify his sense of the irrevocable nature of the enterprise, he engaged himself to Sarah Fricker. It did not matter that only a month before he had written of Mary Evans that 'her image is in the sanctuary of my heart, and never can it be torn away but with the strings that grapple it to life.'

It had been superseded for the moment by another and surely more tangible image, or rather by a beautiful but empty frame which it was agreeable to fill with the concrete figure of a pantisocratic wife to be.

§ 8

The rest of August Coleridge spent at Bristol with 'thoughts of the day and visions of the night' centred on America. These thoughts and visions, however, do not seem to have advanced the 'Imitations from the Modern Latin' which were to produce his quota to the funds. It was more fitting for a good pantisocrat to collaborate even in authorship and to select a topical theme. Lovell's 'sportive' suggestion therefore of 'Robespierre' as a dramatic subject was enthusiastically accepted, and Coleridge, Southey and himself each agreed to produce an act in twenty-four hours. Such conditions were not calculated to produce anything of artistic significance. But though Coleridge's sole aim was 'to imitate the empassioned and highly figurative language of the French Orators,' a style which he parodied in loose dialogue about violence, conspiracy, the popular voice, liberty and expediency, he did express himself in two passages; in the lines in which he spoke of a character as

'one
Who flies from silent solitary anguish,
Seeking forgetful peace amid the jar
Of elements. The howl of maniac uproar
Lulls to sad sleep the memory of himself.
A calm is fatal to him – then he feels
The dire upboilings of the storm within him.'

a passage which, divested of melodrama, is illuminating self-confession; and in that song:

'Soft nurse of pain, it soothes the weary soul
Of care, sweet as the whisper'd breeze of evening
That plays around the sick man's throbbing temples,'

which embodies the hunger for domestic harmony which deluded him into attaching himself to Sarah Fricker.

'Tell me, on what holy ground
May domestic peace be found?
Halcyon daughter of the skies,
Far on fearful wing she flies,
From the pomp of scepter'd state,
From the rebel's noisy hate,
In a cottag'd vale she dwells
List'ning to the Sabbath bells!

Still around her steps are seen
Spotless honour's meeker mien,
Love, the sire of pleasing fears,
Sorrow smiling through her tears,
And conscious of the past employ,
Memory, bosom-spring of joy.'

Despite, however, a very suitable dedication to Mrs.
Hannah More, the Bristol bookseller to whom the play
was offered would have none of it, and it was not until later
that it was accepted by a charitable Cambridge publisher.

In London, however, to which Coleridge journeyed at
the end of August, 'pantisocracy' found much cheering
support. Dyer, to whom he was introduced by a Cambridge
friend, was 'enraptured' by his exposition of the system
and pronounced it 'impregnable.' And if the value of the
opinion of the absent-minded author of *The Complaints of
the Poor* was uncertain, 'a most intelligent young man'
who had spent the last five years of his life in America
corroborated it. He came regularly every evening to
'benefit by conversation,' assured Coleridge that £2,000
would do, that the land could be bought a great deal
cheaper on the spot, and that twelve men could easily
clear 300 acres in four or five months, while for an additional 600 dollars a thousand acres could be cleared and
houses built on them – a plan which in the interests of
'social converse' he thought worth considering.

As for Susquehanna, it justified its name. Its beauty
was 'excessive' and it was immune from hostile Indians.
Moreover, he had never seen a *bison* in his life, though
he had heard of them. But they were 'Quite backwards,'
while the mosquitoes were 'not as bad as our gnats.' In
addition there were visions of limitless credit: every possible assistance would be given, though by whom it was
not specified, and – most enigmatic reassurance of all –

'literary characters made money there.' It was surely a miraculous land.

Primed with such encouragement Coleridge returned to Cambridge and immediately wrote in a perfect frenzy of enthusiasm:

'I am at last arrived at Jesus. My God! how tumultuous are the movements of my heart. Since I quitted this room what and how important events have evolved! America! Southey! Miss Fricker! . . . Pantisocracy! Oh! I shall have such a scheme of it! My head, my heart, are all alive. I have drawn up my arguments in battle array: they shall have the *tactician* excellence of the mathematician, with the enthusiasm of the poet. The head shall be the mass; the heart, the fiery spirit that fills, informs and agitates the whole. SHAD GOES with us: HE IS MY BROTHER!! . . . I am longing to be with you: make Edith my sister. Surely, Southey, we shall be *frendotatoi meta frendous* – most friendly where all are friends. She must, therefore, be more emphatically my sister.'

Shad was the manservant of Southey's rich Aunt Tyler, whom, unknown as yet to her, as indeed was the whole scheme, the pantisocrats intended ruthlessly removing to America to assist in the clearing of the 300 acres. But Coleridge in his fraternal orgy smothered in abstract embraces not only the members of the prospective brotherhood, but even a young jackass which browsed on Jesus Piece; and while Southey and Shad moved him to prose, he hailed this 'Innocent foal' as 'Brother' in verse, protesting his love of 'the languid patience' of its face and his longing to take it with him

'In the Dell
Of Peace and mild equality to dwell,
Where Toil shall call the charmer Health his bride,
And Laughter tickle Plenty's ribless side!'

protesting that its 'dissonant harsh bray of joy' would there be more 'musically sweet' to him

'Than warbled melodies that soothe to rest
The aching of pale Fashion's vacant breast!'

Even Titania was not more immoderately bewitched.

But while Southey was agreeably affected by these freaks of frantic enthusiasm, there was one matter which disturbed his inherent correctness. The touch of personal attention was strangely lacking in Coleridge's addresses to Sarah Fricker. He had not written to her for a full fortnight after his departure, and when admonished for his neglect he excused himself a little too effusively to be convincing and ended with the rather ominous remark — 'my heart is very heavy, much more so than when I began to write.'

The news which reached him in October was calculated to make it heavier. Southey's mother, who at one time had been reported to be 'fully convinced of the propriety of our resolution,' admiring the plan and enrolling herself in the company, had now announced that her son was not to entertain it. But there was worse to come. Southey had hinted that Aunt Tyler might prove a somewhat refractory critic when their intentions were disclosed to her. But her anger exceeded his gloomiest expectations. It was not merely that she objected to the abduction of 'Shad.' She treated the whole scheme as preposterous, and to prove her sincerity expelled her nephew from her house on a stormy night and declared that she would never see him again nor open a letter of his writing. During the four-hour walk back to Bath which this inhuman treatment necessitated, in pelting rain and the company of a drunken old man of sixty, it may be conjectured that the tide of 'new life, new hope, new energy' which had been running so strongly before began to ebb, and that 'the

faculties of his mind' ceased to be so genially dilated.
For Aunt Tyler was their financial hope. Of course
Southey continued to write jauntily; only so could he
preserve his self-respect, but the gradual descent towards
a complete surrender of the scheme had begun, and he
was soon to make the shocking suggestion that co-opera-
tive farming in some retired part of Wales should be substituted for Paradise by the Susquehanna.

A reaction from such a debauch of enthusiasm as Coleridge had indulged in was due, and this news hastened it.
He was alone in Cambridge. People would listen to his
pantisocratic talk and admire the performance, but they
would laugh too. Was it true, as one of them had said, that
the strength of his imagination had intoxicated his reason,
and that the acuteness of his reason had given a directing
influence to his imagination? Perhaps precipitance was
wrong, perhaps he had once again, as in his military venture, been the 'slave of impulse, the child of imbecility.'
Suddenly the light went out which had illuminated his
cloudy palaces: they seemed like the framework which
had upheld overnight a firework set-piece. He felt limp
and incapable, nerveless and unreal. His very faith in
fraternity failed him! He was once again thrown back
upon himself and submerged in solitary self-disgust.

Even a company of actors who were visiting Cambridge,
which included six sisters 'said to be the most literary of
the beautiful, and the most beautiful of the literary,' with
whom he drank tea and to one of whom he addressed a
poem, could not divert him. His faculties and discern-
ment were 'so completely jaundiced by vexation that the
Virgin Mary and Mary Flanders, alias Moll, would appear
in the same lines.' His fraternalism was so summarily
quenched that he could confess to Southey that he was
'out of love with everybody.'

Inevitably he returned to his old narcotic of self-pitying

verse. A friend, he told Southey, had lately departed this
life in a frenzy induced by anxiety. Poor fellow, 'a child of
frailty like me!' – so like, that he could commemorate him
by mourning over himself in elegiac strains:

'As oft in Fancy's thought thy grave I pass,
And sit me down upon its recent grass,
With introverted eye I contemplate
Similitude of soul – perhaps of fate!
To me hath Heaven with liberal hand assign'd
Energic Reason and a shaping mind,
The daring soul of Truth, the Patriot's part
And Pity's sigh, that breathes the gentle heart –
Sloth-jaundiced all! and from my graspless hand
Drop Friendship's precious pearls, like hour-glass sand.
I weep, yet stoop not! the faint anguish flows,
A dreamy pang in Morning's feverish doze.'

But such introversion he knew to be deadly. It was true
that 'like a sick physician, feeling the pang acutely' he yet
'derived a wonted pleasure from examining its progress
and developing its causes.' But the pain exceeded the
pleasure. He must escape it, and if 'pantisocracy' had
failed as a means, perhaps Mary Evans would not. The
glimpse of her at Wrexham tantalized his memory. She
had started and looked wonderingly before he hid himself,
and passed and repassed the inn with mute inquiry. Had
he cruelly misjudged the situation in abruptly ending his
correspondence with her? Had rumour lied? Was there
still a chance that his 'Evening Star' would shine again,
that his 'bleeding Heart' – as he fancied it in the sudden
revulsion from a mistress who was a detail in a clouded
system—might be healed?

'Faint was that Hope, and rayless! – Yet 'twas fair
And soothed with many a dream the hour of rest.'

Surely he should have 'nursed it with an agony of care' instead of rejecting it so summarily.

The problem was now how to convey to Southey the revolution which had occurred in his sentiments, to Southey, who was repeating his reproaches for his neglect of Sarah Fricker with a tiresome persistence, and who, unless an adequate reason was given, must condemn as the basest disloyalty his withdrawal from the pantisocratic venture. He did it by quoting a letter, presumably fictitious, which he claimed to have received three weeks before unsigned, but which he immediately recognized as from Mary Evans. In it she conjured him earnestly and solemnly to consider long and deeply, before he entered into any rash schemes. 'There is an eagerness,' the letter continued, 'in your Nature, which is ever hurrying you in the sad Extreme. I have heard that you mean to leave England, and on a Plan so absurd and extravagant that where I for a moment to imagine it *true*, I should be obliged to listen with a more patient Ear to suggestions, which I have rejected a thousand times with scorn and anger. Yes! whatever Pain I might suffer, I should be forced to exclaim: "O what a noble mind is here *o'erthrown*, Blasted with ecstasy." You have a country, does it demand nothing of you? You have doting Friends! will you break their Hearts! There is a God – Coleridge! Though I have been told (*indeed* I do not believe it) that you doubt of his existence and disbelieve a hereafter – No! You have too much sensibility to be an Infidel.'

The letter which Mary Evans was really to write Coleridge two months later – sober, tactful and matter-of-fact as he himself testified – no less than the familiar pulpit style of this theatrical invention, is proof enough that it emanated from himself. And it served a double purpose. It threw doubt by proxy on the scheme in which Coleridge had lost faith, and it provided him with material to which, if his renewed sentiments for Mary Evans should after all evoke a response, he could point as the cause and in some sense the justification of his unaccountable change of mood.

Not that he confessed to Southey as yet his treason. He needed to be sure of the new love before he denied the old. And at the moment he was sure of nothing. His thoughts were 'floating about in a most chaotic state.' But Southey would realize how disturbing such a letter would be. 'I loved her,' he wrote, 'almost to madness. Her image was never absent from me for three years. My resolution has not faltered, but I want a comforter.'

And Sarah Fricker was no longer a comforter. She was only one 'whom by every tie of reason and honour I ought to love.' 'I am resolved,' he added, 'but wretched! But time shall do much. You will easily believe that with such feelings, I should have found it no easy task to write to – (he could not even bring himself to write her name). I should have detested myself, if after my first letter I had written coldly – how could I write as *warmly?*'

And now for the first time differences of opinion appeared between himself and Southey over the details of 'pantisocracy' itself. The critical judgment was no longer in abeyance and abstract arguments helped to divert his mind from introspection. Southey's suggestion, for example, that 'Shad' should be employed in the toil of the field while they were pursuing philosophical studies was surely as bad an inequality as that of 'Earldoms or Emperorships.' He was introducing servitude into the society, a statement to which doubtless 'Shad' would have assented if he had had to listen to Coleridge's metaphysics. And though his 'feeble and exhausted heart' regarded even this 'with a criminal indifference,' he must protest.

What woman too was really loyal to libertarian principles? Even a sympathetic Cambridge critic had warned

him that he would never give his *women* 'sufficient strength
of mind, liberality of heart, or vigilance of attention.
They would spoil it.'

And then in a feverish rebound from doubt and dejection he would feel almost confident, until his thoughts
turned to Mary Evans and he swooned at the remembrance
of her. 'Whatever of mind we *will* to do, we *can* do!
What, then, palsies the will? The joy of grief. A mysterious pleasure broods with dusky wings over the tumultuous
mind. . . . She *was very* lovely, Southey! We formed
each other's minds; our ideas were blended. Heaven
bless her! I cannot forget her. Every day her memory
sinks deeper into my heart.'

How hatefully the female contingent of pantisocrats
intruded upon such dreams. '*That* Mrs. Fricker!' for
example. 'We shall have her teaching the infants *Christianity* – I mean that mongrel whelp that goes under its
name – teaching them by stealth in some ague fit of superstition!' . . . 'Have our Women been taught by us habitually to contemplate the littleness of individual comforts
and a passion for the *novelty* of the scheme rather than a
generous enthusiasm for Benevolence? Are they saturated
with the Divinity of Truth sufficiently to be always weakful?' Will 'the *Mothers* tinge the minds of the infants with
prejudications?' And was not the addition of children
'subversive of *rational* hopes of a permanent system? . . .
the little Frickers, for instance, and your brothers – are
they not already deeply tinged with the prejudices and
errors of society? Have they not learned from their
schoolfellows *Fear* and *Selfishness*, of which the necessary offsprings are Deceit and desultory Hatred? How
are we to prevent them from infecting the minds of *our*
children?'

Such were some of the querulous questions which he
rained upon Southey in the attempt to conceal from him

and from himself the fact that his longings had turned in another direction, although he still professed his willingness to accompany him on 'an imperfect system.' But his condition was too hysterical to be eased even by arguing about fixed principles. He could no longer endure the isolation of Cambridge, heightened as it was by stabs of coldness and reproach from home, and on November 8 he drove up to London in the phaeton of a Mr. Potter, of Emmanuel.

There at least he was near 17 Sackville Street, and to that address, 'after infinite struggles of irresolution,' early in December he despatched a letter, in which he asked Mary Evans whether or no she was engaged to Mr. – . 'Read this letter,' he wrote, 'with benevolence – and consign it to oblivion.' And after describing the course of his attachment for her and how brotherly affection had imperceptibly changed into 'a Passion which he felt neither the power or the courage to subdue,' he added – 'Indulge, Mary, this my first, my last request, and restore me to Reality, however gloomy. Sad and full of heaviness will the intelligence be; my heart will die within me. . . . I will not disturb your peace by even a *look* of Discontent, still less will I offend your ear by the whine of selfish Sensibility. In a few months I shall enter at the Temple, and there seek forgetful calmness where only it can be found – in incessant and useful activity.'

'The Temple' was the last fiction which Coleridge was able to associate with Mary Evans. Her reply, though it was compassionate and even self-accusatory, was decisive. It restored him to some sense at least of reality. Divested of hope, his 'passion' lost 'its disquieting power.' No one knew better than he, who seldom achieved it, what comfort was to be derived from this sense. Even a desolating fact was a straw, to which, drowning in the pool of his own emotions, he could cling. 'The workings of one's imagination,' as he was to write, 'go beyond the worst that Nature afflicts us with; they have the terror of a superstitious circumstance.' And now one superstitious circumstance was removed and he could enjoy the pose of moral self-denial, writing that far distant from her he would journey through the vale of Men in calmness, since he could not 'long be wretched who dared to be actively virtuous.' Philosophy, too, offered its compensations; for 'Had I been united to her, the excess of my affection would have effeminated my intellect.'

Mary Evans was, with one possible exception, the only woman who entered Coleridge's life for whom he really felt more than a brotherly fondness. Yet even for her it was only in absence that his self-indulgent feeling faintly approximated to passion. And now her removal as an incitement to dreaminess of mind and sense induced a calm as pleasing 'as an autumnal day, when the sky is covered with grey moveless clouds.' It was rather the prospect of being actively virtuous, as Southey interpreted it, that pained him. 'To lose her!' he wrote to him, 'I can rise above that selfish pang. But to marry another. O Southey! bear with my weakness. Love makes all things pure and heavenly like itself – but to marry a woman whom I do *not* love, to degrade her whom I call my wife by making her the instrument of low desire, and on the removal of a desultory appetite to be perhaps not dis-pleased with her absence! Enough! These refinements are the wildering fires that lead me into vice. Mark you, Southey! *I will do my duty.*'

The pronouncement seems to have contented Southey, but in his heart he must have begun to suspect that Cole-ridge was as incapable of doing his duty as of experiencing a low desire. He had too faint a grasp on things for either.

§ 9

Nevertheless towards the end of December he was resolved, whatever the consequences, to be at Bath by the following Saturday. But a new comforter interposed, 'a man of uncommon genius,' once his schoolfellow and now a clerk in the East India House. Like himself Charles Lamb was at this time 'a Unitarian Christian, and an advocate for the automatism of man.' But it was not so much his opinions as his suffering sensibility that attracted. He too was haunted by an inveterate subjectivity, felt isolated and neurotic. He even dreaded insanity, not having yet achieved that close contact with and so understanding of life which was later to enable him to sweeten tragedy itself with serenity. He was 'sore galled with disappointed hope' and, like Coleridge himself, inclined to make the most of it, 'Sickly Hope with waning eye' being 'well content to droop and die.'

In the little smoky room at the 'Salutation and Cat' the two hypochondriacs, eating welsh-rabbit, drinking 'egg-hot' and 'smoking Oronooko,' beguiled the cares of life by completely forgetting them. Coleridge, of course, had no intention of ever returning to Cambridge. It was too full of painful memories, too much the stage of an impossible dilemma. Yet it was pleasant to drug himself against the thought that in so doing he was rejecting the possibility of a conventional career and attaching himself to what, amid the human bustle of the London streets, seemed a painfully cold and distant creed.

As usual he drugged himself with talk. Lamb, whose stutter encouraged brevity in his own utterance, was a very sympathetic listener, and, if he failed him, there were always customers to the house, appreciative idlers who enjoyed the display so much as a sort of musical undertone to their libations that the innkeeper even offered him free quarters if he would become a permanent entertainer. And he drugged himself with poetry and with metaphysics too, reciting, as Lamb put it:

'Many an holy lay
That, mourning, soothed the mourner on his way,'

and completing a poem on which he had been working ever since his military escapade, a desultory effusion in which he sought, as unsuccessfully in verse as he was to do in life, to materialize his pantisocratic idealism.

'Thought,' he was to write later of an ode, 'is the body; enthusiasm the soul; and imagination the drapery.' The phrases are too abstract to be really enlightening as criticism, but they do in a general way describe the constituents of such of his verse as that of which 'Religious Musings' is the first ambitious example. They explain, too, its failure as poetry. For philosophic verse is really a contradiction in terms. Poetry may, great poetry must, express a philosophy, but it must express it in the immediate and plastic terms of poetry. Its body of thought and its soul of enthusiasm must be fused in an imaginative act. With Coleridge this fusion seldom occurred. And so his enthusiasm floated like a beautiful or merely dimming vapour about a body of ideas, which, instead of being converted into images, were merely draped in a loose garment of metaphors.

Not yet did he recognize where his fundamental incapacity lay, that it lay in a constitutional inability to cut into the world of fact, without which his imagination could never function healthily, but only sail like an enchanted ship or drift like a derelict in the unmapped seas of the miraculous or the abstract. Later indeed he was to recognize it and experience the despair only possible to a poet who knows in theory the creative principles which some disorganization of temperament prevents him from practising. But for the time he imputed his dissatisfaction to the 'body of thought,' which crowded his poetry and made it 'sweat beneath a heavy burden of ideas and imagery,' admitting it 'elaborate and swelling,' yet 'the heart not owns it.'

'Religious Musings,' like its companion poem 'The Destiny of Nations,' was certainly crowded with such unassimilated notions and with a typical array of personified attributes, partnered according to their moral or immoral tendencies with graceful or opprobrious epithets. In purpose it was a hymn of worship to Love as a creative, harmonizing spirit, through which the self was annihilated and the creature might achieve identity with the Creator. But the young neo-Platonic, pantisocratic Unitarian could scarcely claim to be a poet in such lines as:

> 'There is one mind, one omnipresent Mind
> Omnific. His most holy name is Love.
> Truth of subliming import! with the which
> Who feeds and saturates his constant soul
> He from his small particular orbit flies
> With blest outstarting!'

The poem had been begun a year before, when the offer of a treaty with the French Republic had been rejected on the now familiar grounds that the preservation of the Christian religion depended on the continuation of the war. It was therefore a political as well as a metaphysical tract, passing from a high-flown enunciation of transcendental principles to their practical application as the force which 'fraternizes man' in contrast with the 'embattling Interests' which divide him. Erring Priests, property and 'the low puppetry of thrones' were ranged against enlightened philosophers and scientists and 'the vacant Shepherd' who in a conveniently 'dateless' age cultivated all

the pastoral virtues; until in a final burst of exotic rapture
the poet saw earth once more occupied by the 'vast family
of Love,' the massy gates of Paradise thrown open,

> 'and forth come in fragments wild
> Sweet echoes of unearthly melodies,
> And odours snatched from beds of amaranth.'

The final rapture was as unreal as the preceding rhetoric.
Once again Coleridge was flying from a teasing world to
drug himself with 'strange beatitudes.' His philosophy
was the servant of his temperament. He longed for 'the
plenitude and permanence of bliss' and he thought it was
to be captured by a vague sensational excess. For this,
despite all his metaphysical jargon, was what his conception of love amounted to.

To annihilate self was not for him to purify and humanize instinct by intelligence and so to pierce through the
actual to the real, but to dissolve in a featureless ecstasy.
It was not to heighten and deepen consciousness, but to
lose it or at best to wander over

> 'Heights most strange,
> Whence Fancy falls, fluttering her idle wing.'

Such an escape is no solution of discord either for mankind or, as he was to learn, for the individual. At most
it can only afford a moment's respite and render more
grievous the return to the actual. Coleridge was as incapable of facing the facts of his own as of human nature, and
so his religious philosophy, like his political idealism, his
poetry and his life, was to prove a fugitive activity, and
'the whole' for which he hungered was always to elude him
where he stood, not indeed 'blinded by lusts' as he pictured
the 'disinherited soul' in this poem, but blinded by the

want of them, and for an exactly opposite reason to the
sensual egotist, having 'no common centre,' a

> 'solitary thing
> Mid countless brethren with a lonely heart.'

For the universal cannot be satisfactorily experienced as a
pure abstraction. As such it can only be discoursed upon.
And just as Coleridge was all his life to long for that vital
communication with men and things, which he knew to
be necessary to health and happiness, so as a thinker he
was to move in involved circles of argument about a
reality which he could never seize because he could not
relate it to fact.

Yet when he directed his flight to Nature and not to
'Nature's essence,' he drew at least within reach of poetry,
as when he wrote:

> 'Beneath some arched romantic rock reclined
> They felt the sea-breeze lift their youthful locks;
> Or in the month of blossoms, at mild eve,
> Wandering with desultory feet inhaled
> The wafted perfumes, and the flocks and woods
> And many-tinted streams and setting sun
> With all his gorgeous company of clouds
> Ecstatic gazed! then homeward as they strayed
> Cast the sad eye to earth, and inly mused
> Why there was misery in a world so fair.'

Coleridge never went beyond such transitory musings,
since to do so conflicted with the desires which he mistook
for convictions; and then the problem of evil and of pain,
being to some extent at least a problem of fact, was difficult
to grasp for one who 'soaring aloft' breathed

> 'the empyreal air
> Of love, omnific, omnipresent Love.'

It was easier to indulge in phantom horrors, to describe for example one whom

> 'Some Fury fondled in her hate to man,
> Bidding her serpent hair in mazy surge
> Lick his young face, and at his mouth inbreathe
> Horrible sympathy!'

Few indeed could have foretold that these qualities of relaxed sensuousness and fanciful hysteria should in three years be transmuted into magic.

Towards the end of 'Religious Musings' however there is a reference to one

> 'of mortal kind
> Wisest, he first who marked the ideal tribes
> Up the fine fibres through the sentient brain,'

who was to supply Coleridge with a staple subject of conversation for the rest of his life. At the moment he was as enthusiastic an admirer of Hartley's empirical philosophy as he was later to be an interminable critic. His opinion of Godwin, whom he had met since coming to London and described as a 'necessitarian,' underwent a similar revolution, but not until he had acclaimed him in a sonnet which he sent to the *Morning Chronicle*, with whose editor and proprietor he had dined. This sonnet was one in a series of no great merit contributed to the same paper in praise or vituperation of public characters so various as Burke and Mrs. Siddons, Pitt and the Reverend William Bowles.

§ 10

Meanwhile the Bristol pantisocrats were growing impatient. No letter had been received for weeks either by

Southey or Sarah Fricker, and they began to think that
Coleridge's family had placed him somewhere in confinement. At last, information being received that the fugitive
was residing at the 'Angel' Inn in Butcher Hall Street,
Southey presented himself like an officer of the pressgang
and bore him off to Bristol.

Coleridge made no resistance. It was nice to be cap-
tured, and a day or two in company with the brotherhood
restored his enthusiasm. At least they provided him with
a variable audience to whom, seven times a week, with the
smallest excuse, he could discourse on the idealism of
Bishop Berkeley and the infamies of that 'dark scowler'
Mr. Pitt, or eulogize those three indispensable books,
Simpson's Euclid, Hartley 'On Man,' and Bowles' Poems.
He, Southey and Burnett lodged together at 48 College
Street, and for the moment quite fraternally. If Southey
had begun to suspect that 'no dependence could be placed
on Coleridge,' he concealed the fact and was proud to
declare that 'our names are written in the book of destiny,
on the same page.'

But the possibilities of theory were now for all but
Coleridge almost exhausted. March was drawing near.
Aunt Tyler preserved a morose silence, *Robespierre* and
Joan of Arc had not sold, and *The Imitations from the
Modern Latin* was merely a forgotten advertisement. It
was necessary to explore other financial avenues. They
might lecture, they might produce a magazine, they might
publish some more poetry. An introduction to a young
Bristol bookseller named Cottle led them to favour the
third alternative. It was true that he seemed disinclined to
join the 'social colony' on the banks of the Susquehanna,
abstract ratiocination making little impression on his
business instinct. But he was very appreciative when
Coleridge and Southey read him their poems, offered
each of them twenty guineas for the copyright, increased

it in Coleridge's case to thirty, and kindly assisted
when the landlady pressed for payment or the larder
was bare.

Coleridge set to work at once, but it was fortunate that
Cottle was so impressed by 'an eye, a brow, and a forehead, indicative of commanding genius,' that he made
every allowance. The printer, however, had no such
impression to support his patience. He objeﬅed to having
his types locked up week after week 'to his great detri-
ment' through long continued delays in the delivery of
copy. It seemed so unnecessary too since the procrastinat-
ing poet had repeated to Cottle almost all the poems he
intended colleﬅing; they needed only transcribing. But,
as Coleridge pathetically pleaded, he had very little 'finger
industry'; the very aﬅ of writing things down made them
so painfully material and put the bridle on a mind which
needed to be 'always at full stretch.' And even if his
fingers would work, circumstances were 'brain-crazing,'
or he was ill, or it only wanted another day or two
and a fat bundle of manuscript would, he felt sure, be
ready.

The projeﬅ of leﬅures, however, did materialize without delay. It was the one aﬅivity which, with a necessary
reminder as to date and time, he could be relied upon to
perform, since his leﬅuring was as involuntary and usually
as unprepared as his conversation, and he enjoyed the
one exaﬅly as he enjoyed the other. Both enabled him,
not so much to express, as to relieve himself. The advertised theme of the leﬅures might be political, his professed
aim a polemic against the war with France, for example, or
the Pitt and Grenville Aﬅs for gagging the Press, but it
was not for one whose mind 'soared above the present
state of humanity' and might be 'justly said to dwell in
the presence of the Most High' to be bound by petty
detail.

The audience which gathered in the Corn Market or the vacant house in Castle Green discovered a lay-preacher, not a stump-orator, one who continually asserted 'the propriety and utility of holding up the distant mark of attainable perfection,' who urged the cultivation of the 'sympathetic passions' and of 'moral taste,' who spoke of benevolence as 'the silken thread that runs through the pearl-chain of all the virtues,' and looked forward 'to that glorious period when justice shall have established the universal fraternity of love.'

Possibly these 'soul-ennobling views' would have more quickly wearied the Bristol Radicals had not the lecturer on occasions leavened his idealism with ingenious humour, as when he recited a letter from 'Liberty' to his dear friend 'Famine' or discoursed on the Hair Powder Tax with inimitable archness. A series of lectures on Revealed Religion, its Corruptions and its Political Views, led to an invitation to preach in a Unitarian chapel at Bath, but here unfortunately humour could not be indulged. And when, to the dismay of the gentleman who had issued the invitation, he insisted on appearing in the pulpit with his blue coat and waistcoat undraped, and then proceeded to inflict on the congregation a previously delivered lecture on the Corn Laws, his reception was somewhat chilly. It was even chillier when, stimulated by his dinner, he compelled them to listen in the afternoon to his old lecture in reprobation of the Hair Powder Tax, divested of its whimsical frolics. Yet, despite their fatuities and their facile edification, his preaching and lecturing did reveal an attitude to life essentially religious. He was still vital and true enough to insist that Christian values should inspire politics and economics as well as private conduct, and to realize the frequent insignificance of dogma.

Meanwhile, however, the 'silken thread of benevolence' that had run through the pantisocratic brotherhood began to wear perilously thin. A 'marked coolness,' for example, had appeared between Coleridge and Lovell, who was far from being convinced by Coleridge's attentions to his sister-in-law. Southey too, as Coleridge confided to Burnett, was curiously distant at times, if not estranged. Could it be that he was losing sympathy, that practicality was undermining the fraternal faith which it had once so attractively graced? Why, he asked himself, must people change? Why could they not preserve their enthusiasms in simple disregard of circumstance? It was true that neither lecturing nor poetry seemed likely to bring the realization of 'pantisocracy' nearer; he even admitted that its realization was 'distant – perhaps a miraculous millennium,' but that did not alter its essential, its wholly satisfying rightness.

Southey, however, derived little satisfaction from the 'thing in itself': he was not mystically inclined and he liked his friends to be dependable, so that when Coleridge, after undertaking to deliver a lecture in a series of his 'On the Rise, Progress, and Decline of the Roman Empire' unaccountably failed to appear, all the latent dislike of his friend's vagueness and verbosity rose to the surface. The expedition to Tintern Abbey, upon which Cottle tried to heal the breach, proved 'a detestable party of pleasure,' a most un-pantisocratic altercation ensued, and the suggestion that such a lapse was not likely to occur again was received with frank incredulity.

And the rift went deeper than accidentals. Ironically enough Coleridge himself now appeared to Southey the strongest argument against the 'pantisocracy' he preached. The scheme shared in the discredit of his grandiloquent, undependable nature. The idea of offering any of his expected annuity to so improvident a partner grew increasingly distasteful. He could not tell Coleridge this, but he could hint it by opposing his principles, by pleading

with pertinacity 'for the wisdom of making self an undi-
verging center'; he could assume a 'cold and gloomy'
manner, and he could break up the joint lodging in College
Street on the grounds of economy and return to his mother
at Bath. Even Coleridge began to suspect that Southey
'meditated a separation.' 'Pantisocracy,' he noticed, was
avoided as a topic of conversation, and then there was a
dark rumour that an uncle was urging him to enter the
Church, a course which, as he wrote to him, 'would argue
imbecility and a latent wickedness in myself, if for a
moment I doubted concerning your purposes and final
determination.'

Southey rejected the Church, but he dallied with the
Law, and although Coleridge himself had dallied with it
too, the parallelism was scarcely comforting. For even
Southey's dallying was purposeful. If only he could have
demanded openly his intentions, the situation would not
have been so wretched. But he hated scenes, hated above
all surrendering a cherished idea and a delightful conversational topic. Something at least must be preserved
from the ideal shipwreck, and surely domestic happiness
was pantisocracy in miniature, 'the greatest of things
sublunary, and of things celestial it is impossible, perhaps,
for unassisted man to believe anything greater.'

Southey was failing him; but Sarah, plump, smiling
and imperturbable, remained. To marry her was no
longer a baseness or even a duty. It was the consecration
of a faith threatened on all sides by treason, it provided
also an escape from lonely lodgings to an Elysium which
he had never known – the Elysium of a home. He needed
some one to heal his soul 'sickening at the world,' he felt,
as he confessed in the lines he addressed about this time
'To an Infant,' his own infantile helplessness, his own
need of the maternal attentions of a wife and the maternal
support of a creed:

'A babe art thou – and such a thing am I!
To anger rapid and as soon appeased,
For trifles mourning and by trifles pleased,
Break Friendship's mirror with a tetchy blow,
Yet snatch what coals of fire on Pleasure's altar glow!

'O thou that rearest with celestial aim
The future Seraph in my mortal frame,
Thrice holy Faith! whatever thorns I meet
As on I totter with unpractised feet,
Still let me stretch my arms and cling to thee,
Meek nurse of souls through their long infancy!'

Sarah was motherly; she could tend him like a child, and 'in soft impassioned voice, correctly wild' could, as he fancied, 'raise the Poet's kindred strain' in eternal tribute to 'pantisocracy,' and eternal scorn of 'purple Pride, that scowls on wretchedness.'

A visit to Poole at Stowey confirmed him in his purpose. He told him, with tears stealing down his cheeks, of Southey's defection, of a friend

'Who erst, as thou dost say, was wondrous kind,
But now, unkind, forgets.'

Poole was visibly affected and was so excited by his visitor's moods of indignation for the unfeeling world and adoration of 'Religion, white-robed Maid of Peace,' that he recorded his impressions in verse, hailing a 'soul to heavenwards towering' that culled celestial sweets 'amid the flowerets of the milky way.' Coleridge returned with his idealism reinforced, and when Cottle, possibly as a further inducement to 'finger industry,' offered to buy an unlimited number of verses at the fixed rate of a guinea and a half for every hundred lines, he no longer hesitated. If any scruples existed, this offer removed them. To so genial an improvisatore the prospect of producing a hundred thousand lines of poetry a year for the upkeep of a home had no terrors.

And so in the full conviction that his subsistence was assured, Coleridge on October 4, 1795, married Sarah Fricker at the Church of St. Mary Redcliffe, Bristol.

CHAPTER THREE

THE DOMESTIC DREAM

§ I

ONE of the most unfortunate results of Coleridge's indifference to material concerns was that when material things did affect him, they affected him quite out of proportion to their importance, while his imagination, which was only too far-sighted in its own abstract sphere, was incapable of concrete foresight. His marriage to Sarah Fricker was the outcome of similar trivialities to those which had made him wish to be a cobbler and masquerade as a dragoon. Yet each of these actions was also provoked by the same basic need, the need to anchor himself to something solid. It was easy for him to transfer his idealism from Mary Evans to Sarah Fricker, because she was part of a formula, an element in a system based on first principles. In marrying her he attached himself less to a person than to an array of personifications, to

> 'Freedom's UNDIVIDED dell,
> Where *Toil* and *Health* with mellow'd *Love* shall
>   dwell,
> Far from folly, far from men,
> In the rude romantic glen.'

Any imperfection of face or character counted for nothing beside that immaculate 'perfectibility' upon which he had expended so much eloquence, and in the radiance of which she stood. Yet addresses which, in his own words, were 'first paid from principle, not feeling,' and which 'met with a reward more than proportionate to the greatness of the effort,' were scarcely a promising form of courtship. They certainly did not flower into poetry in such lines as:

'The tears that tremble down your cheek,
Shall bathe my kisses chaste and meek
    In Pity's dew divine;
And from your heart the sighs that steal
Shall make your rising bosom feel
    The answering swell of mine!'

Admittedly for one who craved in woman less beauty
and vivacity than an indulgent sympathy, the want of
immediate passion was no cardinal defeſt. He was not
physically sensuous. 'Nothing,' as he wrote, 'affeſts me
much at the moment it happens. It either stupefies me
. . . or I am simply indifferent.' He was sensuous only
in meditation, when he could invest the physical with a
delicate enchantment, as in the description of 'Such light
as lovers love, when the waxing moon steals in behind a
black, black cloud, emerging soon enough to make the
blush visible which the long kiss has kindled,' or of the
voices in opera, – 'one and not one, they leave, seek, pursue, oppose, fight with, strengthen, annihilate each other,
awake, enliven, soothe, flatter and embrace each other
again, till at length they die away in one tone,' than which
there seemed to him in later years 'no sweeter image of
wayward yet fond lovers.'

But generally his conception of love was even more
remote from the particular and more diffused than this.
Once when reading *Troilus and Cressida* he emphasized
the distinſtion between the *affeſtion* of Troilus and the
passion of Cressida, remarking that only the former
deserved the name of love, and when he spoke of the
'religion that is in all deep love,' it meant, as religion
always meant to him, something which 'soothes misfortune' even more than it 'buoys up to virtue.' Sarah
Fricker was, in short, a 'pillow of sorrows,' on which he
hoped to wake to virtue. He was lonely and worried:

he dreaded a return to apathy, to that sense of flabby impotence he knew so well. To marry was to escape momentarily from the foreknowledge of failure. 'In the tumultuous evil hour' . . . 'Peace with Sara came.' But it was a peace sown, had he known, with discord.

To attribute however to Coleridge's marriage, as some critics have done, the tragedy of his broken life is surely a mistake. In a sense his life was always broken. To appreciate the unity of his career necessitates a recognition of the essential disunity of his character, a disunity which affected him physically, mentally, and spiritually. This, and not the unfortunate marriage to which it incidentally contributed, was the root cause of disaster. Yet although Coleridge's destiny was almost certainly beyond any woman's control, he could scarcely have done worse than to drift into marriage with one so little capable of understanding the nature or the needs of genius.

Years later, in writing of marriage as satisfying more than any other relationship the need of man 'to transfuse from himself into others, and to receive from others into himself,' he cited among the necessary pre-conditions for such a state, 'an understanding proportionate to thine, that is, a recipiency at least of thine,' and 'a natural sensibility and lively sympathy in general.' Sarah Fricker may have possessed the latter of these qualities, but it was quickly deadened by her want of the former. Love, for a man of intelligence, as Coleridge was speedily to discover, can never really 'transform the soul into a conformity with the object loved' unless that object has some intellectual affinity. To him, with his appealing sensibility, such a transformation was the breath of life. Without it he languished and all the festering traits in his character, his indolence, self-indulgence, cant, and ineffectuality emerged. Without it too

'With cruel weight these trifles press
A temper sore with tenderness
When aches the void within.'

Yet it is as unreasonable to blame Sarah Fricker for
being a commonplace woman as it is to blame Coleridge
for not being content with her many practical virtues.

That she should have allowed Coleridge to marry her
was also inevitable. Strange though she must have
thought his silences in the early days of their engagement,
his renewed enthusiasm must have completely reassured
her. Even Southey had only begun to read the reality
beneath the captivating illusion, and it was not till later
that Coleridge began to favour his friends with those
portraits of himself, so exasperating in their insight
because by confessing his weaknesses he excused himself
from trying to eradicate them; as for example – 'Indeed I
want firmness. I perceive I do. I have that within me
which makes it difficult to say, No! . . . my face, unless
animated by immediate eloquence, expresses great sloth,
and great, indeed, almost idiotic good nature. 'Tis a
mere carcass of a face; fat, flabby, and expressive chiefly
by inexpression. . . . As to my shape, 'tis a good shape
enough if measured, but my gait is awkward, and the
walk of the whole man indicates *indolence capable of
energies.*'

Dimly Sarah Fricker may have perceived this; but in
the flush of immediate contact, even his weaknesses were
extraordinarily attractive. He was so ardent, expansive
and bewildering, and though so little animal in his instincts, he irradiated a strange magnetism. His very
tenderness was voluptuous, his amiability breathed a
yielding, a docile, charm, just because they were self-
indulgent, because he loved the love of others rather than
themselves. But an inexperienced girl could not trace

an eloquence and an affluent generosity, so apparently disinterested, to its source, could not guess that without the genius which justified it all, his impulse was not dissimilar to that which induces the garrulous bore to make himself, in self-absorbed obliviousness, a burden to his friends and acquaintances.

And beneath the melodious speech there was a pathos. He so obviously needed his audience. Alone in the centre of his amazing utterance, and ineffective in all else, he appealed to them, as a child would to his elders, to hear his story and accept him as one of themselves. The pitiful lot of Sarah Fricker was to respond to that appeal for sympathy as any woman would, without sufficient understanding however to supply it indefinitely. The excessive unworldliness which attracted her in the genius was exactly that which, as a conventional woman, she was incapable of tolerating in the man. She could not make allowances because genius meant nothing to her; for the same reason she could not truly appreciate, and her inability to do so served only to exaggerate in Coleridge the self-pitying impotence which in the end fully justified her petulance.

§ 2

For the moment, however, all was bliss. One detail at least of the pantisocratic dream had achieved the dignity of reality. 'We are settled,' he wrote to Poole three days after their marriage, 'nay, quite domesticated, at Clevedon our comfortable cot! *Mrs. Coleridge!* I like to write the name. . . . The prospect around is perhaps more various than any in the kingdom. Mine eye gluttonizes the sea, the distant islands, the opposite coast! I shall assuredly write rhymes, let the nine Muses prevent it if they can. . . .'

Rhymes he did write, since he was in harmony with

himself and so with nature, and they reveal how quickened his sensibility was. Sara, plump, pretty, and
methodical, was not calculated to renew the note of
'Lewti,' but she made Coleridge feel at home not only in

'our cot o'ergrown
With white-flowered Jasmin, and the broad-leaved
    Myrtle,
(Meet emblems they of Innocence and Love!)'

but with the scent of bean-fields and the 'murmur of the
distant sea.' His desire had found 'a local habitation and
a name'; he was no longer an alien in a world of things; he
could sink deliciously into a natural world, which accepted
him for a short while as one of her family.

The luxury of this sense of identity with life was more
rich and stable than his dreams of Mary Evans. It regenerated like music trembling along the nerves; his passive
pleasure-loving instincts ceased to cloy, ceased to require
justification from his conscience, and the unreal seemed
real. He was like the Æolian harp which he hung in the
cottage casement, and addressed in what he called the
most perfect poem he ever wrote:

'How by the desultory breeze caressed,
Like some coy maid half yielding to her lover,
It pours such sweet upbraiding, as must needs
Tempt to repeat the wrong! And now its strings
Boldlier swept, the long sequacious notes
Over delicious surges sink and rise,
Such a soft floating witchery of sound
As twilight Elfins make, when they at eve
Voyage on gentle gales from Fairy-Land,
Where Melodies round honey-dropping flowers,
Footless and wild, like birds of Paradise,
Nor pause, nor perch, hovering on untamed wing!

O! the one life within us and abroad,
Which meets all motion and becomes its soul,
A light in sound, a sound-like power in light,
Rhythm in all thought, and joyance everywhere –
Methinks, it should have been impossible
Not to love all things in a world so filled;
Where the breeze warbles, and the mute still air
Is Music slumbering on her instrument.

'And thus, my love! as on the midway slope
Of yonder hill I stretch my limbs at noon,
Whilst through my half-closed eyelids I behold
The sunbeams dance, like diamonds, on the main,
And tranquil muse upon tranquility;
Full many a thought uncalled and undetained,
And many idle flitting phantasies,
Traverse my indolent and passive brain,
As wild and various as the random gales
That swell and flutter on this subject lute!'

And since love was this infinitely indolent surrender, there was satisfaction even in surrendering a philosopher's freedom of thought, those 'shapings of the unregenerate mind' which provoked a 'mild reproof' in the more serious eyes of the 'meek daughter in the family of Christ' who had saved him from dark bewilderment, and now expected him to be correct in his views and to 'walk humbly with his God.'

So agreeable was it to please Sara by his correctness, so delightful to cross his lotus mood with practical projects, that he even proposed to become a pedagogue. 'In the course of half a year,' he wrote, 'I mean to return to Cambridge . . . and taking lodgings there for myself and wife, finish my great work of "Imitations," in two volumes. My former works may, I hope, prove somewhat of genius and erudition. This will be better; it will show great industry and manly consistency; at the end of it I shall publish proposals for School etc.'

It was all fiction of course, but it was pleasant to fancy himself a conventional professional man on a conventional honeymoon. Even a letter from Southey announcing his abandonment of 'pantisocracy' and his immediate intention of sailing for Lisbon did not really stab him to the heart as he pretended. It gave him the opportunity of delivering a moving funeral oration over the corpse of the scheme and of his friendship. Still better it enabled him to forget his own treachery and disillusionment in denouncing that of Southey. He did not wish to admit that 'pantisocracy' was in itself unrealizable, because in condemning it as such he condemned himself and incidentally his marriage.

The enormous attraction which the scheme exercised over him was due to its exact reflection of his own nature. To disown it was indeed to confess that he was 'drunk with principle,' but by attributing its non-realization to Southey's defection, he preserved his dream and his self-approval intact. 'When you broke from us,' he argued, 'our prospects were brightening; by the Magazine or by poetry we might and should have got ten guineas a month.' But alas! by a 'system of prudentials' and qualifications Southey had gradually 'sloped his descent from virtue' to the abyss of apostasy. His own vacillation in the previous year was a very different matter. He took honour to himself for the 'convulsive struggles of feeling' he then underwent, inferring that he had sacrificed Mary Evans to his pantisocratic loyalty. What indeed could be more dastardly than that Southey should play false to 'the plan for which he abandoned his friends, and every prospect and every certainty and the woman whom he loved to an excess' which Southey 'in his warmest dreams of fancy could never shadow out'?

It was exceedingly affecting to pose as one who had given his all and only asked in return a like generosity from his friend and a little bread and cheese; it was even more ironically apposite when he attacked Southey for contemplating the very profession which he himself had proposed to Mary Evans. 'For the sake of mankind' he claimed to have tried to argue Southey out of his baseness, but it was of no avail. He had 'fallen back into the ranks,' he had turned from 'the ocean of Universal Redemption.' With 'trembling hand' he accused him of 'falsehood and duplicity.' 'You are *lost* to *me*,' he wrote, 'because you are lost to Virtue. . . . O selfish, money-loving man! What principle have you not given up ? . . . O God! that such a mind should fall in love with that low, dirty, gutter-grubbing trull, Worldly Prudence!'

Full of self-deception as this letter is, it is possible to sympathize with Coleridge's standpoint. His indignation was that of a child refusing to be robbed of an illusion. It hurt him, with his devotion to theory, even more that Southey should reject a word-proof scheme than that he should reject himself. But the impossibility of the scheme, as Southey saw, was one with the impossibility of Coleridge's character. Coleridge could quote examples of his energy and helpfulness in rebuttal of the charge of indolence. But this did not alter the fact that, with the best intentions, he would have made a hopeless partner in any concern which called for effectual organization. He was clearly incapable of 'disciplining his body and mind' to the extent required by pantisocratic, no less than by creedless, pioneers. And then the whole scheme had no material foundation, and, so far as could be seen, never would have. For Southey it had ceased even to serve a purpose by generating enthusiasm. All he could say was that 'the plan you are going upon is not of sufficient importance to justify me to myself in abandoning a

family who have none to support them but me.' It was a
cruel, but necessary candour.

The cottage on the banks of the Severn was, however,
no poor substitute for a conjecture on the banks of the
Susquehanna. Burnett and one of Sara's sisters were
visitors for a time and gave a pantisocratic flavour to the
housework, while the excellent Cottle was at hand to
supply such necessary articles as a cheese-toaster, a riddle-
slice and a carpet-brush, and such necessary comestibles
as coffee, currants, rice and a keg of porter. When he
added to his services by sending an 'upholsterer' to white-
wash the walls of the cottage, Coleridge's gratitude overflowed into a set of verses in which, blind to Cottle's very
modest poetical powers, he prophesied fame for the verse
'concise yet clear,' which

'Tunes to smooth melody unconquer'd sense.'

Indeed for six months he had dilated with gratitude
towards everything and every one except Southey. The
nightingale on the high bough

'Within whose moon-mellow'd foliage hid
Thou warblest sad thy pity-pleading strains,'

the simmering landscape, the grey clouds

'that shadowing spot the sunny fields;
And river, now with bushy rocks o'erbrowed,
Now winding bright and full, with naked banks;
And seats, and lawns, the abbey and the wood,
And cots, and hamlets, and faint city-spire;
The Channel *there*, the Islands and white sails,
Dim coasts, and cloud-like hills, and shoreless Ocean' —

were all in league with Sara to console. Surely divinity
was Omnipresent in such peace, surely a love which drew

from him such sighs of content was 'pure and spotless'! 'Blest hour! It was a luxury – to be!'

Yet strangely enough Sara herself did not inspire him to poetry, The nightingale did, but when he tried to compare its voice with Sara's, the result undeniably was bathos, and although she was certainly the 'best beloved of human kind,' his attempts to express his devotion proved rather maudlin and uxorious. Even the fact that they were composed during illness could scarcely justify for example such lines as:

'Dim hour! that sleep'st on pillowing clouds afar,
O rise and yoke the Turtles to thy car!
Bend o'er the traces, blame each lingering Dove,
And give me to the bosom of my Love!
My gentle Love, caressing and carest,
With heaving heart shall cradle me to rest!
Shed the warm tear-drop from her smiling eyes,
Lull with fond woe, and medicine me with sighs!
While finely-flushing float her kisses meek,
Like melted rubies, o'er my pallid cheek.'

And as the novelty wore off the situation, the excitement did too. It no longer thrilled him quite so pleasantly to see 'a wealthy son of commerce saunter by,' consumed surely with envy for his peaceful lot. The landscape, once so 'green and woody,' refreshed him less; so did the skylark

'Viewless, or haply for a moment seen
Gleaming on sunny wings.'

Thus satiety began to settle on 'The Valley of Seclusion.' Friends and the Bristol City Library recovered their attractions for one 'in a remote village among apathists and ignorants.' Even Sara had her limitations. For although 'good temper and habitual ease are the first

ingredients of private society . . . wit, knowledge, or
originality, must break their even surface into some
inequality of feeling, or conversation is like a journey on
an endless flat.' Sara's surface was unexceptionably even,
and the fact recalled him rather surprisingly to a sense of
public duty.

'Was it right,
While my unnumbered brethren toiled and bled,
That I should dream away the entrusted hours
On rose-leaf beds, pampering the coward heart
With feelings all too delicate for use?'

that he should be of

'The sluggard Pity's vision-weaving tribe!
Who sigh for wretchedness, yet shun the wretched,
Musing in some delicious solitude
Their slothful loves and dainty sympathies!
I therefore go, and join head, heart, and hand,
Active and firm, to fight the bloodless fight
Of science, freedom, and the truth in Christ.'

§ 3

The plan of battle eventually decided upon was to
publish a weekly paper, but it was rather financial anxiety,
aggravated by the prospect of fatherhood, than any moral
purpose that dictated the step. For after a week or two
at his mother-in-law's house in Bristol, Coleridge began
to long again for unobtrusive Clevedon. The Frickers
were very suburban, their conversation an 'endless flat,'
and their minds, as he had feared, 'deeply tinged with
the prejudices and errors of society.' Fortunately Poole
understood the situation. He was a trifle sententious, but
he understood. 'In their moments of mind,' he wrote of
men of genius, 'they form plans which would be practic-
able only if those moments were of continued duration;

but in their career they feel like other mortals the sad burdens of mortality . . . they ought imperiously to command themselves to think *without* genius of the common concerns of life. If this be impossible – happy is the genius who has a friend ever near of *good sense.*' He was such a friend and he showed it by asking Coleridge to bring his wife to Stowey.

The change proved most salutary. Poole himself was so 'active and firm' and he stood for 'science and freedom,' while Sara's virtues had no longer to wage a losing battle with her family's respectability. Early in 1796 they both returned to lodgings in Bristol, and Coleridge braced himself to a practical effort. He took up again the idea, originally mooted by Southey, of starting a magazine, and gathered a number of friends and potential subscribers one evening to the Rummer Tavern to lay proposals before them and sketch preliminaries. A few days later the inevitable prospectus appeared under the motto:

'That All may know the Truth;
And that the Truth may make us Free!!'

The journal was to combine the functions of the modern newspaper, a literary review and Hansard, and was to be called 'The Watchman,' since its editor offered himself to the Public 'as a faithful WATCHMAN, to proclaim the state of the Political Atmosphere, and preserve Freedom and her Friends from the attacks of Robbers and Assassins!!'

To avoid contributing through the Stamp Tax to the guilt of a war against Freedom, it was to appear every eighth day, a systematic irregularity well calculated to appeal to Coleridge himself and to irritate a methodical public. Despite this, however, three hundred and seventy promises of subscription were obtained in Bristol, and to swell the number Coleridge determined to combine

the functions of a missionary and an advertising agent
in an expedition to the Midlands and the North. The
possibility of a prolonged exposition of first principles
was exceedingly inviting. And so, with a blue coat and
white waistcoat to proclaim his utter independence 'of
the woman of Babylon' and a number of recommendatory
epistles, he set out.

He went to Worcester, Birmingham and Nottingham,
to Lichfield, Derby, Manchester, Sheffield and Liver-
pool, and he talked incessantly. If he was not canvassing
tradespeople, he was preaching in Unitarian chapels.
He did not stoop to adapt himself to his audience: the
same stream of radical eloquence descended upon all
and sundry, upon the Calvinist tallow-chandler at Birmingham, 'a tall dingy man,' lean and desiccated, who was
supposed to have 'proved to the satisfaction of many
that Mr. Pitt was one of the horns of the second beast in
The Revelations, that *spake as a dragon*,' but who excused
himself from becoming a subscriber on the grounds that
one copy of the proposed paper was as much as he read
in a year; or upon the 'stately and opulent Manchester
cotton dealer' who replied curtly enough that he was
'overrun with these articles.'

Yet generally people were exceedingly friendly, and
although it was noticeable that they all tried to dissuade
him from proceeding with his enterprise, he was too
absorbed in his oratory to guess that most of them regarded
him as a very amiable eccentric. Certainly there were
moments when his spirits flagged, when he was inclined
to complain, 'Ah, what a weary way! my poor crazy ark
has been tossed to and fro on an ocean of business, and I
long for the Mount Ararat on which it is to rest.' But his
journey was full of compensations. The space in the
coach to Worcester, for example, might be villainously
restricted 'by a lump of a man, who would want elbow

room if he were walking on Salisbury Plain! a most
violent Aristocrat to boot,' and the city, when he reached
it, might prove to lie under the heel of the Clergy, but at
least it contained the hospitable Mr. Barr, whose lovely
children sat round after church singing hymns so sweetly
that with great difficulty he abstained 'from weeping
aloud,' while a baby in Mrs. Barr's arms 'looked like a
young spirit just that moment arrived in Heaven.'

Yet Heaven seemed far enough off when it came to
bandying business with booksellers. 'Like a prisoner,
who in his dreams has enjoyed the freedom he has
imagined,' he began to suspect that he was sleeping and
feared 'to dispel the illusion by waking.' With a rush
his sense of freakish isolation came upon him again. 'I
verily believe no poor fellow's idea-pot ever bubbled up
so vehemently with fears, doubts, and difficulties, as
mine does at present. Heaven grant it may not boil over,
and put out the fire! I am almost heartless! My past
life seems to me like a dream, a feverish dream! all one
gloomy huddle of strange actions, and dim-discovered
motives! Friendships lost by indolence, and happiness
murdered by mismanaged sensibility!'

It was reassuring to return to Bristol and Sara. She at
least existed, even if her condition inclined her to be tearful and reminded him cruelly of his responsibilities. He
had collected, too, a thousand names, if not a thousand
subscribers, and the propagandist in his travels had served
to advertise the poet, if ever his work should struggle into
print. But when Cottle, knowing how harassed he was,
pressed for copy, the pathos of his situation was really
too affecting. 'I have left my friends,' he wrote, 'I have left
plenty; I have left that ease which would have secured a
literary immortality, and have enabled me to give the
public works conceived in moments of inspiration, and
polished with leisurely solicitude, and alas! for what have

I left them? for – who deserted me in the hour of distress,
and for a scheme of virtue impracticable and romantic!
So I am forced to write for bread! write in flights of poetic
enthusiasm, when every moment I am hearing a groan
from my wife. Groans and complaints, and sickness!
The present hour I am in a quick-set hedge of embarrassment, and whichever way I turn a thorn runs into
me! The future is cloud and thick darkness! Poverty,
perhaps, and the thin faces of them that want bread,
looking up to me! Nor is this all. My happiest moments
for composition are broken in upon by the reflection that
I must make haste. I am too late! I am already
months behind! I have received my pay beforehand!
Oh wayward and desultory spirit of genius! Ill canst
thou brook a taskmaster! The tenderest touch from
the hand of obligation wounds thee like a scourge of
scorpions.'

It is comforting, however, to know that a timely bank-
note from Cottle completely lifted the 'cloud' and extracted the 'thorn.' The 'hand of obligation' apparently
had no power to wound when it made such winning
gestures, and his conversation became once more as brilliant and as edifying as ever.

And at last, on March 1, nearly a month behind the
scheduled date, the first number of *The Watchman* was
published. Almost immediately he was assailed by disappointed subscribers. Despite his attack on contemporary methods of criticism, his own reviews were wordy
and worthless; there was little news, and the staple substance of the paper, the Parliamentary Debates, had been
reported at length elsewhere. One subscriber objected
to his 'democratic scurrility,' another to the amount of
original composition, and quite a number of sensitive
readers were outraged when in the second number he
attached to an essay on 'National Fasts' the too pictur-

esque motto 'Wherefore my Bowels shall sound like an Harp.'

And while there was abuse from without, there was slovenliness within. Burnett proved a most incompetent assistant, and the printer multiplied 'injurious blunders.' Between the two of them and Sara's increasing danger, Coleridge's eyes became alarmingly inflamed and his mood utterly distracted. Three years before, in a letter to Mary Evans, he had confessed to taking 'rather a strong dose of opium'; now, since journalism, unlike poetry, was proving an irritant instead of a sedative, he was obliged to take laudanum almost every night. Week by week the subscribers fell off, debts accumulated, and in a tenth and farewell number he was compelled to admit 'O Watchman! thou hast watched in vain.'

Like Southey, it seemed, the 'patriot and the philanthropist' had failed him. They preferred to be taught 'RATIONAL LIBERTY' by the *New Monthly Magazine*, which more adroitly than he 'strengthened the intellect by SCIENCE and softened the affections by the GRACES.' But as usual Poole was there to break the fall. On the last day of publication the editor's 'sorrow-sallowed cheeks' were cheered by a cheque and an almost fulsome testimonial. Poole, who had foreseen disaster, had persuaded half a dozen of Coleridge's friends to contribute five guineas each to a sustentation fund, which he hoped to continue for six years. They were 'irresistibly impelled to make this offer by recollecting the disinterested traits in his character' and because he presented in himself 'an object which awakens every tender and noble sensation of the soul.'

Coleridge received the gift with a 'burst of affectionate feeling,' admired the 'excess of delicacy' which dictated 'some grossness of flattery,' and vowed that he would make every possible exertion. He succeeded at any rate

in completing his poems for the press and at last in April
they appeared.

§ 4

They were, as he later admitted, full of faults. There
was in them for example 'a rage and affectation of double
epithets . . . *truly* ridiculous,' and they were full of those
'shadowy nobodies of personifications.' He confessed
suspiciously enough to a 'conscious aptitude for many
poetic styles and an incapacity to determine which should
be definitely adopted and cultivated to perfection.' He
had too 'such a high idea of what poetry ought to
be that he could not conceive that such things as his
natural emotions might be allowed to find a place in
it.' The result was artificiality and strain, 'a garishness
and swell of diction' also, which he hoped in future to
avoid.

But these, after all, were superficialities. Every young
poet may be forgiven for deviating from 'Nature and
simplicity' until he has found himself. In estimating his
possibilities it is wise rather to examine those elements
in his early work which are typical not of his youth but of
his personality. Even Coleridge's early verse is abun-
dantly typical in this sense, and already imperfectly he
himself knew the flaw in his consciousness. 'I feel
strongly,' he wrote, 'and I think strongly, but I seldom
feel without thinking or think without feeling. Hence
though my poetry has in general a hue of tenderness or
passion over it, yet it seldom exhibits unmixed and simple
tenderness or passion.'

This intermingling as distinct from fusion of thought
and feeling had its origin in a physical incapacity. The
artist's sensibility, as a modern critic has said, is one
upon which objects and episodes in the life about him
produce not only a deeper but a more precise impression

than they do upon the ordinary man. In Coleridge they produced an impression which was agitating but not precise. 'Of all men I ever knew,' he was to write, 'I have the faintest pleasure in things contingent and transitory'; and again, – 'In looking at objects of Nature . . . I seem rather to be seeking, as it were *asking* for, a symbolical language for something within me that already and for ever exists, than observing anything new.' Lacking a normal sensuous response to things his perception was utterly disorganized. He could not project his feeling into things, and so it fermented within him, and at best he could only diffuse it over objects dimly perceived and never crystallized by insight into significance. Similarly his mind, starved of real forms to criticize and define, was compelled to fabricate forms, to build an abstract world of argument over a concrete void.

Again, the great artist's attitude to life, his perspective of values, is formed from an accumulation of exact and instinctive impressions out of which eventually emerges a unity of idea, a universal criterion to which the particular is subconsciously referred. This metaphysic he may in his maturity translate into terms of thought, or it may remain implicit in his handling of his artistic medium. But in either case its origin is not rational but instinctive. His abstract ideas are the interpretation of concrete experiences, his moments of vision the fusion of sense, thought and feeling.

But from childhood Coleridge lacked this sense of the concrete: often as he preached the necessity of a union of feeling and thought for both the poet and the philosopher, he himself could never really unite them, because for him they lacked a common denominator in primary experience. Consequently the superstructure of his writing had the most tenuous foundations; its complexity did not derive, as it should have, from an essential simplicity, and his sense of the infinite remained amorphous for want of achieving contact with the finite.

The more therefore he desensualized his nature by purely abstract thought, the more discursive that thought became; and the more he enveloped the world of men and things in an emotional mist, the more, as a poet, in a vain attempt to objectify, did he multiply metaphors and personifications, while the inevitable image eluded him. Instead of the symbolical language of art he resorted to allegory and 'dim similitudes in moral strains.'

His early poetry like his later metaphysics reveals this constitutional defect, a defect which must be emphasized since his failure to focus his experience was at once the cause and effect of his neuroticism. More and more he was to long for the poet's complete realization of ideas in concrete expression, more and more he was to struggle to become a conscious, effective soul, to escape from himself into a pure imaginative act. For one short period he did launch himself upon a magnificent voyage into the unreal and make it real. It was his one hour of pure creative satisfaction, but it was a miracle that hung upon the hazard of circumstance and which circumstance did not allow him to repeat.

Valueless therefore as most of his early poetry was in itself, its qualities were prophetic. Its lack of organic cohesion or impulse, its self-indulgent romanticism, its dreamy exoticism, touched by ecstasy in 'Lewti' to enchantment, and elsewhere occasionally by fever to a sort of ghostly delirium, its involuntary assimilation of the style of other poets, are all conditions of the later miracle. But above all it foretold that 'indescribable sweetness and fluent projection' of versification, that flowing form which he himself, in speaking of Spenser, distinguished from the deeper and more inwoven harmonies of Shakespeare. He preferred music among the arts because it seemed most completely to resolve the conflict which troubled him between a world of form and of motion, of matter and idea, to enable him as it were to float upon the languor which clogged him. He described music, too, as 'lubricating' his inventive faculty, and his own highest achievement as a poet approaches a condition of pure music. It was never perhaps the greatest music of which poetry is capable, because, even when most animated, it was the music of surrender and escape, not that in which the facts of life are nobly mastered and harmonized; but it was the most bewitching and seductive.

In his early verse it is seldom even that. The surrender was too much of a swoon, but in several passages where prose became poetry simply by virtue of its deliquescent syllables and sliding cadences, the later music, so melting and impalpable, so sweet and buoyant too at its best, was foreshadowed. And as with other romantic poets his sense-perceptions intermingled, colour in particular suffusing sound and movement, as in the line 'Bathed in rich amber-glowing floods of light'; although only in 'Lewti' had he yet conjured that mild iridescence which plays over his greatest verse like suave moonlight on the ripples of a stream.

Of his tendency, never outgrown, to moralize nature, he himself was his best critic, when later he wrote of Bowles that 'never to see or describe any interesting appearance in Nature without connecting it, by dim analogies, with the moral world proves faintness of impression. . . . A poet's heart and intellect should be *combined*, intimately combined and unified with the great appearances of nature, and not merely held in solution and loose mixture with them, in the shape of formal similes. . . . The truth is Bowles has indeed the sensibility of a poet, but he has not the *passion* of a great poet.'

It was because, though morbidly sensitive, he lacked

the passion of a great poet, that when he wrote of simple human things, of love and domestic peace, and even at times of Nature, he was either sentimental or moralistic. His imagination was only vitally kindled by the strange and far, by drifting dream-scenes, and homeless, unlocalized desires.

He did himself however less than justice in pinning all his poetical credit on the 'Religious Musings,' doubtless mistaking an apparent universality of theme for imaginative power. Yet even in this effusion there were passages, such as that already quoted, where he escaped from moralized landscapes to such characteristic nature reflection as he wove into the poems written at Clevedon. And although few could have divined the possibilities of an 'Ancient Mariner' or a 'Christabel' in the relaxed verse of this early volume, it showed a progressive advance in technique. In the later poems the blank verse was broken up and was less florid and emptily sublime, while in the shorter lyrics, sickly as the feeling generally was, it had superseded the elaborate and artificial. The deft weaving too of some of the verse-patterns, learnt from such various poets as Spenser, Crashaw and Thomson, foreshadowed both the inspired selective artistry of his great poems and the deft verbal simplicity that still gave distinction to many of his verses long after inspiration had failed.

§ 5

Although however 'The Monthly . . . cataracted panegyric . . . the Critical cascaded it, and the Analytical dribbled it with civility' the poems did not ease the financial situation, rendered desperate, but for Poole's testimonial, by the failure of The Watchman. A fortnight at Stowey in May soothed his sense of defeated hope and even restored his spirits, but a plaintive wife and a sentinel mother-in-law awaited him on his return. Something he must do, and when towards the end of June he was offered the assistant editorship of the *Morning Chronicle*, despite his aversion to 'local and temporary politics' which 'narrow the understanding and at least acidulate the heart,' he was prepared to bid 'farewell to the Muse and his literary Fame.'

Almost immediately, however, a suggestion was made to him by a Mrs. Evans, of Matlock, whom he had met on his missionary tour earlier in the year, that he should act as tutor to her sons. Accordingly he and Sara went to Darley Abbey to arrange the matter and the visit proved a great success — 'a sunny spot,' as they spoke of it later, 'in their lives.' Coleridge 'was the first fiddle: — not in the concerts — but everywhere else.' At Matlock he 'dined in a cavern at the head of a divine little fountain, and returned to Darley, quite worn out with the succession of sweet sensations.' Unfortunately, however, the trustees ended by vetoing the transaction, and the visit ended with a gift of baby-clothes to Sara and a consolation prize of £95 to her husband.

But another missionary acquaintance, a Dr. Crompton, stepped into the breach, proposing that the 'Watchman' should open a school in Derby. Coleridge went so far as to engage an unfinished house which was to be completed by October, before going to stay with a friend at Moseley, where he preached on Faith. Here he renewed his acquaintance with a neurotic young man named Charles Lloyd, the son of a banker. Coleridge's personality and propaganda appealed to him so strongly that the prospect of a commercial career became utterly distasteful. Indeed so great was the fascination that he offered to contribute £80 a year to household expenses in return for the privilege of his conversation. It was a pity that he was subject to epileptic fits, but the prospect of so appreciative a paying guest attracted Coleridge.

It seemed a god-sent opportunity, and one which, with £40 earned by himself in reviewing, might relieve him of the necessity of bidding 'farewell to literary fame.' Lloyd's banker father, 'a mild man . . . and in religion an allegorizing Quaker,' was induced to agree, and it was in the midst of these negotiations that Coleridge was informed of the birth of a son.

He had, of course, miscalculated the date, was 'quite annihilated with the suddenness of the information,' and when he retired to his room to address himself to his Maker, 'could only offer up to Him the silence of stupefied feelings'! To be first numbed by experience and then to overflow with feeling was characteristic enough. The feeling he enshrined in three sonnets, the second of which, composed on the way back to Bristol with Lloyd, contained the luxurious notion of weeping 'idly o'er thy little bier!' Finding the infant, however, alive, he had to content himself with the melancholy – and indeed in the issue relevant – thought of 'all I had been, and all my child might be.' 'I looked on it with a melancholy gaze; my mind was intensely contemplative, and my heart only sad. But when two hours after, I saw it at the bosom of its mother – on her arm – and her eye tearful and watching its little features – then I thrilled and melted, and gave it the kiss of a father.' He gave it too the names David Hartley, trusting 'that his head would be convinced of, and his heart saturated with the truths so ably supported by that great Master of Christian Philosophy' – a master whose arguments he was incidentally to spend many hours of his later life in refuting.

For the moment the joy of paternity renewed his sense of domestic satisfaction:

'for the mother's sake the child was dear,
And dearer was the mother for the child.'

Lloyd's delight also in 'the circumstances of his domestication' was most gratifying, the more so as he now spoke of the arrangement as a permanency; and when Southey, who had returned from Portugal, made a gesture of reconciliation, it was eagerly accepted. The 'blasted oak' of friendship might not perhaps 'put forth its buds anew,' but it was not for a father to cherish feelings of hostility towards any man.

All these events, however, had been very agitating, and a reaction was inevitable. Something, he realized, must be done, and the thought worried and depressed. On nearer consideration pedagogy attracted as little as journalism. Was it really necessary? he asked himself, and appealed to Poole to confirm his own unuttered negatives. 'Can you conveniently receive Lloyd and me?' he wrote. 'I have much, very much to say to you, and to consult with you about; for my heart is heavy respecting Derby.'

After a week's visit to Stowey the very thought of Dr. Crompton was too painful to entertain. By November he had wiped him from his memory. 'To live in a beautiful country,' as he wrote to Poole, 'and to enure myself as much as possible to the labour of the field, have been for this year past my dream of the day, my sigh at midnight. But to enjoy these blessings *near* you, to see you daily, to tell you all my thoughts in their first birth, and to hear yours, to be mingling identities with you as it were, – the vision-weaving fancy has indeed often pictured such things, but *hope* never dared whisper a promise.'

The rumour of a possible vacant house near Stowey only increased his agitation. Once again a dream seemed realizable, a new pantisocracy with Poole and Lloyd and Sara amid the Quantock Hills, 'not wearisome and bare and steep,' but soft and gradual as was his temper, mossed over with 'coloured lichens' and sprayed by 'summer torrents.' There beneath the 'red clusters of the ash':

'Calm Pensiveness might muse herself to sleep;
  Till haply startled by some fleecy dam,
That rustling on the bushy clift above
With melancholy bleat of anxious love,
  Made meek enquiry for her wandering lamb.
  Such a green mountain 'twere most sweet to climb,
E'en while the bosom ached with loneliness –
How more than sweet, if some dear friend should bless
  The adventurous toil, and up the path sublime
Now lead, now follow: the glad landscape round,
Wide and more wide, increasing without bound.'

There he pictured himself wandering, arm linked in
friendly arm . . . the world's vain turmoil left, until

              'eve the valley dims
  Tinged yellow with the rich departing light'

or cheating the noons

              'in moralizing mood,
While west winds fanned our temples toil-bedewed:
  Then downwards slope, oft pausing, from the mount,
To some lone mansion, in some woody dale,
Where smiling with blue eye, Domestic Bliss
Gives *this* the Husband's, *that* the Brother's kiss!'

But would 'Heaven realize this vision bright'? He had
been so cruelly disillusioned before. Fancy, as he wrote
in 'The Destiny of Nations' – an effusion closely akin to
'The Religious Musings' upon which he was working
at the time – might unsensualize

              'the dark mind,
  Giving it new delights';

but could the delights ever have any substance? Between
desire and doubt he suffered agonies. Life itself, he felt,

hung upon the issue. 'I so ardently desire it,' he wrote, 'that any disappointment would chill all my faculties, like the fingers of death'; and four days later – 'Disappointment! disappointment! dash not from my trembling hand the bowl which almost touches my lips.'

Such hysteria brought the inevitable physical consequences and what was now to prove the inevitable anodyne. He was seized 'with an intolerable pain from the right temple to the tip of the right shoulder. . . .' He was 'nearly frantic, and ran about the house naked, endeavouring by every means to excite sensations in different parts of his body, and so to weaken the enemy by creating diversion.' It continued from one in the morning till half-past five, and left him 'pale and fainting.' On its recurrence the next day he 'took between sixty and seventy drops of laudanum, and *sopped* the Cerberus, just as his mouth began to open.' The next day, a Friday, 'it only *niggled*, as if the thief had departed from a conquered place, and merely left a small garrison behind. . . . But *this morning* he returned in full force, and his name is Legion. Giant-fiend of a hundred hands, with a shower of arrowy death-pangs he transpierced me, and then he became a wolf, and lay a-gnawing at my bones!' His medical attendant, he added, decided it to be altogether nervous, and that it originated 'either in severe application, or excessive anxiety.' He took twenty-five drops of laudanum every five hours and gained 'ease and spirits' by it.

Coleridge was always to be remarkable as the poet and analyser of pathological states, because these were the only physical conditions from which he could not escape, save by narcotics, into a dream world. Of them he was, until they were artificially assuaged, concretely aware, abnormally so because of his strange insensitiveness to normal stimuli. 'I hear in my brain,' he was to write, 'sensations . . . of various degrees of pain, even to a strange sort of uneasy pleasure . . . I hear in my brain, and still more in my stomach.'

It was the poet's pleasure in imaging for once an actuality, that led him to describe experiences of this kind so vividly, but it was also his constitutional aversion to actuality that made pain so much more intolerable to him than to the ordinary man and drove him without a thought of consequences to the drug which brought relief. Laudanum supplied the same refuge from physical pain as first poetry and then metaphysics from mental pain. But the two were of course intimately connected. The neuralgic symptoms which he here described were always to coincide with periods of acute mental anxiety and emotional stress.

Physical distress, however, was at the moment an additional argument on behalf of a move which he now desired with utter abandonment. It would surely banish any doubts which Poole might still entertain of the wisdom of the step, make him realize that even the thought of frustration endangered not only his friend's hopes but his health. Meanwhile he grew more and more frenzied. 'With a gloomy wantonness of imagination I had been coquetting with hideous *possibles* of disappointment. I drank fears like wormwood, yea, made myself drunken with bitterness; for my ever-shaping and distrustful mind still mingled gall-drops, till out of the cup of hope I almost *poisoned* myself with despair. . . . My anxieties eat me up. . . . I want consolation – my Friend! my Brother! write and console me.' Even Poole's sister was caught in the deluge of his feelings: – 'I felt my heart overflowed with such tenderness for her as made me repeatedly ejaculate prayers in her behalf.' And then from despair he would rebound to hope, and even to a facetiousness that rang false as the hysteric's laughter.

'Will you try,' he asked, 'to look out a fit servant for us –
simple of heart, physiognomically handsome, and scientific in vaccimulgence?'

At last Poole announced that a small, unattractive
cottage on the street had fallen vacant. He emphasized
its disadvantages, but Coleridge snatched at it deliriously.
The news was so glorious as to be scarce endurable. In
gratitude he multiplied resolutions. – 'I mean to work
very hard – as Cook, Butler, Scullion, Shoe-Cleaner,
occasional Nurse, Gardener, Hind, Pig-protector, Chap-
lain, Secretary, Poet, Reviewer, and *omnium-botherum*
schilling-Scavenger.' There was no end to his prospective
activities or to the motives which determined and justified
the step. He saw himself as a 'horticulturist and a
farmer' managing half an acre of land, and raising on it
with his own hands all kinds of vegetables and grain,
enough for himself and his wife, and sufficient to feed a
pig or two with the refuse.

Unfortunately the cautious Poole was troubled with
second thoughts. A better residence was obtainable
near Bristol. Was Coleridge wise to retire to a cramped
cottage in a remote village, far from libraries and stimu-
lating friends? His agricultural enthusiasm was of course
very charming, but how little would it stand the test of
fact. These doubts he embodied in a second letter which
crossed that containing Coleridge's acceptance. Upon
his enthusiastic expectancy it fell like a hammer. At first
he was numbed and replied in terms of reasonable argument, but as the day advanced he was seized with panic.
The edifice of rural enchantment, which for three months
his fertile fancy had been raising, seemed to tumble about
his ears. He was as one 'falling from the summit of his
fondest desires, whirled from the height just as he had
reached it.'

The result was a second letter, penned in the evening

and continued the next morning, that approximated to
the ravings of lunacy. 'There is one Ghost,' he wrote,
'that I *am* afraid of . . . the hideous Ghost of departed
Hope. O Poole! how could *you* make such a proposal to
me? . . . Surely, surely, my friend! Something has
occurred which you have not mentioned to me. Your
mother has manifested a strong dislike to our living near
you – or something or other. . . . My God! my God!
what if . . . my most beloved friend has grown cold
towards me. . . . I shall be again afloat on the wide sea,
unpiloted and unprovisioned. . . . Nothing remains possible but a School, or Writer to a newspaper, or any
present plan. I could not love the man who advised me
to keep a school, or write for a newspaper. He must have
a hard heart! . . . Surely, surely you do not advise me to
lean with the whole weight of my necessities on the Press?
Ghosts indeed! I should be haunted with Ghosts enough
– the ghosts of Otway and Chatterton, and the phantasms
of a wife broken-hearted, and a hunger-bitten Baby! O
Thomas Poole! Thomas Poole! if you did but know what
a Father and a Husband must feel who toils with his
brain for uncertain bread! I dare not think of it. The
evil face of Frenzy looks at me. . . . Indeed, indeed, I
am very miserable.' The whole letter covered many pages.

Poole of course surrendered. A poet so hysterical and
so theatrical could not be argued with. Even so his nerve
storm necessitated a further resort to the laudanum bottle,
the effects of which may perhaps be traced in the 'Ode on
the Departing Year' which he wrote hastily for the *Cambridge Intelligencer* in the last week of December. It was,
like all but one of his political verses, a brittle composition
echoing the ghostly violence of Burgher's 'Leonore,'
which he had been reading, and in a hollow fashion
Milton's 'Nativity Ode.' Doubtless his own recent nightmares dictated the passage:

'Yet still I gasped and reeled with dread.
And ever, when the dream of night
Renews the phantom to my sight,
Cold sweat-drops gather on my limbs;
    My ears throb hot; my eye-balls start ;
My brain with horrid tumult swims;
    Wild is the tempest of my heart;
And my thick and struggling breath
Imitates the toil of death.'

But it ended on a very personal note of relief and expect-
ation:
                'Away, my soul, away !
    In vain, in vain the birds of warning sing –
And hark! I hear the famished brood of prey
Flap their lank pennons on the groaning wind!
        Away, my soul, away!
I unpartaking of the evil thing,
    With daily prayer and daily toil
    Soliciting for food my scanty soil,
    Have wailed my country with a loud Lament.
Now I recentre my immortal mind
    In the blest sabbath of meek self-content.'

So on the 30th of December, 1796, he moved to Stowey.
The dream had materialized after all. And considering
how much it was to mean to English poetry, Coleridge's
satisfaction must find an echo in many hearts.

CHAPTER FOUR

THE POETIC DREAM

§ I

'A GREEN and silent spot' it was 'amid the hills' even in winter, through the feathery moss that clung to the stripped boughs and carpeted the airy ridges. A pastoral spot, where sheep-bells mingled with the gush of streams and the woodman wound along the deep lanes with laden pony. And inland up the heathy Quantocks ran broken coombs, half glens, half gorges, lined with fir and oak and forest undergrowth, with many a 'quiet spirit-healing nook' where silence was companionable even without the hum of insects, 'that noiseless noise which lives in the summer air,' or the larks that filled the sky.

When spring came, a wanderer amid the golden furze on the upper slopes could look northward across a level of moor and marsh and meadow to the heaped mounds of the Mendip Hills or beyond to the Welsh mountains faintly pencilled in blue along the sky-line, while behind him stretched and, when the breeze blew inland, sounded, or seemed to sound, the sea. Thus like a girl between two Titan lovers Stowey lay, a girl too tender to be wild, too virginal to be profuse. It was the feminine genius of the place which appealed to Coleridge. With his homeless mind he yearned for a homely, a caressing environment. And he yearned for beauty too. Stowey with its cool foliage and swelling slopes provided both. The same need compelled him to write – 'My poetic vanity and my political furor have been exhaled, and I would rather be an expert self-maintaining gardener than a Milton, if I could not unite both.'

In the outsider of course the avowal must have excited derision. Never was there a man less capable of getting up before breakfast to work in the garden or of cleaning out a pigsty. And yet the assertion was tragically sincere. Coleridge, than whom no man was more capable of self-analysis or less capable of self-reform, knew himself unbalanced, knew obscurely that only physical experience could cure him of the disease of himself, knew too what awaited him if he failed to adjust his body to his mind. 'O this unutterable dying away here,' he was to write in a few months, 'this sickness of the heart!' Every decisive action which he had taken was directed unconsciously towards remedying an abnormality which tortured him between excitement and inertia. In a regular practical life at Stowey he hoped yet again to achieve balance, to cease to be 'depressed by weight of musing Phantasy,' to 'tame himself down to living purposes,' to become the master of his moods. For thirteen years he continued however fitfully to struggle for that balance, and then, almost with relief, he abandoned the attempt.

He began at Stowey happily enough. He was determined to be idyllic, and the little cottage was far from being 'the old hovel' which it later became. Certainly it was small, dark and drab, but its strip of kitchen garden and orchard opened into Poole's land, and it was only a step to his house, or, on warm mornings, to an 'arbour' that invited composition. 'We are *very* happy,' he wrote in the spring, 'and my little David Hartley grows a sweet boy. . . . I raise potatoes, and all manner of vegetables. . . . Our house is better than we expected. . . . Before our door a clear brook runs of very soft water (he did not mention that it was in the street) and in the backyard is a nice *well* of fine spring water. We have a pretty garden . . . and I am already an expert gardener.' . . . Nevertheless he had to admit later that the garden was covered with weeds, but this was due rather to his equalitarian principles, since he thought it unfair to prejudice the soil towards roses and strawberries. Sara may possibly have thought otherwise, but neither she nor the Bristol librarian who dunned him for five shillings for not returning books, nor the mice which took advantage of his aversion to setting a trap, succeeded in quenching his impish humour, a humour which won the hearts of 'a number of very pretty young women in Stowey, all musical.' With them, he announced, he was 'an immense favourite; for I pun, conundrumize, *listen*, and dance,' while in the intervals Hartley 'laughs at us till he makes us weep for fondness.'

It may be that Coleridge was scarcely as blissful as his correspondence suggests, since he had so long indulged over-statement that it had become a habit. For example, he told a friend at this time that after hearing of his wife's illness, 'Sara burst into an agony of tears that she *had* been so ill' – an improbable outburst in a woman of marked common sense.

Certainly a more chastened note, a 'moody murmur' sounded in the dedicatory lines to his brother George, which at Cottle's suggestion he wrote for a second edition of his Poems. In these he spoke of friendships and hopes that had failed him, and while describing his present happiness, confessed that at times his soul was sad because he stood as an alien to his own kin. Once again too 'anxieties and slothfulness in a combined ratio' caused the printer exasperating delays. The revision of his Poems which should have been completed in a fortnight, dragged on until near midsummer when, supplemented with poems by Lamb and Lloyd, they limped into print. It was a task all the more grievous because his judgment was rapidly maturing. He began to see how flaccid much of his early poetry was. 'The Monody on Chatterton' for example and the 'Pixies' Parlour' contained less than five lines 'which might not have been written by a man who had lived and died in the self-same St. Giles' cellar, in which he had been first suckled by a drab with milk and gin.' The Pixies was the least disgusting, 'because the subject leads you to expect nothing, but on a life and death so full of heart-going *realities* as poor Chatterton's, to find such shadowy nobodies as cherub-winged *Death*, Trees of *Hope*, blue-bosomed *Affection* and simpering *Peace*, makes one's blood circulate like ipecacuanha.'

Long walks and Poole's sound sense were beginning to take effect, and when in March Sheridan invited him to write a play for Drury Lane he was so anxious to avoid muffled pieties that he plunged helplessly into melodrama. Incapable of human characterization or 'heart-going realities' he could do nothing else. The only alternative to the jejeune was the violent and *macabre*. But he was not satisfied. Encouraged by Charles Lamb and by that 'divine and nightly-whispering voice, which speaks to mighty minds, of predestinated garlands starry and un-withering,' he dreamed of a great Epic on the Origin of Evil. The work was of vast design, as was to be expected of one to whom evil in the particular and the concrete was an unknown quantity. He contemplated devoting not less than twenty years to it, ten years 'to warm his mind with universal science. . . . Mathematics, Mechanics, Hydrostatics, Optics, Astronomy, Botany, Metallurgy, Fossilism, Chemistry, Geology, Anatomy, Medicine, the mind of man, the minds of men in all Travels, Voyages and Histories,' five years for composition and five for correction. It was an inebriating prospect, and as such it sufficed, materializing only in a desultory reading of certain books of travel, which threw little light on the origin of evil but did in a few months' time quite unexpectedly redound to the glory of poetry.

Meanwhile Charles Lloyd was far from blessing 'the adventurous toil' or leading up 'the path sublime.' His fits were frequent and severe. Once they occurred three

times in the space of seven days and he remained in 'one
continued state of agonized delirium . . . from twelve
o'clock at night to five in the morning.' No wonder after
such a bout that Coleridge paid for his guest 'with aching
temple and a feeble frame'; no wonder that, try as he would,
Osorio, as he called his play, refused to be anything but
morbid and overstrung, and that he could write in it

'All men seemed mad to him,
. . . In this world
He found no fit companion.'

He seemed to be dogged by failures. George Burnett
was another frequent visitor, another victim to pantisocracy, mourning in his listless way over a lost illusion
for which he could substitute no other aim, and, to stress
his incapacity, developing jaundice.
Soon enough the old depression 'too dreadful to be
described' was to return, 'a sort of calm hopelessness' to
diffuse itself over his heart. But on the downward path
a magnetic influence was first to interpose, an influence
so potent that for a few dazzled months he was to mount
to heights which float for ever in a kind of ether above the
deepening morass of his life.
Earlier in the year he had wished to send some verses to
the poet Wordsworth, whom, it seems probable, he had
met quite formally two years before, and who was now
living with his sister Dorothy at Racedown, only forty
miles away. The wish persisted, but instead of sending
verses he decided to present himself. And so on June 6 he
went on foot from Taunton. The Wordsworths were out
walking, and when he recognized them at a distance he
broke from the high road, 'leapt over a gate, bounded
down the pathless field by which he cut off an angle,' and
introduced himself all fire and eagerness and disarray.
The manner of his meeting was symbolical. He had

discovered two beings to whom he could give himself, not, at first at least, as a sick soul but as a vital one, not as a pantisocrat but as a poet. And the gift was possible because both could return it in kind: Wordsworth thriftily as was his wont, but Dorothy with the adorable unreserve of a nature even more finely sensitive than his own. For three minutes only did she stand aside, doubting, assessing with wild and rapid glances. He was plain and pale and thin. He had thick lips and imperfect teeth. And then the tide of his talk began and she thought no more of such things. 'His eye,' she wrote, 'is large and full, and not very dark, but grey – such an eye as would receive from a heavy soul the dullest expression; but it speaks every emotion of his animated mind; it has more of "the poet's eye in a fine frenzy rolling" than I ever witnessed. He has fine dark eyebrows, and an overhanging head.'

It was such appreciation Coleridge needed to take fire, to prove himself indeed 'a wonderful man.' Insensitive affection could not work the miracle; a tolerant kindness could comfort, it could not quicken. But this was 'a woman indeed, in mind . . . and heart . . . her manner . . . simple, ardent, impressive. In every motion her most innocent soul outbeams so brightly, that who saw her would say

"Guilt was a thing impossible in her."

Her information various. Her eye watchful in minutest observation of nature; and her taste a perfect electrometer. It binds, protrudes and draws in, at subtlest beauties and most recondite faults.'

Such was Wordsworth's 'exquisite sister'; and she who gave her brother eyes and ears, gave Coleridge a year of faith in his own wonder-working genius, and paid, it seems probable, for her power to do so in the melancholy vacuity of after years.

§ 2

But Wordsworth himself too contributed to the miracle. Two years older than Coleridge, he was just twenty-eight. Gaunt, narrow-shouldered and prematurely prim, the impression he made was in strong contrast with that of his sister, whose ardent sensibility proclaimed itself with a certain gipsy wildness in every motion and glance, in quick flushing and impulsive speech. Her instinct was so plainly, so fiercely, yet delicately vital. But in him the same fire seemed bleakly incased. It smouldered in the eyes, but the face as a whole was too strong, austere, and uncouth to reflect a flow of feeling. It suggested a nature more capable of spiritual solemnity than responsive sympathy.

Yet in several ways Wordsworth's experience had paralleled that of Coleridge. From childhood his vision was abnormal. 'I was often,' he wrote, 'unable to think of external things as having external existence, and I communed with all that I saw as something not apart from, but inherent in, my own immaterial nature. Many times while going to school have I grasped a wall or tree to recall myself from this abyss of idealism to the reality.' For him too therefore as a poet the absorbing problem was how to relate this subjective radiance, this

'something in myself, a dream,
A prospect in the mind,'

to the facts of life. Recent events had made a solution of this problem absolutely imperative. With far more sincerity than Coleridge he had indulged the hopes generated in every young and liberal heart by the French Revolution, and when the 'pyre' that he had raised 'upon the basis of the coming time . . . fell in ruins' round him, disillusionment struck down to the roots of his nature and reduced him to impotence. For his enthusiasms had not been, like Coleridge's, the mere vapours of an indulgent sensibility. His mysticism might play strange tricks with his sense-perception, but this was not due to any lack of animal instinct, but only to an excessive self-absorption. Similarly Nature for him was not an abstraction, but an intimate sensation of force, freedom and life, which he wished to realize and justify in his own creative expression, and men and nations to realize in their social and international relationships.

He had not succeeded in realizing it in the poetry which he had yet written – 'Descriptive Sketches,' 'Guilt and Sorrow' and the 'Borderers' – because he had entangled his creative powers in the emotional individualism of Rousseau and the rational of Godwin. And when France had declared war upon England four years before, it was not France that seemed disproved, but the very instinct of Nature which quickened him to expressiveness. The shock to his moral nature, aggravated by a bitter personal experience of frustration in a romantic attachment, paralysed his creative powers. He could not, like Coleridge, temper the shock by sophistry. If Nature, as he understood her in the fibres of his being, was a blind, destructive agency, he had no right to sentimentalize her in poetry. The one outlet for his fierce, retentive egotism seemed closed and the gloom of impotence settled upon him.

It was thus at a time when

'Nature within me seemed
In all her functions weary of herself,'

when even Dorothy could not quicken faith, but only sharpen sensibility, that Coleridge bounded down the pathless field and opened a way to self-escape. And the service was reciprocated, not so much through any generosity on Wordsworth's part (it was Dorothy who gave),

as because his stability, his very limitations of character
were in themselves for a time a reinforcement to Coleridge,
provided him with a foundation of confidence and understanding from which he could take his amazing leap into
the enchanted unknown. Coleridge needed some one positive and practical to spur him to activity, Wordsworth
needed another's emotional faith to enable him to master
creatively the bitter knowledge of fact he had acquired.
It was thus, as he later gratefully acknowledged, that
Coleridge gave:

> 'O capacious soul!
> Placed on this earth to love and understand,
> And from thy presence shed the light of love,
> Shall I be mute, ere thou be spoken of?
> Thy kindred influence to my heart of hearts
> Did also find its way. Thus fear relaxed
> Her overwhelming grasp; thus thoughts and things
> In the self-haunting spirit learned to take
> More rational proportions.'

The fruit of this alliance was in Wordsworth a ten years'
wonder of human achievement, in Coleridge little more
than a ten months' wonder of inhuman witchery. Both
were egotists, both were fighting inertia, but with a difference. Both had found that mere individualism led only to
disillusion; Coleridge for example was projecting at this
very moment 'a book of morals in answer to Godwin,'
while the villain of the 'Borderers' was a Godwinian
rationalist. But while Wordsworth discovered release in a
profoundly sympathetic and detailed study of Nature and
of unsophisticated men, Coleridge could only escape by
unworldly ecstasy. Wordsworth read the real into the
commonplace, Coleridge made the fantastic real; the one
illuminated actual life before coming prosaically to terms
with it, the other but faintly touched it either in the

morning moment of his romantic rapture or the long cloudy afternoon of his philosophic compromise.

This fundamental difference existed from the beginning and revealed itself in their first plan as collaborators, in which it was agreed that Coleridge should endeavour to give 'a human interest and a semblance of truth' to things supernatural, and Wordsworth 'the charm of novelty to things of every day'; but it was not until later when differences arose and Coleridge suffered from being identified with certain of Wordsworth's critical opinions, that he would admit how fundamental the difference was. He needed and profited too much by Wordsworth's friendship, and was himself too gratefully sympathetic to acknowledge it for many years. And meanwhile he infused into Wordsworth his own idealism when he was about to lapse into a materialist conception of the universe, from which no poetry could flower, without making him the helpless transcendentalist he was himself.

Wordsworth's matter-of-factness – the uninspired commonplace which alone survived when ten years later the fire had almost burnt itself out – ensured him against the unsubstantial ecstasy which was all that Coleridge himself had to give. But it was Coleridge, with his feminine generosity and infinitely subtler mind, who kindled the fire which Wordsworth's masculine limitations were to make effective. For, as he was to write – 'Of all the men I ever knew, Wordsworth has the least femineity in his mind. He is all man. He is a man of whom it might have been said – It is good for him to be alone.' It was disastrous for Coleridge to be alone. His powers at once dissolved in self-pity. He began to whine about his condition or philosophize his failure. Wordsworth and his sister between them gave him for a season a sense of partnership in poetic enterprise, and fortified by it he suddenly floated into pure poetic achievement.

'I find an unmixed pleasure in esteeming and admiring,' wrote Coleridge, and he indulged it to the utmost in these first days of intercourse with Wordsworth. He found the 'Borderers' 'absolutely wonderful,' vowed it rose to the level of Schiller and Shakespeare without their 'inequalities,' and spoke of his friend now as 'the Giant,' and soon as 'the only man to whom *at all times* and *in all modes of excellence* I feel myself inferior.'

Brother and sister came on a fortnight's visit to Stowey in July, and on the 7th Charles Lamb, sad, shy, but to whom no sound was 'dissonant which tells of life,' came too. Suddenly Coleridge found himself more profoundly in harmony with things than he had ever known. It did not matter that Sara accidentally emptied a skillet of boiling milk on his foot which confined him to house and garden He had found 'the sympathy of human faces' which he needed, and he could feed on his contentment only the more blissfully when its originators were momentarily away. Sitting in Poole's arbour one evening he followed them in fancy and put his fancy into verse:

'Well, they are gone, and here must I remain,
This lime-tree bower my prison! I have lost
Beauties and feelings, such as would have been
Most sweet to my remembrance even when age
Hath dimmed mine eyes to blindness! They meanwhile
Friends, whom I never more may meet again,
On springy heath, along the hill-top edge
Wander in gladness, and wind down, perchance,
To that still roaring dell, of which I told

.   .   .   .

'Yes! they wander on
In gladness all; but thou, methinks, most glad,
My gentle-hearted Charles! for thou hast pined

And hungered after Nature, many a year,
In the Great City pent, winning thy way
With sad yet patient soul, through evil and pain
And strange calamity ! Ah! slowly sink
Behind the western ridge, thou glorious Sun!
Shine in the slant beams of the sinking orb,
Ye purple heath-flowers! richlier burn, ye clouds!
Live in the yellow light, ye distant groves!
And kindle, thou blue Ocean! So my friend
Struck with deep joy may stand, as I have stood,
Silent with swimming sense; yea, gazing round
On the wide landscape, gaze till all doth seem
Less gross than bodily; and of such hues
As veil the Almighty Spirit, when yet he makes
Spirits perceive his presence.
      A delight
Comes sudden on my heart, and I am glad
As I myself were there!'

The relaxed note was there, but it was informed with
'lively joy.' The consequence was first a finer focus of
vision. His senses were quickened. Indeed, judging by
such passages as the following, for example, it might seem
that Dorothy, of whom in the first version of the poem he
spoke as 'my sister,' had already given him eyes kindred
to her own:
      'the sea,
With some fair bark, perhaps, whose sails light up
The slip of smooth clear blue betwixt two Isles
Of purple shadow!'

or
      'and I watched
Some broad and sunny leaf, and loved to see
The shadow of the leaf and stem above,
Dappling its sunshine.'

And secondly his idealism was for the moment almost

pinned to earth. His benevolent, visionary mind on this lovely July evening had established a real contact with the richly-tinged walnut-tree, 'the dark green file of long lank weeds' and the bat that wheeled in the twilight. The life directly about him had at last an existence of its own. It was not completely overlaid by the unreality of himself. And so he could cry:

> 'Henceforth I shall know
> That Nature ne'er deserts the wise and pure;
> No plot so narrow, be but Nature there,
> No waste so vacant, but may well employ
> Each faculty of sense, and keep the heart
> Awake to Love and Beauty!'

It was a knowledge which he could help Wordsworth to acquire but could not retain himself. In these lines, among the finest of all his communings with Nature, he put in to the haven from which he was soon to be driven on homeless wanderings. A sense of 'the kind "charities"' of relationship, as the gentle-hearted Charles called it, a relationship that came as near to physical expression as ever he required, enabled him to do so, set him right, as it were, with the human world, and through it with the inanimate. Instead of being suffocated by his own tenderness, it opened a way for him to the heart of life.

Such was the first transient fruit of this phenomenal friendship, and when, before the fortnight's visit was over, the Wordsworths secured a house at Alfoxden, only three miles distant, its continuance was assured. Henceforth Coleridge and they saw as much of one another 'as if the width of a street, and not a pair of coombes' had separated them. They were 'three people but one soul.' Later in the month too the neighbourhood was outraged by the arrival of a notorious Jacobin, named Thelwall, who had suffered imprisonment for his views and so attracted

Coleridge's sympathy. The ultimate consequences of this visit both to Coleridge and Wordsworth were considerable, since Citizen Thelwall's presence brought even Wordsworth under suspicion, and although Poole assured the owner of Alfoxden of his tenant's entire respectability, he refused to extend the lease of the house beyond a year.

But the supposed conspirators had no thought of the future as they rambled among the plantations, passing sentence on the productions and characters of the age, bursting forth in poetical flights of enthusiasm, and philosophizing their minds into a state of tranquillity. They agreed that it was 'a place to reconcile one to all the jarrings and conflicts of the wide world.' Coleridge was quite naïvely charmed by the fact that Thelwall should prove a great favourite with Sara, for the energetic activity which was his 'master feature,' and doubtless Sara herself, exposed to a rather invidious comparison 'with a more intellectual person' and naturally a trifle jealous of her husband's long walks with Dorothy, was nothing loth to emphasize her appreciation.

Meanwhile the work on *Osorio* advanced, and in October he sent the play to Sheridan. He had little hope of its 'success or even of its being acted'; for he knew his weakness as a dramatist. He could not create character because he was not intimate enough with humanity, could not lose himself impersonally in men and women. The 'sentimental moralist' which his hero represented was certainly more real because more personal than the sophisticated villain, but both were incapable of natural action. And metaphysical speculations, which are not inwoven into a play's action or significantly related to an actor's character, as in Hamlet, are irrelevant. *Osorio* had some poetical but little dramatic merit. At best Coleridge could only project his own sentiments like a ventriloquist into puppets or knock their heads violently together.

And at moments, even in this halcyon period, the fact
depressed him. He began to feel that the harmony with
Nature which he had boasted was a passing illusion.
Within him at least she seemed again 'in all her functions,
weary of herself.' But, as he wrote, 'God remains,' and,
what was more important, Wordsworth did. He could
forget his failure in daily conversation. In talk he had the
sensation of drifting, and his liking for the sensation led
him to plan a great poem on Man, Nature and Society
which should flow like a brook in its course from upland
source to the sea. But even a brook was too confined. If
only 'along some ocean's boundless solitude' he could
'float for ever with a careless course'!

Sometimes his talk with Wordsworth as they rambled
along the top of the Quantocks did float about such ulti-
mates. How was personality to be reconciled with
infinity? Was a sheet of paper, as a thing in itself,
separate from the *phænomenon* or image in the perception? Granted the existence of a Being, the ground of
all existence, was He necessarily a moral Creator and
Governour?

But Wordsworth's metaphysical range was limited.
He preferred to confine his theorizing to poetry and not
then to stray too far into abstractions. It was therefore on
the relations of actuality and imagination, of the natural
and the supernatural in poetry that their conversation
most frequently turned. They were both convinced of the
sterility of pseudo-classical verse, but while Coleridge
was particularly alive to its commonplace content, its
failure to give 'the interest of novelty by the modifying
colours of imagination,' Wordsworth stressed the artificiality of its diction. He argued that poetry should employ
'the language of ordinary,' or, as he sometimes described
it, 'of real life,' and should choose simple and even collo-
quial subjects. What he inferred by 'ordinary' or 'real' was

somewhat doubtful and scarcely satisfied Coleridge's taste for metaphysical definition, but it was enough that he wished to inject reality into poetry from below as Coleridge himself did from above. His statement of principle might be confused, though Coleridge was too sympathetic to stress the point, but it was his practice which mattered, and there was no doubt that in that he was beginning to achieve a reality which transcended altogether the elegant correctness of Pope and his school.

Coleridge was so convinced of it that on reading an account of the effects of witchcraft on the Negroes in the West Indies he made it the basis of what he called a common Ballad-tale supposed to be told in homely diction by an old sexton in a country churchyard to a traveller whose curiosity had been awakened by three graves. The story of 'The Three Graves,' as it was later named, was certainly too fantastic and *macabre* for Wordsworth, but Wordsworth's influence is evident enough in the diction, although Coleridge was later to deny that the poem was in any way connected with his views on diction. With his views indeed it may not have been, but one so sensitive to any influence as he, could not associate with Wordsworth for some weeks and listen to his poetry without reflecting its tone and accent. Wordsworth affected his style; he made it simpler and purged it of superfluous epithets without affecting in any way the nature of his poetical experience.

When Coleridge tried to be homely, as he did occasionally in this ballad, the result was a parody of Wordsworth's worst manner:

> 'But Ellen, spite of miry ways
>   And weather dark and dreary,
> Trudged every day to Edward's house
>   And made them all more cheery.

'Oh! Ellen was a faithful friend,
   More dear than any sister!
As cheerful too as singing lark;
And she ne'er left them till 'twas dark,
   And then they always missed her.'

The error in Wordsworth's theory concerning the inherent poetical virtue of 'the language of ordinary life' could not be better exemplified. But when Coleridge, while echoing Wordsworth's manner, sought to express his own morbid, necromantic consciousness, the result was not poetry perhaps, but the first crude vibrations of a poetry which in the next few months was to sound in perfection. It is not difficult for example to parallel such stanzas as the following in 'The Ancient Mariner':

"'Tis sweet to hear a brook, 'tis sweet
   To hear the Sabbath-bell,
'Tis sweet to hear them both at once
   Deep in a woody dell.'

Or:

'A tiny sun, and it has got
   A perfect glory too;
Ten thousand threads and hairs of light,
Make up a glory gay and bright
   Round that small orb, so blue.'

Or these in 'Christabel':

'Dear Ellen did not weep at all,
   But closelier did she cling,
And turned her face and looked as if
   She saw some frightful thing.'

Or:

"'Twas such a foggy time as makes
   Old sextons, Sir, like me,
Rest on their spades to cough; the spring
   Was late uncommonly.'

The strange blending of the supernatural element in himself with the natural diction of Wordsworth had begun. He was exciting his visionary mind by reading and emulating Swedenborg and Böhme. He suspended for some hours of the day 'all communication with sensible objects' and he confided to his note-book – 'Certainly, there are strange things in the other world, and so there are in all the steps to it; and a little *glimpse* of Heaven . . . any communication from the spirit of Comfort, which God gives to his servants in strange and unknown manners – are infinitely far from illusions.' And to Thelwall he wrote: '*All things* appear *little*, all the knowledge that can be acquired child's play. . . . My mind feels as if it ached to behold and know Something *Great*, something *one* and indivisible. . . . But in this faith *all things* counterfeit infinity. . . . It is but seldom that I raise and spiritualize my intellect to this height. . . . I should much wish, like the Indian Vishnu, to float about along an infinite ocean cradled in the flower of the Lotus, and wake once in a million years for a few minutes just to know that I was going to sleep a million years more.'

But fortunately Wordsworth, the pedestrian, was at hand to save these dreams from the void of somnambulism and induce Coleridge to convert them into feelings of vivid sense in a poem which has not its like, nor can have its like, as its author later claimed, in the English tongue.

On November 13, at half-past four on a dark and cloudy afternoon, Coleridge, Wordsworth and Dorothy set out on a walk to Watchet, intending from there to explore the coast as far as Linton and the Valley of the Stones. Their expenses were to be defrayed by a poem jointly composed on the way, for which they hoped that the editor of the *Monthly Magazine* would offer them £5. As they plodded along the Quantock Hills they searched after a possible theme. Coleridge had recently had a dream described to him by a friend in which a skeleton ship figured, manned by a ghostly navigator, and with this dream he associated incidents from various strange voyages of which he had been reading in books of travel, particularly an Epistle of Saint Paulinus to Macarius, telling of a miraculous shipwreck. Wordsworth, more interested in fact than fantasy, remembered that Shevelocke reported in his *Voyages* that he had frequently seen an albatross while doubling Cape Horn. 'Suppose,' said he, with a typical desire to blend the moral even with the miraculous, 'you represent him as having killed one of these birds on entering the South Sea, and that the tutelary spirits of these regions take upon them to avenge the crime.'

The idea fired Coleridge. He wanted something to justify the purely spiritual experience with which he knew his poetical powers to be most at home, and the ideas of vengeance and remorse appealed to him the more easily for their recent embodiment in *Osorio*. The two poets began composing together, or rather Coleridge uttered the first stanzas with the certainty of one repeating an incantation, and when he drew breath Wordsworth began to furnish a line or two. He furnished:

'He holds him with his glittering eye – '

he furnished:

'And listens like a three years' child
The Mariner hath his will.'

And after that, save for the lines:

'And thou art long, and lank, and brown
As is the ribbed sea-sand,'

the Mariner *had* his will.

For Coleridge was launched on strange seas where

Wordsworth could not follow him; his sails were caught in the wind of creative ecstasy:

'I moved, and could not feel my limbs
I was so light – almost
I thought that I had died in sleep,
And was a blessed ghost.

'And soon I heard a roaring wind:
It did not come anear;
But with its sound it shook the sails,
That were so thin and sere.'

The act of walking and in such company had released him. All the horrors which his uneasy nerves had stored, the apparitions that he had glimpsed, the strange reptiles he had read of, the sweet sounds of the June countryside so luxuriously absorbed, even the bassoon that had been added to the Stowey choir were suddenly caught in and overmastered by the need and delight of expression, an expression almost as involuntary as the movement of his body in walking. He had discovered 'the pleasurable activity of mind excited by the attractions of the journey itself. Like the motion of a serpent . . . or like the path of sound through air; – at every step he pauses and half recedes, and from the retrogressive movement collects the force which again carries him onward.' It was as if the vague images some still pool had reflected in its weedy depths suddenly rose to the surface when its waters were stirred to motion and floated there exquisitely clarified.

It is surely significant that Coleridge's finest poem and perhaps the finest descriptive passage in his letters should have been rooted in physical activity. Bodily movement enabled him to escape the stagnation which entangled his faculties. It was that stagnation which he imaged in the becalming of the ship while Death and Life-in-Death diced for the Mariner. This and the subsequent effortless movement of the ship were symbols of his own spiritual experience, of his sense of the lethargy that smothered his creative powers and his belief that only by some miracle of ecstasy which transcended all personal volition, he could elude a temperamental impotence. Impotence was the dæmon that he feared:

> 'Like one, that on a lonesome road
> Doth walk in fear and dread,
> And having once turned round walks on,
> And turns no more his head;
> Because he knows a frightful fiend
> Doth close behind him tread . . .'

It was the sense too of death haunting his own creative desire that made so poignant his love of gliding, glittering, tensely animated and tireless things, or that urged him to fling himself with a nightmare feverishness into the wild elements of nature, as in

> 'The upper air burst into life!
> And a hundred fire-flags sheen,
> To and fro, and in and out,
> The wan stars danced between.

> 'And the coming wind did roar more loud,
> And the sails did sigh like sedge;
> And the rain poured down from one black cloud;
> The Moon was at its edge.'

Like the Mariner 'in his loneliness and fixedness he yearneth towards the journeying Moon, and the stars that still sojourn, yet still move onward; and everywhere the blue sky belongs to them, and is their appointed rest, and

their native country and their own natural homes.' For
the moment he had himself found that natural home when
he wrote:

> 'The moving Moon went up the sky
> And nowhere did abide:
> Softly she was going up,
> And a star or two beside.'

In such lines he was one with the elements he worshipped
for their buoyancy as he was with the water-snakes that

> 'moved in tracks of shining white
> And when they reared, the elfish light
> Fell off in hoary flakes.

> 'Within the shadow of the ship
> I watched their rich attire:
> Blue, glossy green, and velvet black,
> They coiled and swam; and every track
> Was a flash of golden fire.

> 'O happy living things! no tongue
> Their beauty might declare:
> A spring of love gushed from my heart,
> And I blessed them unaware.'

It was by this creative communion with living things that
Coleridge, like his 'Ancient Mariner,' sought the absolu-
tion he longed for.

Fully to live is not merely to reflect but to create,
whether in life or art or thought, and Coleridge, being
essentially a poet, hungered for such a life in sickly defiance of a slothful nature. As he was to write later: 'all
the products of the mere reflective faculty partook of
death, and were as the rattling twigs and sprays in winter,
into which a sap was yet to be propelled from some root

to which I had not penetrated, if they were to afford my soul either food or shelter.'

In 'The Ancient Mariner' even his indolence trembled with life and motion:

> 'Oh sleep! it is a gentle thing
> Beloved from pole to pole!
> To Mary Queen the praise be given!
> She sent the Gentle Sleep from Heaven,
> That slid into my soul.'

And finally, what an allegory of his own longing to escape from the solitude of an abnormal consciousness the conclusion of the poem is!

> 'I pass, like night, from land to land;
> I have strange power of speech;
> That moment that his face I see,
> I know the man that must hear me:
> To him my tale I teach,'

is himself seeking relief throughout his life in endless monologues, because

> 'this soul hath been
> Alone on a wide wide sea:
> So lonely 'twas that God Himself
> Scarce seemed there to be.'

It is his own never-satisfied need of simple, devout human relationships which speaks in

> 'O sweeter than the marriage-feast,
> 'Tis sweeter far to me
> To walk together to the kirk
> With a goodly company!'

and his own childlike affection for everything without distinction in

'He prayeth best who loveth best
All things both great and small;
For the dear God who loveth us,
He made and loveth all.'

Finally in

'It is the Hermit good!
He singeth loud his godly hymns
That he makes in the wood.
He'll shrieve my soul, he'll wash away
The Albatross's blood,'

he strangely forecasted the conventional religious sanctuary to which he himself was at last to resort, when a wreck, with warped planks and sere sails, he drifted over the harbour-bar of Highgate.

To emphasize these personal parallels may seem a trifle superfluous, since Coleridge, of course, could not have achieved the imaginative triumph of the poem without projecting himself into every tone and gesture of his Mariner. But it is perhaps well to do so, if only to show why the poem reaches a higher level of reality than any other which he wrote.

It was no mere miracle of inventive fantasy, but an involuntary but inevitable projection into imagery of his own inner discord. The Mariner's sin against Nature in shooting the Albatross imaged his own morbid divorce from the physical: and the poem was therefore moral in its essence, in its implicit recognition of creative values and of the spiritual death which dogs their frustration.

Imagination can only be moral in this ultimate sense, and the explicit moral inserted at the end of the poem was a descent from the pure imaginative level. Coleridge knew that imagination was distinguished from fancy by its deeper loyalty to the creative principles, to the positive truth of life, and that this was its only moral obligation. But he knew also how slight a hold he himself had upon such principles and such truth, how often his dreams were vague and disorganic, how insecurely he lived beyond good and evil. And so as 'The Ancient Mariner' drew to a close, his fears returned. Had he been after all a mere romancer? Was the illusion, which he had achieved, true or false, arbitrary or necessary? Troubled, as he always was in his passive moments, with the sense of a vital moral obligation which he could not meet, he concluded his poem, as he was to conclude his life, with a conventional one.

But to emphasize the personal reference of the poem shows also that the miracle which had occurred had its roots in everything which had gone before. Coleridge's nature was not changed by his association with the Wordsworths or by the walk to Watchet, but his powers were suddenly co-ordinated. His whole spirit was at last engaged in an experience, which harmonized the passive and active tendencies of his nature, concentrated emotions previously diffused and charged the whole with creative delight. The very defects of his nature, its obscure discords, were unconsciously fused, as in a dream, and involuntarily dramatized in the person of a Mariner outlawed in a silent, festering sea.

The cause of this sudden transmutation of weakness into strength was perhaps the physical stimulus of walking with such companions and the fact that the theme and form of the poem was exactly suited to release his imagination from self-consciousness. For the form he was considerably indebted to Wordsworth, not so much for any details of ballad metre, as for the simple, natural diction which, with his amazing powers of speedy assimilation, he had spontaneously acquired and employed for effects which were quite alien to Wordsworth's experience.

Eight miles of the journey were enough to convince Wordsworth of that. It was evidently an undertaking, whatever its ultimate value might be, upon which he could only be 'a clog.' That 'willing suspension of disbelief,' which constituted Coleridge's poetic faith, was not his. How little it was his may be judged from his later criticism of the poem in which he wrote that it 'has indeed great defects; first that the principal person has no distinct character, either in his profession of Mariner, or as a human being . . .: secondly, that he does not act, but is continually acted upon: thirdly, that the events having no necessary connection do not produce each other; and lastly, that the imagery is too laboriously accumulated.'

This formidable and rather foolish indictment was due to his inability to allow that imagination could dispense with fact, or to recognize a pure poetic value which transcended human dimensions and transported human emotion into an unmapped region of sea and air. Regarded as a sequence of lyrical moods 'The Ancient Mariner' was perfectly related. It had its own higher logic, and Wordsworth's censures were as irrelevant as a literal application of the Aristotelian canon of the dramatic unities to 'The Tempest' or a play of Maeterlinck. Genius, as Coleridge was later to remark, is constituted in 'the power of acting creatively under laws of its own organization.' And the laws are necessarily modified by the nature of the subject matter which they govern.

If Coleridge had attempted to make the poem more concrete or humanly intelligible, it would have sunk immediately to the level of 'The Three Graves.' His imagination flagged at the touch of fact: it only moved coherently and vitally in a dream world, and 'the obtrusion of the moral sentiment' later seemed to him, and rightly, a fault in a work of such pure imagination.

Coleridge was drawn to Wordsworth because he possessed the moral and local sense of life which he himself lacked, because he sought to penetrate deeper into life as it was lived by ordinary men, and to make the world yield a meaning. At first companionship with such a man sustained him, helping him, as has been shown, to simplify and more adequately materialize his own very different experience. But little by little it depressed him. The finer flame was quenched by the stronger. Wordsworth's solider sense of things, of human beings and moral relations, served only to intensify his dissatisfaction with his own dream-shadowed, introspective genius. Unfortunately he was too moral and metaphysically minded himself to be content to be a purely lyrical poet, communicating immediate experience valued only for itself; and yet he lacked the faculty to be anything else. Ought he, he increasingly asked himself, to reject the actual to enjoy the ideal? Had such an ideal any desirable reality? Was he harmonizing his own experience merely by avoiding its discord? Had poetry of this kind only the superficial charm of strangeness?

That was his dilemma, and Wordsworth's virtues aggravated it. To use the terms of a distinction made by a modern critic, Wordsworth's aim as a poet was that of interpretation, Coleridge's that of refuge, and the fact made him ashamed of taking flight from a world of distress and discord into that peculiar world of his own which was under a spell. It made him long for self-command when all his hopes of realizing his genius lay in self-surrender.

The process of disillusion had begun which was to end in his writing to Godwin: 'If I die and the booksellers will give you anything for my Life, be sure to say, "Wordsworth descended on him like the γνῶθι σεαυτόν from heaven; and by showing him what true poetry was, he made him know that he himself was no poet."'

§ 3

The rejection of *Osorio* by Sheridan in December must have increased his doubts, and when in the same month he was invited to preach at a Unitarian chapel at Shrewsbury as a prospective candidate for the Ministry, he accepted the offer. He disliked 'preaching God's holy word for hire,' but literature promised to bring him nothing, except pain and unrest, while these were as 'the fertilizing rain' to a professionally 'religious benevolent man' whose life was 'an April day.'

It was true that the 'hey-day of hope' and enthusiasm in which absolute religious and political liberty seemed so necessary and desirable was already passing. He was half disgusted with the 'absurdities of sectarian and democratic fanaticism,' and no longer derived any pleasure from mounting 'his darling hobby-horse, "the republic of God's own making" ' or from scattering 'levelling sedition.' The very freedom which Unitarianism claimed for the individual, the emphasis it laid on rational judgment, failed to satisfy both his mystical bent and his need of substantial support. Secretly he began to feel that the Established Church was more likely to satisfy his requirements. It was a venerable and respectable institution, which offered to its inmates, with a very small sacrifice of personal conviction, a solid sense of security.

But it did not offer a yearly stipend of £150, and so he went by coach to Shrewsbury and was entertained by Mr. Rowe, whom he contemplated succeeding. Among the congregation on the Sunday morning was one William Hazlitt, the son of a neighbouring minister, who had walked ten miles in the mud to hear him preach, a young man whose mind was full of thoughts which he could not express and who was therefore the more amazed at the volubility of the 'round-faced man in black,' with nevertheless 'a strange wildness in his aspect,' who rose and gave out as his text, 'And he went up into the mountain to pray, HIMSELF ALONE,' in a voice, too, which, as he described it in days no longer inarticulate, ' "rose like a stream of rich distilled perfumes"; and when he came to the last words, which he pronounced loud, deep, and distinct,' it seemed to his listener 'as if the sounds had echoed from the bottom of the human heart, and as if that prayer might have floated in solemn silence through the universe.'

Doubtless it was the soul of the Mariner so recently 'alone on a wide wide sea' that gave to Coleridge's voice so reverberating an intonation. And the sermon upon peace and war was a kindred incantation. 'I could not have been more delighted,' wrote Hazlitt, 'if I had heard the music of the spheres. Poetry and Philosophy had met together. Truth and Genius had embraced under the eye and with the sanction of Religion.'

On the following Tuesday the enchanter called on Hazlitt's father, and while he 'glanced over a variety of subjects' the same observer had an opportunity of marking more closely his features. 'His complexion was . . . clear, and even bright. His forehead . . . broad and high, light as if built of ivory, with large projecting eyebrows, and his eyes rolling beneath them, like a sea with darkened lustre. . . . His mouth was gross, voluptuous, open, eloquent; his chin good-humoured and round; but his nose, the rudder of the face, the index of the will, was small, feeble, nothing. . . . It might seem that the genius of his face as from a height surveyed and projected him . . . into the world unknown of thought and imagination, with nothing to support or guide his veering purpose. . . . His person was rather above the common size, inclining to the corpulent. . . . His hair . . . black and glossy as the raven's . . . fell in smooth masses over his forehead.'

The next morning, however, a letter arrived which

promised both to support and guide his veering purpose.
Among Poole's friends, with whom Coleridge had become
acquainted, were two brothers, Thomas and Josiah Wedgwood, sons of the famous potter. They had inherited a
considerable fortune, of which they regarded themselves
'rather as Trustees than Proprietors.' Thomas suffered
from an obscure disease, which he was incessantly struggling to cure or relieve, but which was in fact incurable.
He was an excellent chemist, but this unfortunately
induced him to experiment continually with drugs in the
hope of recovering his health. He was also deeply interested in metaphysics and this was the chief bond between
Coleridge and himself. When the two brothers heard that
Coleridge intended abandoning poetry and philosophy for
the Ministry, they sent him £100 in the hope of dissuad-
ing him. Coleridge thanked them but returned the cheque.
It offered no security for the future. But on the Wednes-
day morning at the Hazlitts' house he received another
letter offering him on the same terms a regular yearly
annuity of £150, an annuity 'to be independent of
everything' but the wreck of his benefactors' fortune. It
arrived with a covering letter from Poole, who wrote to
his 'dearly beloved' that 'it would be palsying that benevolence, which, God be praised, does exist in the human
breast, to think of refusing it.'

Coleridge decided to accept the offer while he was tying
on one of his shoes. It relieved both his financial and
mental embarrassments. For he had already decided, as
he confided to Hazlitt, that he could not accept the
Shrewsbury situation. He realized that his sympathies
were no longer with Unitarianism, and although, as he
went on his way accompanied for six miles by his young
admirer, he condemned that erstwhile 'great and good
man, Archdeacon Paley' as a 'mere time-serving casuist,'
his feet were really set towards the Church and the faith

of which that syllogistic divine was to be the perennial apologist.

§ 4

The Wedgwoods' gift gave a new impulse to Coleridge's poetic faith. Perhaps after all, instead of being a Dissenting Pastor, he was really 'to inhabit the Hill of Parnassus, to be a Shepherd on the Delectable Mountains.' And if Wordsworth strode on so far before that he 'dwindled in the distance,' Dorothy was glad to walk with him on the lower slopes. So for the first three months of 1798 she walked with him incessantly. With her encouragement the perfect telling of a fairy tale did not seem so unworthy an aim. It was not until March 23 that he could bring 'The Ancient Mariner' to her complete in its final form, but meanwhile he was working on another poem the idea of which he had derived from Spenser, and possibly from Mrs. Radcliffe's *Romance of the Forest*. He intended to describe in it the bewitching of a maiden 'Christabel' by a fiend, disguised as a lady in distress; and to emancipate himself the more from mundane consciousness, he planned to found the metre on an accentual principle, which gave a greater variation in the number of syllables to a line.

But as he walked to and fro from Alfoxden with Dorothy their talk had little reference to prosody. She showed him the first strawberry flower under the hedge, the locks of wool, spotted with red marks, that the sheep had left upon the paling, the vapour sliding in one mighty mass upon the seashore, and how the distant country, overhung by straggling clouds that sailed upon it, seemed itself like a bank of darker cloud. She bid him listen to the snow dripping from the holly boughs and the slender notes of a redbreast, or they lay on the turf together, and if her questing eyes captured no 'perfect image of delight,' fancy filled the void. The year advanced and they worshipped the gathering tide of 'soft and vivid green.'

But nights perhaps were even more enchanting than days. On January 27 they walked from seven o'clock till half-past eight, and in a wood, as she wrote in her Journal, 'the moon burst through the invisible veil which enveloped her, the shadows of the oaks blackened, and their lines became more strongly marked. . . . The manufacturer's dog makes a strange, uncouth howl, which it continues many minutes after there is no noise near it but that of the brook.'

And Coleridge, who through her had lived these moments as vividly as she, turned to his poem and wrote:

'Sir Leoline, the Baron rich
Hath a toothless mastiff, which
From her kennel beneath the rock
Maketh answer to the clock,
Four for the quarters, and twelve for the hour;
Ever and aye, by shine and shower,
Sixteen short howls, not over loud;
Some say, she sees my lady's shroud.'

On March 7 she drank tea with her brother at Coleridge's. 'A cloudy sky,' she wrote. 'Observed nothing particularly interesting – the distant prospect obscured. One only leaf upon the top of a tree – the sole remaining leaf – danced round and round like a rag blown by the wind.' March 24 was a dull night: 'a sort of white shade over the blue sky. The stars dim. The spring continues to advance very slowly, no green trees, the hedges leafless; nothing green but the brambles that still retain their old leaves. . . . The crooked arm of the old oak tree points upwards to the moon.' And on the next evening, spent

again at Stowey, she noted – 'The night cloudy but not
dark.' And Coleridge continued his poem:

'Is the night chilly and dark?
The night is chilly, but not dark.
The thin gray cloud is spread on high,
It covers but not hides the sky.
The moon is behind, and at the full;
And yet she looks both small and dull.
The night is chill, the cloud is gray:
'Tis a month before the month of May,
And the Spring comes slowly up this way. . . .

'She stole along, she nothing spoke,
The sighs she heaved were soft and low,
And naught was green upon the oak
But moss and rarest mistletoe.
She kneels beneath the huge oak tree,
And in silence prayeth she. . . .

'The night is chill; the forest bare;
Is it the wind that moaneth bleak?
There is not wind enough in the air
To move away the ringlet curl
From the lovely lady's cheek –
There is not wind enough to twirl
The one red leaf, the last of its clan,
That dances as often as dance it can,
Hanging so light, and hanging so high,
On the topmost twig that looks up at the sky.'

Thus 'Christabel' was born between them. Coleridge's
was the fantastic fancy, the power of enchanting transmutation; Dorothy's was the vivid sense of the sights and
sounds of nature that supplemented his vaguer vision. As
to any definite plot, the poem never had one until in later

years Coleridge invented one to excuse his inability to continue it.

It was the projection of a romantic mood, of a haunted mood also, like 'The Ancient Mariner.' For the fiend of this poem, as of another – written shortly afterwards:

> 'That sometimes from the savage den,
> And sometimes from the darksome shade
> And sometimes starting up at once
> In green and sunny glade,'–

came and looked him in the face, was the phantom of his own despair which haunted even his happiest moments.

But the poem was the fruit also of a tender association. Without the association it could scarcely have come into being; for his magical powers were already being sapped by circumstance, and, save for a moment when they were artificially restored by a narcotic, 'Christabel' was the last poem in which they were fully realized. In two other poems of this year, 'Love' and 'The Ballad of the Dark Ladie,' there are echoes of the same note, but their general level is more conventionally romantic. Both surely are haunted by Dorothy's presence, although it would be misleading to suggest that they were actually addressed to her. Coleridge addressed her, as he had addressed Mary Evans, as 'Sister.' It was for him the perfect relationship and he implied by it something more than brotherly affection. At once feminine and childlike himself he responded to any woman's sympathy with a tenderness devoid of passion but at times almost fulsome in its feeling. For a woman of such subtle sensibility as Dorothy Wordsworth his devotion only differed in degree. At moments it was translated into the poetry of an enchanted communion, and doubtless it was an image of her which floated through the poem 'Love' and underlay the 'Dark Ladie.' She lives, a consoling phantom, in the stanzas:

'The moonshine, stealing o'er the scene
Had blended with the lights of eve;
And she was there, my hope, my joy,
    My own dear Genevieve!

.   .   .   .

'Few sorrows hath she of her own.
My hope! my joy! my Genevieve!
She loves me best, whene'er I sing
    The songs that make her grieve.

'I played a soft and doleful air,
I sang an old and moving story –
An old rude song, that suited well
    That ruin wild and hoary.'

Or in:

'Wait only till the hand of eve
Hath wholly closed yon western bars,
And through the dark we two will steal
    Beneath the twinkling stars.'

In such verses, intermingled with the relaxed sentiment
typical of Coleridge whenever he set himself to write a
love poem, the meetings of which 'Christabel' was born
are unconsciously remembered; and in two other stanzas,
again doubtless unconsciously, more light is shed on his
relationship with Dorothy than by any amount of inference
from later events:

'My friends with rude ungentle words
They scoff and bid me fly to thee!
O give me shelter in thy breast!
    O shield and shelter me!

'My Henry, I have given thee much,
I gave what I can ne'er recall,
I gave my heart, I gave my peace,
    O Heaven! I gave thee all.'

The poet and the dreamer, as modern psychology has demonstrated, are closely akin. The images which come to both are dramatizations of the subconscious. With Coleridge the comparison is particularly relevant, since he was a somnambulist even in his waking hours, and all his purest poetry was written in a state of trance. These two stanzas may be regarded merely as parts of a romantic ballad and doubtless he wrote them as such. But they are surely self-confession too, and the second of them may even reflect the self-accusation which he was far too irresponsible to admit to his conscious mind, but which emerged in this way from the subconscious. Certainly the first embodies in picturesque language the need which Dorothy supplied, and the second, with tragic completeness, the price which she is now recognized to have paid.

And if 'Christabel' was almost the last of his pure incantations, 'Frost at Midnight' was, except for a passage in 'The Nightingale' written two months later, the last of his domestic idylls. Sara's possibilities as a poetic stimulant were never considerable and could not be compared with Dorothy's, but infancy and childhood made a particular appeal to the childlike in Coleridge. For him, who was in his buoyant hours, as Wordsworth recorded, noisy

'and gamesome as a boy;
His limbs would toss about him with delight,
Like branches when strong winds the trees annoy,'

the eager, oblivious, activity of a child was an image of that perfect natural expressiveness which he longed to realize himself. 'They seem,' he wrote later of young children, 'to be the immediate and secreting organ of Hope in the great organized body of the whole human race, in *all men* considered as the component atoms of *Man* – as young leaves are but organs of supplying vital air to the atmosphere.' But poetry told more than such scientific analogies.

> 'A little child, a limber elf,
> Singing, dancing to itself,
> A fairy thing with red round cheeks,
> That always finds, and never seeks,
> Makes such a vision to the sight
> As fills a father's eyes with light.'

'That always finds and never seeks' – such he was himself in his purest poetic moments; and the light that filled his eyes as he watched Hartley at play was often rendered poignant by self-comparison. This was the mood which he extemporized so tenderly in 'Frost at Midnight.' Surely his infant should realize the freedom, physical and spiritual, of which he was ever by some circumstance or some sultry inhibition being balked:

> 'My babe so beautiful! It thrills my heart
> With tender gladness, thus to look at thee,
> And think that thou shalt learn far other lore,
> And in far other scenes! For I was reared
> In the Great City, pent 'mid cloisters dim,
> And saw nought lovely but the sky and stars.
> But *thou*, my babe! shall wander like a breeze
> By lakes and sandy shores, beneath the crags
> Of ancient mountain, and beneath the clouds,
> Which image in their bulk both lakes and shores
> And mountain crags.'

Strangely prophetic the lines were, since at the time he had no prospect of living in the Lake Country; strangely pathetic too in the light of his own future decline beneath those mountain crags!

And indeed a period was already being set to his happiness. Fact was beginning to threaten fantasy, and fear, public and private, to trouble peace. In April there was an alarm of a French invasion and even in 'a green and silent spot amid the hills' it was no longer possible 'in a half sleep' to dream 'of better worlds.' Wordsworth's attitude to life and his own maturing mind had deprived him of that solace, and yet a contrite, but at heart conventional, patriotism and 'the thoughts that yearn for humankind' could not inspire his mind as they did Wordsworth's. Only the supernatural could give it 'a livelier impulse and a dance of thought,' or that 'gentle Maid'

> 'vowed and dedicate
> To something more than Nature in the Grove.'

'Fears might crowd upon him in Solitude' but he forgot them when with Dorothy in the wood, in which day by day through this sunny April they walked together, he listened to the nightingale,

> 'That crowds, and hurries, and precipitates
> With fast thick warble his delicious notes. . . .
> But never elsewhere in one place I knew
> So many nightingales; and far and near,
> In wood and thicket, over the wide grove,
> They answer and provoke each other's songs,
> With skirmish and capricious passagings,
> And murmurs musical and swift jug, jug,
> And one low piping sound more sweet than all –
>
> '. . . she knows all these notes,
> That gentle Maid! and oft, a moment's space,
> What time the moon was lost behind a cloud,
> Hath heard a pause of silence; till the moon
> Emerging, hath awakened earth and sky
> With one sensation, and those wakeful birds
> Have all burst forth in choral minstrelsy,
> As if some sudden gale had swept at once

A hundred airy harps! And she hath watched
Many a nightingale perch giddily
On blossoming twig still swinging from the breeze,
And to that motion tune his wanton song
Like tipsy joy that reels with tossing head.'

It was the last occasion in his poetry in which 'Nature seemed to bless him as a thing of her own.' He was to worship her in the future, but always as a rejected suitor longing for the embrace which once he had known, and it is fitting that the nightingale, of all Nature's voices the most luxuriously buoyant, should have inspired his ecstatic farewell.

§ 5

For April, apart from Dorothy, was a month of troubles. In the first place Sara was shortly expecting a baby. The fact, as before, filled him, despite the Wedgwood annuity, with financial forebodings. And his nervous depression was intensified by a painful rupture with Lloyd, a rupture all the more harrowing because it also temporarily alienated Lamb. 'Alas!' as to relieve his pain, he wrote in 'Christabel':

'they had been friends in youth;
But whispering tongues can poison truth;
And constancy lives in realms above;
And life is thorny; and youth is vain;
And to be wroth with one we love
Doth work like madness in the brain.'

Estrangement with anyone meant anguish to Coleridge: it intensified his sense of loneliness. That the 'gentle hearted Charles' should have been perverted by the diseased tittle-tattle of Lloyd shook his faith in human understanding.

Of course Lloyd had taken full advantage of his engaging confidences and grossly distorted them. He told Lamb that Coleridge had contrasted himself with Lamb in a distinction which he drew between Genius and Talent, that he had said: 'Poor Lamb! if he wants *any* knowledge, he may apply to me,' and Lamb had accepted it all literally. He had abandoned him for a man who, as Coleridge plaintively wrote, 'became attached to you in consequence of my attachment, caught *his* from my enthusiasm, and learned to love you at my fireside, when often while I have been sitting and talking of your sorrows and affliction I have stopped my conversation and lifted up wet eyes and prayed for you.' Even the mock sonnets ridiculing his own and his friend's weaker style, which he had sent to the *Monthly Magazine* six months before under the name of 'Nehemiah Higginbottom,' were now brought up against him, and Southey too affected displeasure.

Finally Lloyd had written a novel of which the chief character was no less than a libellous portrait of his late host, and in which, besides caricaturing his dreamy incapacity, he suggested that he was addicted to laudanum.

Such ingratitude cut deeply into his heart; it also reduced him to a nervous state in which the most trifling thing made him weep. The wound to his sentiments he tried to heal by moralizing. 'Times change and people change,' he wrote, 'but let us keep our souls in quietness,' and 'I pray God that I may sanctify these events by forgiveness and a peaceful spirit full of love.' A peaceful spirit, however, could not ease the toothache. For that, as he told his brother George, 'Laudanum gave me repose, not sleep; but you, I believe, know how divine that repose is, what a spot of enchantment, a green spot of fountain and flowers and trees in the very heat of a waste of sands!'

It was such a spot that he discovered in a lonely farmhouse between Porlock and Linton to which he retired to try and compose his feelings by a change of scene. After taking a dose of opium he fell asleep in his chair while reading the following passage in *Purchas' Pilgrimage*: 'In Xanadu did Cublai Can build a stately Palace, encompassing sixteene miles of plaine ground with a wall, wherein are fertile Meddowes, pleasant springs, delightfull Streames, and all sorts of beasts of chase and game, and in the middest thereof a sumptuous house of pleasure.'

The sleep thus induced lasted for about three hours, during which he was convinced that he composed from two to three hundred lines, 'if that indeed can be called composition in which all the images rose up before him as *things*, with a parallel produćtion of the correspondent expressions, without any sensation or consciousness of effort.' The whole was so vivid in his mind when he woke, that he instantly began to write it down. Unfortunately, however, he was very soon interrupted by 'a person on business from Porlock,' and after being detained by him above an hour, was mortified to find that, save for some eight or ten scattered lines and images, 'all the rest had passed away like the images on the surface of a stream into which a stone has been cast, but, alas! without the after restoration of the latter!'

The simile was exaćt as it was happy. Coleridge's genius was the genius of a stream, a moving mirror that mixed and recombined the images which it passively reflećted. 'Kubla Khan' was only an extreme example of the involuntary and almost automatic process which produced 'Christabel' and 'The Ancient Mariner.' Not only Purchas, but Bartram's *Travels* and Maurice's *History of Hindostan* were brewed in the witches' cauldron. *Paradise Lost*, as a critic has recently pointed out, was also an ingredient. 'Alph, the sacred river,' probably derived from that which

'Southward through *Eden* went. . . .
Nor changed his course but through a shaggie hill
Pass'd underneath ingulft . . . ,'

the 'gardens bright with sinuous rills' from

'Rose a fresh Fountain, and with many a rill
Watered the Garden; thence united fell
Down the steep glade, and met the neather Flood,'

and, most significant of all:

> 'It was an Abyssinian maid,
> And on her dulcimer she played,
> Singing of Mount Abora,'

from

> 'Nor where Abassin Kings their issue Guard,
> Mount Amara.'

Thus images, stored up in the deeps of memory and dissociated entirely from meaning, rose to the surface and were rhythmically blended in unconscious association. 'Kubla Khan' is an extreme example of the process, of the sacrifice of meaning to image, and is for that reason no more than a wonderful narcotic.

All great lyrical poetry has the quality of an incantation, but its sense is merged in, not sacrificed to sound. Coleridge had little originating force or capacity to transmute fact into image. He was unique, as a dreamer, in recombining images which he had accepted without fully assimilating. In 'Kubla Khan' the dreaming process, the imagination's absolute independence of fact, was complete.

But to dream, it was necessary to sleep. And that, without opium, Coleridge could no longer do. The world was too much with him and his nerves were on edge. In an Ode to France, originally entitled 'The Recantation,' a poem which also borrowed a phrase or two from Milton

and the last in which he had sufficient faith in Abstract
Freedom to honour her with fine verse, he had already
expressed his disillusionment that France should have
failed to present 'to the observation of Europe a people
more happy and better instructed than under other forms
of Government.' But now, like Wordsworth, he was paying the price for his early sentimentalism. And with him
realism killed poetry without a hope of resurrection.
Ironically enough he who had renewed Wordsworth's
faith and so his creative powers could not adjust his own.
Compromise, any modification of absolute conceptions by
material considerations, was fatal to his poetic genius as
it always is to the self-indulgent as distinct from the self-
annihilating Romantic.

His imagination could only function amid ideals
remote from contemporary fact, and France seethed with
savage, unavoidable fact. Social man, he was driven to
admit, was too selfishly depraved to realize freedom under
any form of government; and what hope could he place
in individual man after the treatment he had received
from Lloyd?

Little wonder then that he wrote to his brother George,
– 'Of guilt I say nothing, but I believe most steadfastly
in original sin . . . our organization is depraved and our
volitions imperfect.' From this stark acceptance of evil,
poetic idealism such as his offered no longer a refuge, nor
for the time indeed did metaphysics. 'Our quaint metaphysical opinions,' he confided to his note-book, 'in the
hour of anguish like a plaything by the bedside of a deadly
sick child.' They must be reinforced, he felt, by religious
belief – 'the *spirit* of the Gospel is the sole cure,' adding
that 'without religious joys and religious terrors,
nothing can be expected from the inferior classes in
society.'

The conviction had been growing upon him with each

experience of failure. After the collapse of *The Watchman* he had written, 'We have all become more religious than we were' and regretted his 'precipitance in praise of Godwin.' He said the same during the nightmare months which preceded his coming to Stowey and sent Thelwall an earnest, if rather sermonizing, defence of Christianity. And now that both poetical and political faith were failing him ('The Opposition and the Democrats' he denounced as 'not only vicious, they wear the *filthy garments* of vice'), he snapped his 'squeaking baby-trumpet of sedition' and wished 'to be a good man and a Christian,' not a Whig, Reformist or Republican.

Mrs. Coleridge was embarrassed by the change. Her mind ran in simple channels, and if her husband had become respectable, she wished to be able to announce the fact categorically. 'It is very unpleasant to me,' she complained, 'to be often asked if Coleridge has changed his political sentiments, for I know not properly how to reply. Pray furnish me.'

But the change was not a matter of simple definition. It might indeed have been Wordsworth who wrote: 'I devote myself to such works as encroach not on the anti-social passions – in poetry to elevate the imagination and set the affections in right tune by the beauty of the inanimate impregnated as with a living soul by the presence of life. . . . I love fields and woods and mountains with almost a visionary fondness. And because I have found benevolence and quietness growing within me as that fondness has increased, therefore I should wish to be the means of implanting it in others.' But there was a difference between the two men's opinions of what 'a Christian' implied. Coleridge regretted it: he reverenced his friend's powers; he admitted that he was 'a tried good man,' but 'on one subject we are habitually silent; we found our data dissimilar, and never renewed the subject.

. . . He loves and venerates Christ and Christianity. I wish he did more.'

The difference was very significant. Wordsworth was still a free man, evolving a faith for himself out of experience, and so his poetic powers were unprejudiced. For ten years at least they remained so, and then imperceptibly he surrendered to a conventional orthodoxy and to that Sabbatical style which later Coleridge happily described as his 'I and my brother the Dean manner.' But Coleridge was already compromised, had already flinched from standing alone; and so the elevating poetry which he planned was never realized, and most of his metaphysics was fatally prejudiced by religious presuppositions. A clerical conscience interposed between him and the Nature with which he could identify himself only in moments of utter abandon. And even the comparative orthodoxy which he had accepted did not solve his difficulties. Christianity he described as his 'passion,' but 'it is too much my *intellectual* passion and therefore will do me but little good in the hour of temptation and calamity.'

The words were prophetic enough. Neither his faith in Nature nor in Christ was ever complete or concrete enough to brace him for the activities of life. In both he merely took Sanctuary.

His spirits however improved as the summer advanced. In May a second son was born and christened Berkeley; Hazlitt came on a visit, and Coleridge joined Wordsworth in a trip to Cheddar. Arrangements too were made with Cottle to collaborate in a volume of verse to be entitled *Lyrical Ballads*. But behind these pleasant activities loomed the fact that the Wordsworths had to quit Alfoxden in June. It was depressing and unsettling, and the thirty guineas promised for the copyright of the poems suggested a scheme by which the association could be prolonged.

Germany was the home of the Romantic Movement, of its nostalgia and transcendentalism. To Germany they would go, all of them at least save Sara and the children. In August Coleridge followed the Wordsworths to Bristol, and the scheme by that time had assumed the character of a serious mission, the realization of which was 'of great importance' to his 'intellectual activity' and of course to his 'moral happiness.' In September they were in London and a few days before starting, the *Lyrical Ballads* were published anonymously. Mrs. Coleridge wrote later with a blunt honesty which exceeded the truth, that they were 'not liked at all by any'; and that was all the poets heard of them. They embarked at Yarmouth on the 16th and reached Hamburg three days later.

§ 6

Dressed all in black, with large shoes and black worsted stockings, Coleridge might well have passed on board, as he suggested, for a Methodist missionary. But his bearing was in no way Methodistical. Impervious to seasickness, he drank, sang, and danced. And he talked so well that he drew from an intoxicated Dane the following comprehensive tribute: 'Vat imagination! vat language! vat vast science! and vat eyes! vat a milk-vite forehead! O my heafen! vy, you're a Got!'

Characteristically enough his expectation of the sea's immensity far outran the reality, and he was consequently disappointed 'at the narrowness and *nearness* . . . of the circle of the horizon.' Only by night was the ocean 'a whole thing.' But now that Sara and the children were become images in the mind, they inspired a really doting affection. 'Every night,' he wrote to his wife, 'when I go to bed, and every morning when I rise, I will think with yearning love of you and of my blessed babes' and 'after the antique principles of *Religion*, unsophisticated by

Philosophy, will be, I trust, your husband faithful unto death.' After landing at Hamburg, however, he felt 'like a liberated bird that had been hatched in an aviary, who now, after the first soar of freedom, poises himself in the upper air,' and this, despite or possibly because of his eventual claim to have worked harder in Germany 'than I trust God Almighty I shall ever have occasion to work again,' despite too a sorrow that fell upon him during his stay, was the dominant mood of the next nine months.

Fact lends little support to the suggestion that Germany killed the poet in Coleridge. He devoted himself to mastering the language, he attended lectures, and he studied modern German literature. He projected a life of Lessing, but he only dipped into other metaphysicians. His immersion in Kant, so often attributed to these days, did not occur until at least a year after his return. For the time he confessed to finding him utterly incomprehensible, though almost every German professor was a Kantean to some degree. It is true that his letters to Sara were often couched in a pathetic and appealing key, but the home-sickness they embodied was as transient as that of a callow schoolboy and too fulsome in its expression to convince of the anguish which they claimed. By his own account he could not receive a letter without palpitations, yet he begged his wife to write 'all that can cheer me; all that will make my eyes swim and my heart melt with tenderness.'

But at Ratzeburg, where he stayed with a German pastor for four months after parting with the Wordsworths, he was sufficiently master of his feelings to turn them into charming verse, a clear proof of his happier condition, even though the stanzas were not written 'without a yearning, yearning, yearning *Inside*.' They were, as he entitled them, 'Something childish, but very natural,' and as exquisitely typical of the playful pathos and confiding tenderness of his nature as anything which he ever wrote:

> 'If I had but two little wings
> And were a little feathery bird,
> To you I'd fly, my dear!
> But thoughts like these are idle things,
> And I stay here.

> 'But in my sleep to you I fly:
> I'm always with you in my sleep!
> The world is all one's own.
> But then one wakes, and where am I?
> Alone, all alone.

> 'Sleep stays not, though a monarch bids:
> So I love to wake ere break of day:
> For though my sleep be gone,
> Yet while 'tis dark one shuts one's lids
> And still dreams on.'

But Coleridge was on the whole so happy in Germany because he was so little alone. At Ratzeburg, for instance, he was surrounded by children who corrected his pronunciation 'in pretty, pert lisps.' And though he might assure his wife of his longing to be home, he confessed to others that 'no little fish thrown back again into water, no fly unimprisoned from a child's hand, could more buoyantly enjoy its element, than I this clean and peaceful house.'

The Gentry and Nobility too paid him 'almost an adulatory attention,' and then there was a 'sweet little woman' – a Countess Kilmansig – with 'perfectly white, regular, French teeth,' whose heart he quite won by the gift of a German poem. He abandoned vegetarianism too in time to enjoy the German Christmas, and early in the New Year he was skating on the lake and marvelling at the prismatic effects of colour in the ice. Similarly when he went to Göttingen in the following March he was adopted by a group of high-spirited English students, and renewed, between bouts of abstruse speculation, something of the revelry of his early Cambridge days. In abstaining on the whole from writing poetry he was merely following Poole's advice. He was refusing to be diverted from his proposed aim 'to attend to those things which are better attained in Germany than elsewhere.' And he clearly felt the better for it. 'The journey to Germany,' he wrote, 'has certainly done me good. My habits are less irregular and my mind more in my own power.'

His letters justified his claim to greater self-awareness; the fact was indeed in his case not to favour poetry, but it was an inevitable condition of growth which would have occurred, though maybe less rapidly, if he had never crossed the sea. He wrote, for example, of the 'disease' of his mind that 'it is comprehensive in its conceptions, and wastes itself in the contemplations of the many things which it might do.' And later, 'I have at times experienced such an extinction of *light* in my mind – I have been so forsaken by all the *forms* and *colourings* of existence, as if the *organs* of life had been dried up; as if only simple Being remained, blind and stagnant'; and again – 'Love is the vital air of my genius.' In a portrait of Lessing too he saw a great likeness to himself. 'The whole face,' he added, 'seemed to say that Lessing was a man of quick and voluptuous feelings . . . acute; yet acute not in the observation of actual life, but in the arrangements and management of the ideal world, that is, in taste, and in metaphysics.'

The point at which he had arrived in his own development coincided exactly with the change that had affected methods of criticism in Germany. More and more baffled in self-expression, he had begun to examine the nature of his perception – a perception which he felt to be morbid and ineffective. And in the leaders of German criticism he discovered men who were engaged on a similar examination of æsthetic perception, who had broken through the formal and external methods of classical criticism and were studying art less for its own sake than for the light which it threw upon the nature of the intellectual and moral faculties. In the disinterested experience of beauty Kant had harmonized the conflicting kinds of perception of which his system was an extended analysis, and in similar metaphysical study Coleridge hoped to resolve in theory or at least explain the discord in his own perception which foiled his practice as a poet.

It is well to recognize from the start the personal bias of all his metaphysical inquiry, since it explains its genera ineffectuality. The great philosopher is a great poet inverted. He interprets a rich experience in terms of idea, as the poet in terms of image. Significant metaphysics are creative as significant poetry is: both transcend the purely personal and accidental, both are rooted in a physical sense of life. Their axioms, in Keats' words, are 'proved upon our pulses.' On the contrary, both fanciful poetry and fanciful metaphysics are self-sufficient activities of the imagination and mind respectively which avoid reference to the actual. Kant, idealist as he was, did not avoid this reference, but Coleridge did, and was therefore for the most part what he called Rousseau, 'a spinner of speculative cobwebs.' His metaphysics, like his poetry, were possessed by the spirit of evasion, were an escape from the real rather than an apprehension and analysis of reality, although in both he achieved moments of remarkable insight.

What attracted him in German idealism was its proof of the insufficiency of the senses either as the criterion of truth or belief. But while Kant included the senses in his synthesis of *a priori* perception, Colcridge merely used Kant's arguments to excuse his own lack of keen sense-perception. In the metaphysical speculation into which he was shortly to plunge he was engaged in explaining, and so, to some extent, comforting himself in his impotence. At his best too he did distinguish what the elements of ideal expression were, though in terms generally too descriptive to be quite satisfactory. But the first principles which he was to preach with wearisome iteration, and such distinctions as he drew between subjective and objective, were little more than mechanical extemporizations upon borrowed terms in an attempt to forget that he was himself too morbidly subjective to reconcile them in any significant unity.

But although he could conceal the fact more easily in metaphysics than in poetry, he was to fail in the one to the same extent as he had failed in the other. In both he was a transmitter rather than an originator, and his imagination, reduced to its abstract elements in metaphysics, still trafficked with the unreal. Only when he was tied to the particular in the criticism of poetry can he be said to have achieved an analysis of real experience, an analysis in which metaphysical ideas were adequately sustained by psychological insight. It was a kind of criticism which he may be truly said to have originated, and he acquired the faculty from a long and subtle observance of his own pathological states.

But Germany was no more responsible than Plotinus for changing him from a poet into a metaphysician. The needs and defects of his own nature determined that. How inherent his philosophizing tendency was may be measured by the way in which he received from Poole in March the news of his son Berkeley's death. His wife wrote of her own suffering that it was beyond his conception, and his reply to Poole corroborated her. 'I read your letter in calmness,' he wrote, 'and walked out into the open fields, oppressed, not by my feelings, but by the riddles which the thought so easily proposes, and solves never! . . . Fling yourself forward into your immortality only a few thousand years, and how small will not the difference between one year old and sixty years appear! . . . But I cannot truly say that I grieve – I am perplexed – I am sad – and a little thing – a very trifle – would make me weep – but for the death of the baby I have *not* wept! Oh the strange, strange, strange scene-shifter Death! – that giddies one with insecurity and so unsubstantiates the living things that one has grasped and handled!'

To Poole, who had written counselling common sense, such a tone might have been assumed, but it equally characterized his letter to his wife. He bade her remember that the attractions of an infant a few months old were merely instinctive, and that though its life might seem short, considered 'referently to non-existence,' it was 'a manifold and majestic *Thing*.' Certainly the poet spoke in the passage – 'Methinks there is something awful in the thought, what an unknown being one's own infant is to one – a fit of sound – a flash of light – a summer gust that is as it were *created* in the bosom of the calm air, that rises up we know not how, and goes we know not whither!' But it was a poet to whom human flesh was indeed a vapour.

As the spring came, however, he announced that the vital sap of his affections was rising as in a tree and that there were moments in which he had such a power of life within him. He went with a party of students to the Harz Mountains, lived on potatoes and pancakes, slept on straw in village inns, and left some verses behind in one of them on 'Brocken's sovran height.' And although he described himself as working harder than ever in his

life, he found time to conceive a scheme for making money
by extracting sugar from beet. 'My poor Muse,' he confessed, 'is quite gone – perhaps she may return and meet
me at Stowey.' But as a precautionary measure he spent
£30 on metaphysical books 'with a view to the one work
to which I hope to dedicate in silence the prime of my
life.'

On the 23rd of June, 1799, at a farewell supper with one
of the Professors he was in the best of spirits and talked
inordinately 'with the worst German accent imaginable.'
A month later he was back at Stowey. 'The whale,' he
confided to his note-book, 'is followed by waves. I would
glide down the rivulet of quiet life a trout.'

Alas! for him life was to prove no quiet rivulet, but a
sea of which the horizons were perpetually veiled and
over which, in the wake of recurring and diminishing
tornadoes, the air hung limp and stagnant.

CHAPTER FIVE

THE POETIC NIGHTMARE

§ I

'My resolve is fixed,' Coleridge had written to Poole from Germany, 'not to leave you till you leave me!' Nevertheless Stowey without the Wordsworths seemed dreadfully empty. Poole, with all his fine qualities, did not excite to poetry, and even Southey, with whom he was now reconciled as he was shortly to be with Lamb, and who came on a fortnight's visit, could only help him to concoct a piece of satirical doggerel on public life entitled 'The Devil's Thoughts,' which deservedly made something of a sensation when it appeared in *The Morning Post*, but was scarcely a proof of renewed poetic power. It was primarily because he still hoped that the miracle might be renewed, if only to the extent of finishing 'Christabel,' that his movements for the next year were so restless. Further, he craved Dorothy's presence, and yet Poole, who had described him as 'that sort of acquisition which nothing can replace,' had a prior claim upon his loyalty.

He went to Ottery St. Mary and discovered that he had neither tastes nor feelings in common with his clerical and military brothers – a fact which he learnt from their conversation, but tactfully did not suffer them to learn from his. On his return to Stowey he had a rheumatic attack accompanied by its usual symptoms of pain and sleeplessness. Doubtless the Cerberus was sopped too in the usual manner, and somewhat significantly he wrote at the time to Southey that 'the wife of a man of genius who sympathizes effectively with her husband in his habits and feelings is a *rara avis* with me.'

Early in October he went to London. But it was the Wordsworths whom he really wanted: they were staying at Sockburn with relations, and, on hearing a rumour

that Wordsworth was ill, Coleridge followed them and
met Mary Hutchinson, the future wife of the poet, and
her sister Sarah, who was later to take Dorothy's place in
the succession of those who inspired tender sentiments
principally because they supplied a need. 'Few moments
in life,' he remarked complacently in his note-book, 'are
so interesting as those of our affectionate reception from a
stranger who is the dear friend of your dear friend! How
often you have been the subject of conversation, and how
affectionately!'

The whole party immediately set out on a tour of the
Lake Country, and the attractions of Grasmere proved so
strong that Wordsworth decided to settle there, and
before Christmas he and Dorothy had taken Dove Cottage. But meanwhile Coleridge had received a proposal
from Stuart, the editor of *The Morning Post*, to whom the
Wedgwoods had earlier introduced him, that he should
live in London and write political articles for that paper.
The remuneration offered was good and all expenses
were to be defrayed. Coleridge had anticipated his
allowance and so he accepted the offer as a purely temporary expedient to clear off his debts. He took lodgings
in the Strand, and early in December was joined by Sara
and Hartley. From the same motive he engaged to translate Schiller's *Wallenstein* for Longmans, and between
the two activities he cannot have exaggerated when he
wrote, 'I work from I-rise to I-set.'

But both labours irked. The 'Newspaper business,'
in particular, proved 'too, too fatiguing.' Reporting
speeches in the House and writing leaders was indeed sad
work for either a poet or a philosopher, although his
automatic memory was of great service, while in his most
famous report – that of Pitt's speech on January 17 – his
imagination supplied the want of attention. He proved in
fact a very workmanlike journalist just because in such

superficial and transitory writing as political leaders he was never tempted into that diffuseness, over-refinement, and involved ratiocination which metaphysical abstractions invited. But to be an efficient political journalist gave him so little satisfaction that he could claim later to have wasted on it in three months 'the prime and manhood of his intellect!'

Early in the New Year he abandoned it and suggested that after he had given the Wedgwoods some proof in a *Life of Lessing* that he was endeavouring to do well for his fellow-creatures, he should form a pleasant little colony for a few years in Italy or the South of France. Unfortunately the prospect of an addition to his family in the following September compelled him to relinquish both schemes. He indulged himself instead in drawing up prospectuses of the books which Southey might write, and in March took flight to the Wordsworths at Grasmere.

But he was still the slave of a task, an 'irksome, soul-wearying labour, the translation of Schiller.' He needed the £50 promised by Longmans too much to abandon it, and with a rapidity which astonished Wordsworth he completed it before the end of April. In a few years, when English interest in German literature had grown, it might well have proved a financial as well as a literary success. On the testimony of many authorities it was the latter. A reliable German critic spoke of it as doing justice not only to Schiller's mind but to his imagination. Carlyle judged it the best rendering in existence, and Scott remarked that Coleridge had made it far finer than he found it. In old age Coleridge himself considered it 'a specimen of my happiest attempt, during the prime manhood of my intellect, before I had been buffeted by adversity or crossed by fatality,' and it may still appeal to any reader of to-day who can enjoy a play which, like

Coleridge's own, has little interior necessity and which is richer in poetic thoughts than poetry.

But the more Coleridge felt his faculties to be dwindling in the performance of soulless journey work, the more necessary close association with the Wordsworths seemed when, later in the year, his wings should be 'wholly unbirdlimed.' It therefore added to his embarrassment that Poole should show slight signs of jealousy, taxing him with prostrating himself before Wordsworth as a second Milton; and although, when he visited him in May, his friendliness was as staunch and comforting as ever, he could not hide from himself that Stowey without Alfoxden was no longer the horticultural Eden of three years before. Fortunately there was no other house than the 'old hovel' procurable at Stowey, and this supplied him with a pretext for escaping to one at Keswick, which, as he told Godwin, was 'of such a prospect, that if, according to you and Hume impressions and ideas *constitute* our being, I shall have a tendency to become a God, so sublime and beautiful will be the series of my visual existence.'

Certainly Greta Hall, into which he moved with his family towards the end of July after three weeks spent with the Wordsworths at Dove Cottage, seemed as favourable a residence in which to put Godwin's theory to the test as could be found. It was a combination of a manor and a farm-house, which the Coleridges shared with their landlord, a quiet, sensible man, and the possessor of a respectable library. It stood on a low hill and faced 'a giant's camp – an encamped army of tent-like mountains,' which lay about 'massy Skiddaw, smooth, green, high,' and 'by an inverted arch' gave on the right 'a view of another vale' – the 'lovely vale and the wedge-shaped lake of Bassenthwaite.' On the left was Derwentwater, the waterfall of Lodore, and 'the fantastic mountains of Borrowdale.' Behind the house there was an orchard and a small wood falling to the River Greta, which encircled the house and caught the evening lights at its front.

But, as anyone familiar with the Lake Country will know, it was not merely the landscape's architecture which was sublime and all-inclusive, but the changeful artistry of the atmosphere. 'The two lakes,' as Coleridge was quick to observe, 'the vale, the river, and mountain mists, and clouds and sunshine' made 'endless combinations, as if heaven and earth were for ever talking to each other,' while every day had such moments as that recorded from his study window of a 'rich mulberry-purple which a floating cloud has thrown on the lake, and that quiet boat making its way through it to the shore'; or suddenly 'darkness vanished as by enchantment: far off, far off to the south, the mountains of Glaramara and Great Gable and their family appeared distinct, in deepest, sablest blue . . . with a rainbow at their back'; or the moon through scudding rain clouds looked 'as if it had been painted and the colours had run.'

Surely here, in a country that seemed itself to be 'worshipping the power and "eternal link" of energy,' and 'in the way of almost all whom I love and esteem,' he would recapture the poetry of which such verse as he had written since his return from Germany was only the shadow? And surely Poole for his part would understand the need he had of such inspiration, forgive his friend's abandonment, and 'never doubt that I am attached to you beyond all other men'?

That he should begin his residence in the Lakes with another rheumatic attack was ominous. The illness and its inevitable anodyne left him weak and listless, but Grasmere was only twelve miles away and the old intercourse was renewed. Wordsworth was preparing a second

volume of *Lyrical Ballads* for the press. He was to explain his views on poetic diction in a preface, and among
Coleridge's contributions was to be the completed 'Christabel.' Once again Coleridge walked with Dorothy, now
in the Windy Brow woods, now over the Fells. He began
to follow her example and record in his note-book the
'leaves of trees upturned by the stirring wind in twilight
– an image of paleness, wan affright,' or 'the beards of
thistle and dandelions flying about the lovely mountains
like life – and I saw them through the trees skimming
the lake like swallows.'

But autumn drew on and winter followed, and still the
miracle was withheld. Again and again he recited 'Christabel,' again and again he discussed it, and always the
poem excited interest and admiration, but neither it nor
any other contribution to the *Lyrical Ballads* materialized.
It was surely, he ingeniously argued, the deep unutterable
disgust which he had suffered in the translation of that
accursed *Wallenstein* that had stricken him with barren-
ness. 'The wind from the Skiddaw and Borrowdale was
often as loud as wind need be, and many a walk in the
clouds in the mountains' did he take. 'But all would not
do.'

At last, profoundly dejected, he desisted, and in a
typical attempt to save himself from facing the reality of
his impotence reported to a friend that the poem had
grown so long – to 1,300 lines he fictitiously claimed –
and so impressive, that Wordsworth had rejected it from
his volume as disproportionate.

§ 2

But the reality could not be evaded so easily. Under
conditions so favourable to creative effort he could
scarcely claim to be 'buffeted by adversity,' and if in fact
he was 'crossed by fatality,' it was the fatality of himself.

The 'honey dew' and 'the milk of Paradise' which he had drunk had turned into a malign potion that caused him to long for the old hallucination and at the same time know it for what it was. He was 'a cork, flexible, floating, full of pores and openings, and yet he could neither return nor transmit the waters of Helicon, much less the light of Apollo.' He could not, because he had become too self-conscious to be a 'passive vehicle of inspiration, possessed by the spirit, not possessing it,' while to possess it was beyond his powers. If only he could have been magnificent in his disregard of fact, his imagination could have continued to cast its glitter over fictions. But Wordsworth and Lessing had taught him too much for that. The confused conception of poetry, voiced in a later day by critics to whom 'Kubla Khan' was supreme by virtue of its melodious unintelligibility, was no longer entertained by its author, if indeed it ever was. He knew that a poet must be true to his medium, that he was both more and less than a musician, and that words should serve an intelligible as well as an enchanting purpose. 'Idly talk they,' he was to write, 'who speak of poets as mere indulgers of fancy, imagination, superstition. . . . They are the bridlers by delight, the purifiers; they that combine all these with reason and order – the true proto-plasts – Gods of Love who tame the Chaos.'

The power to master and purify the diversity of every-day experience, in that and that only he had begun to see lay the possibility of realizing all the implications of a creative act. The poet should be solving a problem, not composing a narcotic, and in the solution of his art, he would solve also the problem of himself. It was that problem which Wordsworth was solving. He was effect-ing 'a complete and constant synthesis of thought and feeling and combining them with poetic form,' and Coleridge felt himself 'a better poet, in knowing

how to honour *him*' than in all his own 'poetic compositions.'

For with him emotion and thought would not coalesce.
The greatest happiness he had known was in an entirely
irresponsible play of the feelings. But, as he was later to
admit, 'on such meagre diet as feelings, evaporated
embryos in their progress to *birth*, no moral being ever
became healthy.' Emotional indulgence results in spiritual inertness, if not in active discord. For the heart and
the head can only unite by being subordinated to something beyond themselves and centred in an act of disinterested recognition. Such an act he could not achieve,
but the desire to do so soured his life at the source. For
it was his misfortune to be too moral to enjoy and even
exploit his neurosis as other Romantic poets were to do,
to pose as a sensitive plant in a chilly world and luxuriate
in melancholy isolation. He had had enough of the
poet's sense of the eternal freshness and singularity of
things to be utterly miserable, like a sick child, in a life
which seemed exhausted within and without; his emotional longing for brotherhood intensified the ache of
solitude, and his nostalgia was as often barbed, as it was
softened, by self-accusation.

And wherever he turned the same conditions prevailed. The conviction of unity and reality, as he was to
discover, was no more realizable by him in religion and
metaphysics than in poetry. Since Nature failed him as
a radiator and renewer of energy, Christianity, both as a
faith and a philosophy, failed him too, a real act of imagination being as necessary for the capture of an idea and
the living of it, as for the true impersonation of a character
in a play.

Two years later, for example, he was to write – 'It is
easy to clothe imaginary beings with our own thoughts
and feelings; but to send ourselves out of ourselves, to

think ourselves into the thoughts and feelings of beings in circumstances wholly and strangely different from our own, *hic labor hoc opus.* . . . Metaphysics is a word that you . . . are no great friend to, but yet you will agree with me that a great poet must be *implicité*, if not *explicité*, a profound metaphysician. He may not have it in logical coherence in his brain and tongue, but he must have the ear of a wild Arab listening in the silent desert, the eye of a North American Indian tracing the footsteps of an enemy upon the leaves that strew the forest, the touch of a blind man feeling the face of a darling child.'

In short a poet, if he is not, like a lily, to fester, must mature. For a time indeed the unreal is intoxicating enough and has a flavour faint but exquisite of its own. But inevitably this fades, and if it is not succeeded by the flavour of real existence, which recompenses a healthy maturity for its loss, life must become pale and insipid. Coleridge did not for several years, if ever, realize all that was implied by the creative impotence which now so profoundly depressed him. The fanciful had failed him: he could not complete 'Christabel,' but still perhaps he hoped that the power of taking hold of experience, the gift of positive intuition transcending any purely personal projection, would be granted him. Certainly it was not until two years later that he confessed in perhaps the saddest tribute ever paid by one poet to another that his poetic genius was gone.

But meanwhile the conflict between his sense of what great poetry implied and his inability to realize it, undermined his physical as well as his spiritual life. It is of course arguable that ill-health and opium were the cause and not the effect of his imaginative impotence. Similarly his domestic infelicity might be considered rather as generating than accompanying a temperamental discord. But while there can be no doubt that all these

were aggravating conditions, the root cause must surely
have been spiritual. Coleridge was not yet enslaved to
opium or estranged from his wife. His physical sufferings, as his doctor had told him, were nervous in origin,
and always coincided with periods of stress. At the same
time it must be granted that the morbid sensibility which
had already paralyzed his imagination also exposed him
abnormally to climatic conditions, conditions which in
the Lake Country were particularly likely to prey upon a
rheumatic subject. On December 13 of this year 1800
Dorothy noted in her journal: 'Coleridge came. Very ill,
rheumatic, feverish. *Rain incessantly,*' and he himself was
to remark, 'Very hot weather brings me about in an
instant, and I relapse as soon as it coldens.'

§ 3

From the failure then to complete 'Christabel' the
rapid deterioration in Coleridge's health and character
may be dated. His nature did not alter, but it was mastered by its inherent disease. The most noticeable symptom was diminished power to distinguish fact from fiction.
Incidentally he was far too preoccupied with his personal
problem and far too conscious of Wordsworth's healthier
ability, to contest certain points in the preface to the
new *Lyrical Ballads,* 'half a child' though it was of his
own brain, which he must have known to be very misleading. Posterity may be grateful for his neglect, since
fifteen years later it resulted in so splendid a piece of
criticism, but in the interval he was to suffer much from
the supposition that the preface represented his opinions
or corresponded with his practice. It was not, however,
until July 1802 that he troubled even to set a friend right
'with regard to my perfect coincidence with his (Wordsworth's) poetic creed.' Wordsworth, he then wrote, had
not quite justly interpreted his views, and while warmly

agreeing with his attack on artificial diction, he added –
'In my opinion, poetry justifies as poetry, independent
of any other passion, some new combinations of language
and *commands* the omission of many others allowable in
other compositions. Now Wordsworth, *me saltem judice*,
has in his system not sufficiently admitted the former,
and in his practice has too frequently sinned against
the latter. Indeed, we have had lately some little controversy on the subject, and we begin to suspect that
there is somewhere or other a radical difference in our
opinions.'

But indolence and misery were too constantly present
during 1800 and 1801 for him to contest a point of
theory. He was perpetually in flight from an inner conflict, sopping himself with opium or with metaphysics
or with epistolary confession. Impotent to realize or even
yet clearly to explain himself, he could at least pity and
delude himself. He could 'die in a dream of activity,'
balancing the unrealized by prospectuses of the unrealizable, and consoling himself for his practical sterility
by his theoretical fertility.

And so fabrications, adapted to the taste of each correspondent, multiplied in his letters. He even lied to the
Wordsworths, claiming to be contributing articles to
the *Morning Post*, when in fact those appearing were
Poole's. His undertakings for the booksellers, he assured
others, were overwhelming him. There was a huge
geographical school-book of 1,200 or 1,400 pages, an
Essay on Poetry ('in reality a disguised system of morals
and politics'), and a revised *Life of Lessing*. He was
studying the most ancient forms of the Northern Languages and investigating the laws by which our feelings
form affinities with each other, with ideas and words.
That he was trying to lose consciousness in discursive
reading was doubtless the truth, but the booksellers had

no share in the process. Nor had they for many years in the speculations of which this study of the law of Association was to prove the perennial centre.

Coleridge's efforts to refute the empirical philosophers, who referred all the phenomena of the human mind to sensation, were eventually not only to influence the philosophic thought of his age but to prepare the way for a real psychology. He did 'gain great light into several parts of the human mind' in the process of explaining himself; and in the eternal conflict between a mechanistic and vitalist conception of the universe, a conflict which in the nineteenth century was to become particularly acute through the growth of pure science, he was to play, quite unwittingly, his part, though rather as an interpreter of German idealism, a comforter of uneasy consciences, and an idealizer of the Church's dogma, than as either a clear or significant thinker.

But it was as a comforter of himself 'in the twilight of imagination and just on the vestible of consciousness' that he turned now to the study of the highest form of Locke's philosophy, as presented by Hartley, before plunging into Kant. In meditating on 'the relation of thoughts to things . . . of ideas to impressions,' in claiming to have completely extricated the notions of time and space . . . and overthrown all the irreligious metaphysics of modern infidels – especially the doctrine of necessity,' he lightened the burden of time, space and necessity which weighed upon himself. In arguing too that 'deep thinking is attainable only by a man of deep feeling and that all Truth is a species of Revelation,' he tried in terms of philosophy to justify his own evanescent consciousness; while his projected essay 'concerning Poetry and the nature of the Pleasures derived from it,' which was to 'supersede all the books of metaphysics, and all the books of morals too,' was an airy substitute for the poetry which he could not write and the moral effort which he could not make.

But such metaphysics, like the opium and brandy in which he indulged, aggravated the condition which they temporarily relieved. He confessed to Poole that 'the experiments on my own sensations and on my senses . . . did injury to my nervous system,' and resulted in terrible stomach attacks and nephritic pains. The weeks passed in alternations of false cheerfulness, when a dose of laudanum had 'acted like a charm, like a miracle,' and a drowsy self-distrust deepening into loathing as the unusual stimulus subsided and with it the 'hopes, the vitality and cohesion' of his being.

Even Nature seemed to be in league with his own bewildered, outlawed state. 'The night wind,' he wrote, 'pipes its thin, doleful, climbing, sinking notes, like a child that has lost its way and is crying aloud, half in grief, and half in hope to be heard by its mother.' In a letter which he had 'scarce strength to fold up' he proclaimed his resolution to be a 'liver by Rule,' and in one that asked a loan of £20 he promised to 'gird up his loins and disembarrass his circumstances.' 'I have no doubt,' he wrote in typical strain, 'that I could make £500 a year if I liked. But then I must forgo all desire of truth and excellence. . . . Oh, for a Lodge in a land where human life was an end to which labour was only a means, instead of being, as it is here, a mere means of carrying on labour.'

But it was because his sense of life was curdled that he could not labour, and to quote any further from these letters can serve no useful purpose. It is enough to say that his correspondence for the next two years was 'a wildly wailing strain,' hysterical, fantastic, querulous. He was distraught by everything, by his debts, his incapacity, his ideas, his ill-health, by 'pestilent commerce' and 'splenetic politics,' by the destitution and vagrancy he saw

about him like a sordid reflection of himself, by his family
life and what he called the lack of 'moral being' in all
but those who have felt the pressure of actual hard-
ships.

And among these he came to include even Poole. For
Poole's common sense now acted as an irritant. It was
both exasperating and humiliating to have such rhetorical
questions as 'Is it better to die or quit my native country,
and live among strangers?' answered in sober and judicial
tones. 'If,' wrote Poole, 'your disease be really bodily,
and not the consequence of an irritated mind,' a warmer
climate must be tried. The very conditional read like an
accusation, and alas! a true one, and it deprived 'the
poor sufferer of that sympathy which is always a comfort
and, in some degree, a support to human nature.' Poole
with his robust health might try to argue away his fears,
bid him 'have courage, and make Mrs. Coleridge have
courage to live within your income.' He might remind
him that he had staunch friends and was assured of a fixed
annuity, but to his neurotic mind even this was already
held 'perhaps by a very precarious tenure' and the value
of money was sure to decrease. With the kindest intentions Poole failed him. Instead of answering his appeals
for compassion and nursing his self-depreciation, he tried
naturally to brace him to 'set his house in order.' He even
went further and rather sententiously diagnosed the two
weak parts of his friend's mind: 'its tendency to restlessness and its tendency to torpor.' Coleridge derived small
satisfaction from citing in reply what he considered the
two defects in Poole's character, and when later Poole
failed to respond to a request for a loan of £50 or £100,
offering instead to join with others in contributing £20
towards it, he was deeply hurt.

Poverty was after all a blessing, he told Southey; 'No
man's heart can wholly stand up against property'; and to

Poole himself he wrote after two months: 'It is impossible that you should feel as to pecuniary affairs as Wordsworth or as I feel – or even as men greatly inferior to you in all other things that make man a noble being. . . . You deem me, too often perhaps, an enthusiast. Enthusiast as I may be, Poole! I have not passed through life without learning that it is a heart-sickening degradation to borrow of the rich, and a heart-withering affection to owe to the poor.'

Nevertheless the penurious idealist who thus reproved his friend from a superior height of moral sensitiveness was found asking him for another advance in a few months' time.

But such discrepancies between high sentiment and fact could not be concealed from Sara. To Wordsworth he was still 'a great man, and if God grant him life will do great things.' But Sara, to whom greatness as an abstract quality meant little, who possessed Poole's common sense without his insight into genius, could scarcely feel so optimistic. Incapable of appreciating her husband's flights into the empyrean, she had nothing to set against his too obvious flounderings in the mire. She must already have known the immediate cause of his being 'apparently quite well one day, and the next the fit comes on him again with as much violence as ever.' And even the artificial sense of freedom and expansion which he experienced under the influence of laudanum had no practical issue. Ill or well he was in incessant flight from the present, dreaming of the Azores or of a staider pantiso-cracy on a West Indian Island, 'spawning plans like a herring,' as Southey said, or being washed off the rock of convalescence into deeps of mental and physical anguish where she could not follow him.

She could not realize that he was tormented by a sense of death in life: she only saw his pathetic, exasperating incompetence and wondered where it was to end. And try as she would, she could not altogether suppress a sense of injury and even a faint contempt for his sickly plaints. Coleridge, for his part, knew the impossibility of explaining. His malady was too subtle in its origin for his wife to comprehend it. Inevitably she judged by appearances, since these only she could understand. Her gloom and distress was a tacit accusation. He ought to be working and could not. 'To each reproach that thundered from without . . . remorse groaned an echo.' His lot, as he theatrically described it, was 'a prison without ransom, anguish without patience, a sick-bed in the house of contempt.' It made it worse that the discord, at least on his side, was not active. It became so, gradually, on hers, simply because his utter inability to quarrel positively, or passionately, his aimless, amiable futility in all practical matters, tried her nerves beyond endurance. But for him it was rather a dull ache of hopeless unadaptability that 'gangrened' life 'in its very vitals.'

Even a criminal, he wrote in his note-book, finds 'unspeakable comfort' in being understood, and he avowed later in life that he could have been happy with a servant girl 'had she only in sincerity of heart responded to my affection.' It was not subtlety of intellect or accomplishment that he craved, or to know and share a passion, but a cherishing companionship, blindly loyal in its devotion, a placid, doting affection that would appease his loneliness, soothe his mortification, and draw him home from the wild wilderness of his ideas. For 'God said that it was not well for the human Being to be alone; to be what we *ought* to be, we need support, help, communion in good. What, then, if instead of a Helpmate we take an Obstacle, a daily counteraction?'

No helpmate probably could have saved Coleridge from himself, but doubtless a more tolerant and tactful woman than Sara could have strengthened the finer elements in his nature. His response to affection, selfish though it often was, was also lavish and unqualified. How little Sara could inspire it is proved by the desolatingly true analysis which he wrote of their respective temperaments:

'Mrs. Coleridge's mind has very little that is *bad* in it; it is an innocent mind; but it is light and *unimpressible*, warm in anger, cold in sympathy, and in all disputes uniformly *projects itself forth* to recriminate, instead of turning itself inward with a silent self-questioning. Our virtues and our vices are exact antitheses. I so attentively watch my own nature that my worst self-delusion is a complete self-knowledge so mixed with intellectual complacency, that my quickness to see and readiness to acknowledge my faults is too often frustrated by the small pain which the sight of them gives me and the consequent slowness to amend them. Mrs. C. is so stung with the very first thought of being in the wrong, because she never endures to look at her own mind in all its faulty parts, but shelters herself from painful self-enquiry by angry recrimination. Never, I suppose, did the stern match-maker bring together two minds so utterly contrariant in their primary and organical constitution.'

A husband so searching in theory and so flabby in practice was a problem beyond Sara's powers of solution, but his very detachment from the momentary troubles with which she herself was apt to be unnecessarily obsessed angered her every day, drove her to recrimination and a 'love-killing' manner which was not really typical of her nature, with the result that Coleridge could eventually write – 'The most happy marriage I can picture or image to myself would be the union of a deaf man to a blind woman.' His situation could not be better summed up.

But for him who

> 'loved no other place, and yet
> Home was no home to him'

it was a real tragedy. He fled of course to Dorothy. She forgot his faults in the light of his genius, and even his faults were rather 'amiable propensities' than vices. Coleridge confided in her. In many an 'interesting, melancholy talk' he made her believe that he had struggled to bring Sara 'to a change of temper, and something like communion with him in his enjoyments,' that he was convinced it was impossible, and that he must 'reconcile himself to that one great want, an utter want of sympathy.'

The want excited her compassion as his genius drew her love, and he lived on both. He never reckoned the havoc he was working upon her feelings or the bitterness that he was intensifying in the heart of his wife. Sympathy was 'literally medicinal' to him; he needed it as he needed the laudanum-bottle. And so week by week he walked and talked with Dorothy or, when he was away in London or at Stowey, wrote her agonizing letters. It never occurred to him that she suffered, that she opened them in fearful expectation, and that when, as so often, they were couched in terms of gloomy extravagance, she was too agitated to sleep, and yet cherished them as she longed to cherish him.

'Poor C. left us,' she wrote in her Journal, 'and we came home together. . . . Every sight and every sound reminded me of him – dear, dear fellow, of his many walks to us by day and by night, of all dear things. I was melancholy, and could not talk, but at last I eased my heart by weeping – nervous blubbering, says William. It is not so. O! how many, many reasons have I to be anxious for him.' Or – 'Two very affecting letters from

Coleridge; resolved to try another climate. I was stopped in my writing, and made ill by the letters'; or – 'We received a letter from Coleridge. His letter made us uneasy about him. I was glad I was not by myself when I received it.' And though compassion sounded most frequently in her Journal, she confided an intimate tenderness to it too. For example – 'The hips very beautiful, and so good!! and, dear Coleridge! I ate twenty for thee, when I was by myself'; or – 'We broke the seal of Coleridge's letter, and I had light enough just to see that he was not ill. I put it in my pocket. At the top of the White Moss I took it to my bosom, – a safer place for it'; or – 'We parted from Coleridge at Sara's crag, after having looked for the letters which C. carved in the morning. I kissed them all.'

Such were the feelings which Coleridge had come to excite, and incapable himself of any but vague emotions, he had no conception of the corroding intensity with which they possessed a sensibility more exquisitely precise and personal than his own. But Dorothy's devotion could only soothe: it could not heal. It made life often tolerable, and, when health and weather favoured, even cheerful. With her and Wordsworth he would wander over the hills in holiday mood. He would forget the canker-worm and follow her daring eyes about the countryside, about the bays that 'shot into the low fading shores,' and up to the sky where a little fleecy cloud hung above the mountain ridge and was 'rich in amber light.' He could even ponder 'a series of love poems truly Sapphic, save that they shall have a large interfusion of moral sentiment, and calm imagery – love in all the moods of mind, philosophic, fantastic.'

For a fluid temperament had its compensations. He could romanticize not only despair, but also hope. Sentimentalist as he was, even his home beamed promise

when he was away from it. 'Oh, that I were at Keswick
with my darling! My Hartley and my fat Derwent,' he
wrote from London, in an expansive moment; 'God bless
you, my dear Sara! I shall return in love and cheerfulness.'

Doubtless two days at home shattered the dream and
killed the resolve, but he could find a substitute in the
'two years in a mild and even climate' which 'with God's
blessing' were to give him 'a new lease in a better constitution.'

Yet neither dreams nor Dorothy could hide the fact
that he had no heart for poetry, and there were times
when her intense vitality and her brother's 'homogeneous'
industry acted as terrible reminders. So keenly did he
feel the contrast that in April 1802 on an evening when
the misted moon foretold the coming on of rain, herald
to him of 'giddy head, sick stomach, and swoln knees,' his
sense of it overflowed into verse. It was his testament to
the spirit which in days of 'morning freshness' he had
communicated to Wordsworth, but had lost himself.
Once again as at Clevedon the Æolian lute trembled in
the wind, but no longer with a 'floating witchery of
sound.' The 'long sequacious notes' had degenerated
into a dismal drone, 'which better far were mute,' and the
very quietness of the night beyond seemed impregnated
with his own 'dull pain.' For it was the dullness that
galled, the complete failure of the life within to wed itself
to the life without and so, as once it did, 'meet all motion
and become its soul.' Instead there was

'A grief without a pang, void, dark, and drear,
    A stifled, drowsy, unimpassioned grief,
    Which finds no nat'ral outlet, no relief,
        In word, or sigh, or tear —
O Edmund! in this wan and heartless mood,
To other thoughts by yonder throstle woo'd,

All this long eve, so balmy and serene,
　　Have I been gazing on the western sky,
And its peculiar tint of yellow-green:
　　And still I gaze — and with how blank an eye!
And those thin clouds above, in flakes and bars,
That give away their motion to the stars;
Those stars, that glide behind them, or between,
Now sparkling, now bedimm'd, but always seen;
Yon crescent moon, as fix'd as if it grew,
In its own cloudless, starless lake of blue,
A boat becalm'd! a lovely sky-canoe!
I see them all so excellently fair —
I see, not *feel* how beautiful they are!

　　　　'My genial spirits fail;
　　　　　And what can these avail,
To lift the smoth'ring weight from off my breast?
　　　　It were a vain endeavour,
　　　　　Though I shall gaze forever
On that green light that lingers in the west:
I may not hope from outward forms to win
The passion and the life, whose fountains are within.

'O Edmund! we receive but what we give,
And in *our* life alone does Nature live:
Ours is her wedding-garment, ours her shroud!
And would we aught behold, of higher worth,
Than that inanimate cold world, *allow'd*
To the poor loveless ever-anxious crowd,
Ah! from the soul itself must issue forth,
A light, a glory, a fair luminous cloud
Enveloping the earth —
And from the soul itself must there be sent
A sweet and potent voice, of its own birth,
Of all sweet sounds the life and element.

'Joy, virtuous EDMUND! joy that ne'er was given,
Save to the pure, and in their purest hour,
Joy, Edmund! is the spirit and the pow'r,
Which wedding Nature gives to us in dow'r,
    A new Earth and new Heaven,
Undream'd of by the sensual and the proud –
Joy is the sweet voice, Joy the luminous cloud –
    We, we ourselves rejoice!
And thence flows all that charms or ear or sight,
All melodies the echoes of that voice,
All colours a suffusion from that light. . . .

'There was a time when, tho' my path was rough,
    This joy within me dallied with distress,
And all misfortunes were but as the stuff
    Whence fancy made me dreams of happiness:
For hope grew round me, like the twining vine,
And fruits, and foliage, not my own, seemed mine.
But now afflictions bow me down to earth:
Nor care I, that they rob me of my mirth.
    But oh! each visitation
Suspends what nature gave me at my birth,
    My shaping spirit of Imagination. . . .

'O Edmund, friend of my devoutest choice,
O rais'd from anxious dread and busy care,
By the immenseness of the good and fair
Which thou see'st everywhere,
Joy lifts thy spirit, joy attunes thy voice,
To thee do all things live from pole to pole,
Their life the eddying of thy living soul!'

It was natural that in their revised form these lines should
be addressed to Dorothy; for she, more intimately even
than her brother, reminded him of an ecstasy which he
could no longer share. It was natural too that he should

describe this faculty in moral terms, since for him creativeness was the purest form of moral life, a life in which discord was resolved by a continual act of self-forgetful love. If it had been merely an æsthetic problem, his sense of loss would not have amounted to anguish.

But for him failure as a poet meant failure in every relationship of life, and the only satisfaction left to him was to analyse his condition, as he did in these lines with pathetic subtlety. Indeed he never stated his dilemma with greater psychological accuracy. For here, in this deadly, unimpassioned mood, he could see, as Dorothy saw, with a minute accuracy. The world without was no longer intangible, but sharply defined. Yet he saw only as an anatomist dissecting a corpse. 'I *see*, not *feel* how beautiful they are.' There was no vital relation between himself as subject and nature as object, and so there was no joy. He was still 'in a prison without ransom.' And this state was the exact opposite and was logically conditioned by the other mood, the loss of which he now lamented, and which he described in the lines:

'O Edmund! we receive but what we give
And in *our* life alone does Nature live.'

In that mood, which he had expressed at various times in his early verse, Nature as object scarcely existed for him. She was a something without definition, an intangible essence into which he projected himself. In her, as in a moving stream, he saw only his own blurred image. The movement, the sense of luxurious relaxation, deluded him into the belief that he was achieving a creative experience and in the process escaping from himself. But in truth he was only less smothered by egotism in his earlier emotional worship of nature than in the emotionless observance of her which he chronicled in this deeply affecting ode.

The fact strikes to the root of the difference between himself and Wordsworth. Nature's reality for Wordsworth transcended his personal mood. He did not merely give and receive himself back again as Coleridge, speaking from his own experience, claimed. Nature gave herself to him, too; she existed, in her own right, as an organism to be lovingly studied and, in moments of inspiration, to be harmoniously wed. It is this true and equable marriage between a poet's personality and the external world which distinguishes a mystical realization of life from a sentimental impression, a self-annihilating from a self-indulgent romanticism. It is thus that the personal becomes more than personal and the vision disinterested.

Always Coleridge longed for such a realization, and always the fatal flaw in his temperament prevented it. His 'shaping spirit of Imagination' could wed only with phantoms. Between it and things there drifted, in all but unimpassioned moments, a mist of diffused emotionalism.

But so complete an expression, even of impotence, brought relief. It did not renew his poetic faith, because his ideal of expression was something far other than this. To quote his own later words: 'there are men who can write passages of deepest pathos, and even sublimity, on circumstances personal to themselves and stimulative of their own passions; but they are not, therefore, on this account poets.' But it made it easier

'not to think of what I needs must feel,
  But to be still and patient all I can;
And haply by abstruse research to steal
  From my own nature all the natural man.'

Denaturalized metaphysics were not likely to be more significant than pathetically personal poetry or 'poetical prose,' as he perhaps too modestly called it, but they involved less pain. And so he began a systematic study of Kant, drifting in dreamy passivity along the maze of that philosopher's arguments, until words became truly 'elevated into things and living things too . . . like the parts and germinations of a plant.'

The weakness of Coleridge's metaphysics was due to the fictitious life which words as words assumed for him. Like the images of 'Kubla Khan' they were accepted for themselves rather than as vehicles of meaning, and the fact explains his extraordinary literal memory and power of sustained verbal circumlocution. He derived, however, considerable satisfaction from the process, and could shortly confess with some equanimity that 'all my poetic genius (if ever I really possessed any *genius*, and it was not rather a mere general *aptitude* of talent, and quickness in imitation) is gone and I have been fool enough to suffer deeply in my mind, regretting the loss.'

At the same time he came to an understanding with Sara, of which the immediate consequence, as he told Southey, was 'that now for a long time there has been more love and concord in my house than I have known for years before. I had made up my mind to a very awful step, though the struggles of my mind were so violent, that my sleep became the valley of the shadows of Death and my health was in a state truly alarming. It did alarm Mrs. Coleridge. The thought of separation wounded her pride – she was fully persuaded that deprived of the society of my children and living abroad without any friends I should pine away, and the fears of widowhood came upon her, and though these feelings were wholly selfish, yet they made her *serious* and that was a great point gained.'

Doubtless to Sara the situation for the last three years had always been serious enough, but according to her husband's complacent account she now 'for the first time since our marriage felt and acted as beseemed a wife and a mother to a husband and the father of her children,' promised to alter her 'external manners and looks and language and to fight against her inveterate habits of puny thwarting and unintermitting dyspathy'; while he, on his part, engaged 'to be more attentive to all her feelings of pride . . . and to correct my habits of impetuous censure. I have the most confident hopes,' he concluded, 'that this happy revolution in our domestic affairs will be permanent.'

His hopes were of course delusive, but they actually revived his poetic impulse, even if in so doing they intensified a subsequent despair. A visit from Charles Lamb and his sister in August 1802 sustained the illusion. They drove from Penrith in the midst of a gorgeous evening sunshine and thought they 'had got into Fairyland.' The mountains were all dark with clouds upon their heads, as they reached Greta Hall at dusk. 'Glorious creatures,' wrote Lamb, 'fine old fellows. . . . I shall never forget ye, how ye lay about that night, like an intrenchment. . . . Coleridge had got a blazing fire in his study; which is a large, antique, ill-shaped room, with an old-fashioned organ, never played upon, big enough for a church, shelves of scattered folios, an Æolian harp, and an old sofa, half bed.'

Lamb's enthusiasm was infectious. For three weeks they walked 'among the clouds,' climbed Skiddaw and from Scawfell saw the mountains dying away to the sea in eleven parallel ridges. And the exhilaration survived their going. Late in September he could write to a friend: 'The river is full, and Lodore is full, and silver-fillets come out of clouds and glitter in every ravine of all the mountains, and the hail lies like snow upon their tops, and the impetuous gusts from Borrowdale snatch the water up high, and continually at the bottom of the lake it is not distinguishable from snow slanting before the wind – and under this seeming snowdrift the sunshine *gleams*, and over all the nether half of the lake it is *bright* and *dazzles*, a cauldron of melted silver boiling! It is in very truth a sunny, misty, cloudy, dazzling, howling, omniform day, and I have been looking at as pretty a sight as a father's eyes could well see – Hartley and little Derwent running in the green where the gusts blow most madly, both with their hair floating and tossing, a miniature of the agitated trees, below which they were playing.'

Poetical prose might be 'a very vile Olio,' but when he hymned the elements, Coleridge's critical conscience was fortunately put to sleep. And it seems clear that for these few months he did respond vitally to the genius of the Lake Country, ceasing to look on the mountains in Euclidean abstraction 'only for the curves of their outlines,' losing himself in a worship of 'the spirit of unconscious life.'

His appreciation of Nature, when it was not relaxed, is indeed an excellent example of what a psychologist of to-day has termed 'empathy,' the projection of self into the lines and curves of landscape. As he was to write: 'One travels along with the lines of a mountain. Years ago I wanted to make Wordsworth sensible of this. How fine is Keswick Vale! Would I repose, my soul lies and is quiet upon the broad level vale. Would it act? it darts up into the mountain-top like a kite and like a chamois-goat runs along the ridge – or like a boy who makes a sport on the road of running along a wall or narrow fence!'

It was this typically fluent, and to some extent, abstract experience which he now enjoyed. 'A new joy,' as he wrote:

'Lovely as light, sudden as summer gust,
And gladsome as the first-born of the spring,
Beckons me on, or follows from behind,
Playmate, or guide! The master-passion quelled,
I feel that I am free.'

The freedom was in truth precarious and indefinite as the elements:

'He would far rather not be that he is;
But would be something that he knows not of,
In winds or waters, or among the rocks!'

Yet he could claim it as an 'hour of triumph.' It was 'delicious to the soul' if 'fleeting, vain,' and it momentarily quickened his pulse to poetry. On Scawfell he 'involuntarily poured forth a hymn,' later entitled 'Hymn before Sunrise, in the Vale of Chamouni,' and although its resemblance to Frederica Brun's poem of the same name was considerable, doubtless the plagiarism was involuntary too. It was but another example of his characteristic automatism, of that desire for expression 'in which the effort required bears no proportion to the activity enjoyed.' The moment he tried to control, to be master of a spontaneous afflatus, inspiration failed and prose thought intruded. Poetry for him lived only in an unconscious surrender to what seemed some supernatural impulse, but which might be, as it was in this poem, a recollection of another poet's verse.

His exhilaration, however, survived a tour in South Wales with the Wedgwoods, where with Thomas he discoursed metaphysics and dabbled in narcotics, inquiring particularly after one called 'Bang,' the powder of the leaves of a kind of hemp that grew in hot climates, impressively described as 'the Nepenthe of the Ancients,' and said to be taken by criminals in Barbary condemned to suffer amputation. In the absence of this and encouraged by his 'delightful and instructive companion,' he confined himself (daily) to 'half a grain of purified opium, equal to twelve drops of laudanum,' which, he added, was not more than an eighth part of what he took at Keswick, and he further eased his conscience by anathematizing tea and suggesting that 'virtue and genius are diseases of the hypochondriacal and scrofulous genera, and exist in a peculiar state of the nerves and diseased digestion, analogous to the beautiful diseases that colour and variegate certain trees.'

Later in the year he returned to Greta Hall to find that a daughter had been born to him the morning before, but stormy weather and a soaking on Kirkstone Pass broke the spell of comparative health and provoked a return to unregulated laudanum. Not yet however did the sense of ecstasy forsake him, and in a reply to Wedgwood, who had remarked on his imprudence in disregarding the state of the weather, he suddenly launched into as splendid and illuminating a passage of self-expression as ever he penned.

Prudence, he wrote, even if he possessed any, 'least of all things would endure the climate of the mountains. In simple earnestness, I never find myself alone, within the embracement of rocks and hills, a traveller up an alpine road, but my spirit careers, dives, and eddies, like a leaf in autumn; a wild activity of thoughts, imaginations, feelings, and impulses of motion rises up from within me; a sort of bottom wind, that blows to no point of the compass, comes from I know not whence but agitates the whole of me; my whole being is filled with waves that roll and stumble, one this way, and one that way, like things that have no common master. I think that my soul must have pre-existed in the body of a chamois chaser. The simple image of the old object has been obliterated, but the feelings, and the impulsive habits, and incipient

actions, are in me, and the old scenery awakens them.
The further I ascend from animated nature, from men,
and cattle, and the common birds of the woods and fields,
the greater becomes in me the intensity of the feeling of
life. Life seems to me then an universal spirit, that neither
has, nor can have an opposite. "God is everywhere," I
have exclaimed, and works everywhere, and where is there
room for death? In these moments it has been my creed,
that death exists only because ideas exist; that life is
limitless sensation; that death is a child of the organic
senses, chiefly of the sight; that feelings die by flowing
into the mould of the intellect becoming ideas, and that
ideas passing forth into action reinstate themselves again
in the world of life. . . . I do not think it possible that
any bodily pains could eat out the love of joy, that is so
substantially part of me, towards hills, and rocks, and
steep waters.'

If it had been possible always to live and move on
mountain tops, where no action was resisted and so space
was forgotten, where the elements in motion seemed
limitless and the prospect by its remoteness and immensity seemed to forego all restlessness, and anticipate an
infinite repose, Coleridge's difficulties would have been
at an end. He could have exulted all his days in a sensational pantheism instead of, on a humbler and drearier
plane, devoting years of elaborate argument to an uncon-
vincing exposition of theism. Only by such a sensational
ascent, as he here described, could he, without narcotics,
escape the dualism between the infinite and the finite
which tormented him.

But in truth such ecstasy, though far more vital, was
as inconclusive as his later argument, and for the
same reason. Just as his view of an omniscient and
benevolent Creator was compromised by his failure to
face the conditions which governed the material universe,

so his spirit lost amid the elements had no true vision of life, because it was blind to its material aspect.

But down in the valley the material aspect obtruded and the ideal vanished like smoke, unless restored by laudanum. It was probably laudanum that explained the impression of power and activity which he made on an observer who saw him in London in the spring and in describing his talk spoke of the 'brilliant images of greatness' that 'float upon his mind like the images of the morning clouds upon the waters . . . agitated by every breeze, and modified by every sunbeam. He talked, in the course of one hour, of beginning three works, and he recited the poem of *Christabel*, unfinished.' And when in August came heavy wind and rain, he pined as he had exulted with the elements, finding himself unwell at the very hour when the glass changed and dating his relapses and recoveries by its movements.

And so the tide of exhilaration ebbed. Once again his mind was 'strangely shut up,' and when he took paper to write there was 'one blank feeling; one blank idealess feeling. I had nothing to say; – could say nothing.' Even opium filled his nights with terrors. Sleep was his 'tormenting Angel,' dreams were 'no shadows, but the very calamities' of his life, and his night-screams made him 'a nuisance' in his own house. Inevitably his relations with Sara were as strained as ever, and it was from a hell of domestic discord and mental anguish that in the middle of the month he embarked on a tour of Scotland with the Wordsworths.

But his state was too sodden to be bettered even by a journey to remote regions. The weather became very bad; Wordsworth, himself a 'brooder over his painful hypochondriacal sensations,' was scarcely a helpful companion, while Dorothy's quenchless vitality, her endless, minute, appreciative fervour had ceased to stimulate.

Even she confessed in her journal that she had said so much of a certain lake that she had tired herself and feared she must have tired her friends. Coleridge could no longer live on her level. It was painful to be so constantly made to see things which he did not feel. He was often ill; from the time they left Glasgow 'it rained all the way, all the long, long day,' and laudanum, his one refuge, his one hope of animation, could only be secretly and discreetly indulged in, if at all.

After a fortnight of fluctuating misery, he fled. Shoeless and moneyless he was, and suffering from rheumatism, but how gleefully he found himself alone and no longer compelled to admire, 'having Nature with solitude and liberty – the liberty natural and solitary, the solitude natural and free.'

But now as he retraced his steps, once again the horrors of night overtook him. It may be that he was paying for a too sudden break in narcotic indulgence. He tried ether as an opiate, but only to fall down 'precipices of distempered sleep.' He struggled to keep awake, he prayed, he walked nearly three hundred miles in eight days, hoping to outdistance the demons that pursued him, but still they came up with him at night a

'fiendish crowd
Of shapes and thoughts that tortured me:
A lurid light, a trampling throng,
Sense of intolerable wrong,
And those I scorned, those only strong!
Thirst of revenge, the powerless will
Still baffled, and yet burning still!
Desire with loathing strangely mixed
On wild or hateful objects fixed.
Fantastic passions! maddening brawl
And shame and terror over all. . . .

'So two nights passed: the night's dismay
Saddened and stunned the coming day.
Sleep, the wide blessing, seemed to me
Distemper's worst calamity.
The third night, when my own loud scream
Had waked me from the fiendish dream,
O'ercome with sufferings strange and wild,
I wept as I had been a child;
And having thus by tears subdued
My anguish to a milder mood,
Such punishments, I said, were due
To natures deepliest stained with sin:
Still to be stirring up anew
The self-created Hell within,
The Horror of the crimes to view,
To know and loathe, yet wish to do!

'Such griefs with such men well agree,
But I – oh wherefore this *on me?*
Frail is my soul, yea, strengthless wholly,
Unequal, restless, melancholy;
But free from Hate and sensual Folly!
To live beloved is all I need,
And whom I love, I love indeed.'

Child as he was, Coleridge could not understand why
amiable weakness was punished more than vicious
strength, why life should be kinder to the sensualist than
the sentimentalist. He had not yet read nature as heed-
fully as later he did when he spoke of Shakespeare as
knowing 'that courage, intellect and strength of character, are the most impressive forms of power, and that
to power in itself, without reference to any moral end,
an inevitable admiration and complacency appertains,
whether it be displayed in the conquests of a Buona-

parte or Tamerlane, or in the foam and the thunder of a cataract.'

He knew only that he longed to love and be beloved, that he had 'a joy in life that passeth all understanding'; and yet his very virtues undermined his moral being. His joy led to despair, his benevolence to self-indulgence, not to the brutal licence from which grosser natures derive some positive satisfaction and suffer little from afterthoughts, but to a licence which was a dream in the hours of indulgence and a nightmare afterwards, 'counterfeiting as it were the tortures of guilt, and what we are told of the punishment of a spiritual world.'

In this state of haunted self-awareness he remained through the autumn, enslaved by 'streamy associations,' by his 'moral feelings and the state of the atmosphere.' The universe itself seemed often lurid and malign

'And every goodly, each familiar form
Had a strange somewhat that breathed terrors on me!'

Clouds impressed him 'with a demoniacal grandeur' and the moon, as she rose in the sky, 'upboiled a swell of light.'

At best the world was phantasmal in its beauty, curious and cold as it is to the sleepless who watch it emerging in the early hours, as darkness ebbs. 'The voice of the Greta and the cock-crowing,' he noted at two o'clock one November morning; 'the voice seems to grow like a flower on or about the water beyond the bridge, while the cock-crowing is nowhere particular – it is at any place I imagine and do not distinctly see. A most remarkable sky! the moon, now waned to a perfect ostrich egg, hangs over our house almost, only so much beyond it, gardenward, that I can see it, holding my head out of the smaller study window. The sky is covered with whitish, and with dingy cloudage, thin dingiest scud close under the moon, and one side of it moving, all else moveless, but there are two great breaks of blue sky. . . . The water leaden-white, even as the grey gleam of water is in latest twilight. Now while I have been writing this and gazing between-whiles . . . the break over the road is swallowed up, and the stars gone; the break over the house is narrowed into a rude circle, and on the edge of its circumference one very bright star. See! already the white mass, turning at its edge, *fights* with its brilliance. See! it has bedimmed it, and now it is gone, and the moon is gone. The cock-crowing too has ceased. The Greta sounds on for ever. But I hear only the ticking of my watch in the pen-place of my writing-desk and the far lower note of the noise of the fire, perpetual, yet seeming uncertain. It is the low voice of quiet change, of destruction doing its work by little and little.'

More than ever he felt that his nature required 'another nature for its support, and reposes only in another from the necessary indigence of its being.' Yet there was no one in whom he could repose, and more and more what hopes he still had centred on some foreign country where the barometer changed less often.

Meanwhile he pondered much on the problem of evil. He was pained by the 'irreverent' way in which Words-worth and Hazlitt spoke of Nature and 'so malignantly' too 'of the Divine Wisdom.' Bitterly conscious of his own imperfections, he dare not tamper with the idea of Divine perfection. He must create an idea of perfect wisdom and virtue and vitality somewhere in life to oppose to his own sense of failure and degradation. He could scarcely bear to face the fact of discord in himself; far less could he face it in the Universe. 'Never to be friendless, never to be unintelligible!' he was to write in his note-book. 'O to feel what the pain is to be utterly

unintelligible and then – "O God, thou understandest!" '
and again – 'Facts! Never be weary of discussing and
exposing the hollowness of these.'

In December he could endure the atmosphere of Greta
Hall no longer. Starting for London to see Poole by
way of Dove Cottage he had a serious relapse there and
was nursed for a month by Dorothy and Mrs. Wordsworth. He was exceedingly happy. No effort was required of him, and conscience spares an invalid. No
longer was 'his inner being disturbed': he felt 'serene and
self sufficing' since illness had 'taken away . . . the connecting link of voluntary power, always slender, which
continually combines that part of us by which we know
ourselves to be, with that outward picture or hieroglyphic
by which we hold communion with our like – between
the vital and the organic.'

Lying in bed, with 'only strength enough to smile
gratefully on my kind nurses, who tended me with sister's
and mother's love, and often, I well know, wept for me in
their sleep and watched for me even in their dreams,' he
seemed a spirit disencumbered of a corpse; and how
largely psychological his illnesses were is suggested by
'the suddenness and seeming perfectness' of his recovery.
In a single hour he changed 'from a state that seemed next
to death . . . to a state of elastic health.'

But the weather as usual paralleled his recovery, and
such illusory health brought little comfort. Only by a
change of climate, beneath sunny skies, he assured himself, might he yet recapture his being from opium, discover a will to act and in action forget the need of sympathy which Sara could not supply. Perhaps too the
Wordsworths might be tempted to join him in Sicily, and
since 'mortal life' seemed 'destined for no continuous
happiness, save that which results from the exact performance of duty,' he began to lay down 'the whole plan' of his

literary life and 'the exact order' in which he would execute it.

His first work, fittingly enough, was to be one entitled 'Consolations and Comforts from the exercise and right application of the Reason, the Imagination, and the Moral Feelings, addressed especially to those in Sickness, Adversity, or Distress of Mind, from *Speculative Gloom*, etc.' He also advised Poole 'to look steadily at everything and to see it as it is,' and sent Sara, 'the mother, the attentive, and excellent mother of my children,' as he called her in a farewell letter, minute instructions about the game of 'spillekins' which she was to teach Hartley and Derwent.

But he did not sail till March, and although in January he had sufficient spirit to oppose Godwin ('this dim-headed prig of a philosophoside'), when he was incited to attack him by his 'green-spectacled wife,' and 'thundered and lightened with frenzied eloquence for near an hour and a half,' February found him once again 'low and sinking.' Possibly the 'rich and precious wines' which he enjoyed in Lamb's company did not agree so admirably with him as he claimed, but the fact hastened his departure. And when Wordsworth and Sir George Beaumont, another Grasmere friend, each advanced £100 towards his expenses he looked out for a ship to take him to Malta, a convenient stopping place on a voyage to Sicily. He spent his last weeks in London with John Tobin the dramatist, who tired him with earnest advice and had the bad taste to remind him of an unhonoured debt of £10. And then late in March, 'weak and daily tottering into relapses,' he slipped away to Portsmouth. Nearly a fortnight later he sailed in the *Speedwell* for Malta. It was an adventure upon which he staked the last remnant of his hopes.

§ 4

The voyage was far from promising. Except for ten days spent at Gibraltar scrambling about the rock among the monkeys in a pair of silk stockings and nankeen pantaloons, he was uniformly ill and depressed, and when he was not reading through an Italian grammar, he was analysing his 'dimness of feeling.' Only in the last four or five days did his languor begin to lift. Dr. Stoddart, however, the resident attorney-general, to whom he bore a letter of introduction, received him 'with an explosion of surprise and welcome' which was just what he wished, and the mere novelty of his surroundings distracted him for a time, though he found it a dreary place and the Maltese the 'noisiest race under heaven.'

In June he wrote that he was better in health on the whole and hoped in a month or so to be able to give a more encouraging account. 'As it is, I have every reason to be satisfied. The effect of years cannot be done away in a few weeks.' As previously in Germany he was pathetically home-sick. He trembled at the thought of letters from England. 'I should be most *miserable*,' he confessed, 'without them, and yet I shall receive them as a sentence of death! So terribly has fear got the upper hand in my habitual feelings, from my long destitution of hope and joy.'

But at first he was too fully occupied to indulge in 'diseased excess' of sensibility, since soon after his arrival he became an official secretary to the Governor, Sir Alexander Ball, who found his company a delightful feast to his mind, save when he insisted on propounding such distinctions as that between 'an unorganized mass of matter' and 'a mass of unorganized matter.' Early in August too he was sent to Sicily to draw up a political paper on its revenues and resources, and soon after his return, was appointed as the temporary successor of the Public Secretary, who had died. Among his duties, ironically enough, was that of writing drafts in Castlereagh's name, scarcely a congenial task even for a disillusioned Jacobin.

But his real life had little relation to these surface activities; rather the monotony and press of official duties accentuated his introspection. During 1804 his health showed real signs of improvement and his eye was focused upon the beauties of his new world. Yet all the time he remained dishearteningly detached. He saw for example how interestingly 'a brisk gale and the foam that peopled the *alive* sea' combined with the number of white sea-gulls as if 'the foam-spit had taken life and wing and had flown up,' but he saw it like a geometrical proposition, while the sky, 'that soft, blue, mighty arch, resting on the mountain or solid sea-like plain' suggested 'an awful omneity in unity.' He could not, as he longed to do, feel himself into their very being. 'Days and weeks and months pass on,' he noted, 'and the sea, the sea and the breeze have their influences on me, and so, too, has the association with good and sensible men. I feel a pleasure upon me, and I am, to the outward view, cheerful, and have myself no distinct consciousness of the contrary, for I use my faculties, not, indeed, at once, but freely. But oh! I am never happy, never deeply gladdened. I know not – I have forgotten – what the joy is of which the heart is full, as of a deep and quiet fountain overflowing insensibly, or the gladness of joy, when the fountain overflows ebulient.'

He had tasted intoxication and henceforth no other state was really tolerable. And the self-consciousness, which he at once relieved and aggravated by perpetual analysis, rapidly degenerated into morbid self-pity when his hopes of returning home in May 1805 were disappointed. In addition, through a mishap to the mail, he had received no letters from England for nearly ten weeks and his consequent dejection of spirits was intensified by the news of the death of Wordsworth's sailor brother, which he was told at a public reception, and immediately, according to his own account, fell down on the ground in 'a convulsive hysteric fit.' The effect of these accidents was disastrous. 'They have nearly broken my heart,' he wrote, and his health deteriorated rapidly.

He suddenly realized his isolation among hard-headed officials on a dreary island. They had a 'self-betraying side-and-down look of cunning': their only criterion was one of use. He had no one in whom to confide, no one even to whom he could comfortably talk. His work seemed the very prostitution of his powers, his hopes of physical and spiritual recovery a delusion, his future a homeless blank.

In September he escaped at last, setting out for Rome, but staying on the way for four months at Naples. He was too wretched, too resigned now even to be homesick. An American artist who met him often in Rome noted how prematurely middle-aged he looked. Only the large grey eyes remained invincibly childlike, proclaiming, as they were always to do, the one constant and lovable quality in a character already at the age of thirty-four irreparably aged.

For so soon, he now recognized, he had passed 'the *top of the hill*'; the exhilaration, the irresponsibility of youth was gone from him. He found himself a *man* without a man's capacity. 'Dreadful was the feeling – till then life had flown so that I had always been a boy, as it were; and this sensation had blended in all my conduct, my willing acknowledgment of superiority, and, in truth, my meeting every person as a superior at the first moment. Yet if men survive this period, they commonly become cheerful again. That is a comfort for mankind, *not for me!*'

In May he left Rome hurriedly at a rumour that Napoleon, who had already cut him off from Naples, intended to arrest all the English in Italy, and cherished a peculiar animosity towards himself for articles which he had contributed to the *Morning Post*. At Leghorn he arranged for a passage home in an American ship, which was not however to sail for more than a month, a month of increasing anguish of mind and body. Never had he been so paralysed. His head 'felt like another man's . . . so dead was it' and his right side was numbed as if by a palsy stroke.

But at the same time he was feverishly conscious. 'O my children!' he wrote in his note-book, 'whether, and which of you are dead, whether any and which among you are alive I know not, and were a letter to arrive this moment from Keswick I fear that I should be unable to open it, so deep and black is my despair. O my children! My children! I gave you life once, unconscious of the life I was giving you, and you as unconsciously have given life to me.'

Yet he knew now that the only final escape for him from a sense of death in life lay in the possibility of a life in death. Surely in the infinite unknown he might be gloriously quit of his sagging body and at last come face to face with the central reality of things. 'Come, come,' he begged,

'thou bleak December wind,
And blow the dry leaves from the tree!
Flash, like a love-thought thro' me, Death!
And take a life that wearies me.'

But alas! Poole was right in his refusal to believe that 'your diseases come near the silver cord.' An excessive sensitiveness to circumstance and atmosphere could co-exist with great bodily solidity. Indeed it was this very combination which was his tragedy; and though his sufferings on the voyage home were unremitting, the Captain and his fellow passengers had no need to be 'seriously alarmed for his life.'

In this condition he reached Portsmouth early in August, and a week later dragged himself to London and took sanctuary with Lamb. He was 'ill, penniless, and worse than homeless,' and afraid 'even to cowardice, to ask for any person, or of any person.' He had played his last card and lost. He stood face to face with himself, and in the background, distorted by his sense of remorse and self-disgust, hovered the accusing faces of his wife and his friends. It had been easy to say beforehand that if he did not bring back health, he would at least bring back experience, and suffer with patience and silence; but he did not realize then how stark the experience would be or how incapable of silent resignation he was.

There is no moment more terrible to the romanticist than that in which realism is forced upon him. Generally he eludes the full impact of fact, and possibly this was the only moment in Coleridge's life when some sort of evasion was impossible. Neither poetry, metaphysics, religious unction, epistolary self-depreciation nor projects availed him. His genius had faded like a ghost at cock-crow, his body was an unco-ordinated weight of matter, and the faith and sympathy which alone could quicken the blood in his veins could never be his, because he could not pretend to justify it. He dare not turn even to the Wordsworths.

'O the complexities,' he wrote in his note-book, 'of the ravel produced by time struggling with eternity!' But that was merely an abstraction; it was the conflict in his own harassed being of body with spirit that could never, he now realized, be resolved. 'The chestnut,' he wrote, 'is a fine shady tree, and its wood excellent, were it not that it dies away at the *heart* first. Alas! poor me!'

It was not at the heart that his tree was dying, but at the roots.

¶ CHAPTER SIX
# FLUCTUATIONS

§ I

ORTUNATELY however Stuart presided at the *Courier*
office and there for a month he gave himself to
routine work. It was an ill-substitute for that

'abiding place of love
O'er which my spirit, like the mother dove,
Might brood with warming wings!'

but it helped him to forget. A kind and encouraging
letter however from Wordsworth tempted him away, and
a month after his return he wrote for the first time to
Sara (whose 'character in general,' he informed her, he
held 'in more than mere esteem – in reverence') that he
would arrive at Greta Hall in a fortnight.

But his reverence was met by neither sympathy nor
respect. Sara was heartless enough to make him get up
on really freezing mornings in his nightshirt to light the
fire, before she dressed herself and the children, and
according to his own account broke out into outrageous
passions, 'like a wet candle spitting flame,' he aptly noted.
The weather and his health were terrible and opium a
ceaseless necessity. Once again he resolved at all costs
formally to separate, but Sara's conventionality, which
had helped to kill the marriage as a reality, preserved it as
a fact. Her one argument in opposing such a step was
that 'everybody will talk,' although Coleridge's suggestion
that he should take his two boys with him and superintend
their education may have with reason alarmed her. Before
Christmas, however, his patience was exhausted, and
taking Hartley with him, he followed the Wordsworths
to Coleorton.

Even Wordsworth's hopes were damped by his appearance. His own verses, written four years before, must surely have recurred to his mind:

> 'Ah! piteous sight it was to see this Man
> When he came back to us, a withered flower, –
> Or like a sinful creature, pale and wan.
> Down would he sit; and without strength or power
> Look at the common grass from hour to hour.'

But after nearly three years of exile 'the sweet sense of Home' which stole over Coleridge was inexpressibly consoling. His sense of life began to revive. And in Sarah Hutchinson his emotions, so long frozen within him, discovered a new object over which to diffuse themselves. Dorothy was too intimately associated with the days

> 'when we first
> Together wandered in wild poesy.'

Her very sympathy was a reminder of failure, of those awful days when 'Christabel' hung fire; but Sarah Hutchinson could give him 'a sister's and mother's love' uncomplicated by the past. And so desperate was his need, so dim his realization of love as an exclusive attraction that he never stopped to consider the effect which this new attachment might have on Dorothy.

Surely, he thought, even when he first met Sarah Hutchinson at Sockburn he had unconsciously recognized an affinity? 'As when the taper's white cone of flame is seen double, till the eye moving brings them into one space and then they become one – so did the idea in my imagination coadunate with your present form soon after I first gazed upon you.' And although her charm in his eyes was that she did not remind him of extinguished poetry, it was in meditative verse that he wrote of her in his notebook:

'And in life's noisest hour
There whispers still the ceaseless love of thee,
The heart's self-solace and soliloquy,'

or again:

'You mould my hopes, you fashion me within,
And to the leading love-throb in my heart
Through all my being, all my pulses beat.
You lie in all my many thoughts like light,
Like the fair light of dawn, or summer light,
On rippling stream, or cloud-reflecting lake –
And looking to the Heaven that beams above you,
How do I bless the lot that made me love you!'

He blessed it because it restored him to some degree at
least of communion with life and soothed 'the secret pang
that eats away the heart.' Her voice was the

'dear woman's voice to one cast forth,
A wanderer with a worn-out heart forlorn,
Mid strangers pining with untended wounds.'

Like a man who has been near death, and knows he can
never know good health again, he could yet enjoy a comparative convalescence. 'The moulting peacock,' he noted,
'with only two of his long tail-feathers remaining, and
those sadly in tatters, yet, proudly as ever, spreads out his
ruined fan in the sun and breeze.'

That, he had to admit, was beyond his powers of recovery, yet with Sarah Hutchinson's help he felt that he
could faintly emulate it. How much like a moulted peacock he was, was forced upon him by Wordsworth's
recitation of the poem 'On the growth of an individual
mind,' later named 'The Prelude,' upon which, while his
friend's life had been going down in ruins, he had been
steadfastly working, reconciling in the process

'the two natures,
The one that feels, the other that observes"

between which Coleridge himself could find no unifying concord. Yet as night after night the great constructive record unfolded, despite the memory so often recalled

'of that hour
Of thy communion with my nobler mind,'

despite the comparison it so poignantly, so chasteningly, suggested, his mood was strangely tranquil. He had accepted failure as a poet and derived almost a melancholy satisfaction from the

'Sense of past youth, and manhood come in vain,
And genius given, and knowledge won in vain;
And all, which I had cull'd in wood-walks wild,
And all which patient toil had rear'd, and all
Commune with THEE had open'd out – but flowers
Strew'd on my corse, and borne upon my bier,
In the same coffin, for the self-same grave!'

The tide of the poem took him and he lay passive on it

'by the various strain
Driven as in surges now, beneath the stars,
With momentary stars of her own birth,
Fair constellated foam, still darting off
Into the darkness; now a tranquil sea,
Outspread and bright, yet swelling to the moon.

'And when – O Friend! my comforter, my guide!
Strong in thyself, and powerful to give strength! –
Thy long sustained Song finally clos'd,
And thy deep voice had ceas'd – yet thou thyself
Wert still before my eyes, and round us both
That happy vision of beloved faces –
(All whom I deepliest love – in one room all!)

Scarce conscious, and yet conscious of its close,
I sate, my being blended in one thought, –
(Thought was it? or aspiration? or resolve?)
Absorb'd; yet hanging still upon the sound – '

But while he was forgetting one Sara in the person of another, he was forgetting other friends too. Poole doubtless was too understanding to impute this to positive indifference, but Josiah Wedgwood was both hurt and angry. His brother Thomas had died during Coleridge's absence abroad, and yet six months had passed since his return and not even a letter of ordinary condolence had been received. In addition he had sent a message through Wordsworth concerning a proposed Memoir, which would have 'produced a reply from any good man with feeling such as men usually possess,' but even this had failed to break Coleridge's silence. Illness and unhappiness could not excuse such conduct, and he ceased, in his own words, 'to esteem him.' The breach had been made in their relationship, which, despite a temporary healing, was to end in the withdrawal of his share of the allowance.

Meanwhile Coleridge early in 1807 went up to London to visit another friend, Basil Montagu, and there between February and May he planned to deliver at the Royal Institution the first of those series of lectures on the Principles of Art which for the rest of his life were to prove the most congenial and creative activity in which he was ever engaged. In May it had been arranged that he should join Mrs. Coleridge and his other children at Bristol and that they should all go from there on a visit first to Stowey and then to Ottery St. Mary. The rumour, however, of a possible separation was too much for his clerical brother George, and he closed his doors against him.

Doubtless Coleridge was much relieved. For Stowey maintained the revival begun at Coleorton. The 'stout plain-looking farmer' in Poole helped him to view both his poetical and domestic failures in a more mundane perspective. He rode a horse or he wandered about his 'dear old walks of Quantock and Alfoxden'; he abandoned fermented and abstained from spirituous liquors and lessened the daily dose of opium. Poole found his 'mind heightened and better disciplined,' but his health and will-power weaker. Nevertheless he prevailed upon him to write at last to Josiah Wedgwood, and doubtless his plea for pity, the casuistical contention that the faultiest parts of his conduct had 'arisen from qualities both blameable and pitiable, but yet the very opposite of Neglect or Insensibility,' and the fiction that he had 'a paper now on its way from Malta,' in which he had portrayed 'poor Thomas,' was responsible for removing all Wedgwood's feelings of anger.

But Coleridge's comparative happiness lay in the fact that he had now accepted the position of being a mental doctor continually diagnosing his disease. He was to suffer still from circumstances that lacerated his feelings, but never again was he really to agonize over the disintegration of his personality. Rather it was increasingly to supply him with a subject for secret analysis and public exposition, both in the form of lectures and of that copious conversational display which was to be the outstanding feature of his remaining years and the source of much of his posthumous repute.

It was this performance which amazed and gratified an Oxford undergraduate, 'a scholar and a man of genius,' as Cottle described him in an introductory letter to Poole, who, finding Coleridge away for a few days, followed him to Bridgwater. His admiration had been excited eight years before by 'The Ancient Mariner,' 'the greatest

event,' as he called it, in the unfolding of his mind. He
had seen in it 'the ray of a new morning,' but his interest
had been recently renewed by the information that Coleridge was applying his whole mind to metaphysics and
psychology – his own 'absorbing pursuit.'

A small, shy, dreamy imp of a man, a precocious Greek
scholar, yet gifted with a memory vastly retentive and a
taste already nibbling at narcotics, he had indeed many
points of affinity with the burnt-out poet tending to cor-
pulence whom he found standing in a deep reverie under
a gateway off the main street of Bridgwater. Coleridge
took him back to the house where he was staying and
there, after a few courteous preliminaries, 'like some great
river, the Orellana, or the St. Lawrence, that, having been
checked and fretted by rocks or thwarting islands, suddenly recovers its volume of waters and its mighty music,
swept at once, as if returning to his natural business, into
a continuous strain of eloquent dissertation, certainly the
most novel, the most finely illustrated, and traversing the
most spacious fields of thought, by transitions the most
just and logical that it was possible to conceive.'

It is not the place here to discuss the value of Coleridge's talk: that may be more suitably done later in
considering the quality of his metaphysics and of his prose
writing in general, since all of it was dictated conversation. But one point in De Quincey's account may be
countered at once. 'Coleridge,' he wrote, 'to many people,
and often I have heard the complaint, seemed to wander;
and he seemed then to wander the most when, in fact, his
resistance to the wandering instinct was greatest – viz.,
when the compass and huge circuit, by which his illustrations moved, travelled farthest into remote regions
before they began to revolve. Long before this coming
round commenced, most people had lost him, and naturally enough supposed that he had lost himself . . . and I

can assert . . . that logic the most severe was as inalienable from his modes of thinking, as grammar from his language.'

So far as talk can be considered merely as a technical display, this testimony to Coleridge's logical subtlety and coherence was doubtless justified. But the complaints were also justified, since, wonderful as the circuit of his eloquence might be, it was generally a verbal circuit. Like vocal virtuosity it was a triumph of articulation, but it lacked the very essence of effective communication in words, a clear and concrete meaning. 'Words' too often had become 'things.' And if it was logical in detail, it had no central idea to which its details were subordinated.

But De Quincey's admiration of his eloquence and sympathy with his views on the Hartleian theory evoked an immediate response from Coleridge: he even 'entered into a spontaneous explanation' of his opium habits, and he so wrought upon his admirer's feelings that on his return to Bristol he begged Cottle to inquire whether Coleridge would accept a gift from an unknown friend. Coleridge replied that the only serious obstacle to the completion of the works to which he aspired was pecuniary pressure; that he would employ the tranquillity of mind so gained to benefit his fellow-men, and that he hoped to be able to restore the money at the end of two years. The result of these plausible assertions was a gift of £300 which neither hastened the realization of mythical works nor even the lectures 'On Taste,' which he had vaguely promised to deliver at the Royal Institution and which Poole was constantly urging him to prepare. He continued to talk very much like an angel and to do nothing at all.

§ 2

His talk however at this time had undergone a change, not in its characteristics, but in its subject matter. It had

begun to be quite explicitly devout. Having failed to
realize in poetical activity the morality of the creative
artist, he had fallen back upon the creed of the theologian.
He had confessed to De Quincey how profoundly ashamed
he was of Unitarianism and how disgusted to think that
he could at any time have countenanced its tenets; and
doubtless on the many walks he took with Poole after
Sara and the children had returned to Bristol, he discoursed at length on this subject. Certainly his letters
were increasingly preoccupied with it.

The characteristics of the religious views which he now
embraced may be more profitably summarized towards
the end of his life, when they had become his absorbing
interest and had assumed a less crude and credulous form.
At this point it will be enough to stress the personal aspect
of the change from an Unitarian to a Trinitarian creed.
The change coincided with his own loss of the power of
unified experience. For his conception of God as of Nature
was exclusively an idealized conception of himself. The
more he ceased to be able to harmonize his being in an act
of creative expression, the more conscious he became of the
various faculties which should ideally contribute to such
an act, but which in him were imperfectly co-ordinated.

It was these constituent elements which he began and
henceforth never ceased to separate and analyse in himself,
and it was the knowledge derived from such analysis
which made him unique in his day as a psychological
critic. If he could have brought the same psychology to
an analysis of religious experience, the result might have
been equally fruitful. But into this province of inquiry
another and stronger personal element entered.

For while his failure of creative power as a poet sharp-
ened his critical sense, when he turned to examine, in
the light of his own past experience, works of creative art,
his failure to live creatively as a man completely preju-

diced his attitude to religious questions. Christ, as he was to admit later, was 'not primarily a teacher, but a doer,' and no faith has real value which has not been actively experienced. Poetry in its purest and strangest essence as an imaginative act Coleridge had really experienced, and so, as a critic of romantic art, he could break through literary dogma and pierce to reality. But Christianity as a vital and harmonizing faith, rooted in and issuing in action, was the one kind of poetical experience which he could never realize; he turned to it not joyfully and creatively, as one who has discovered a new set of values which resolved an inner discord, but as one harassed by 'sorrow and ill health and disappointment,' who seized despairingly upon a body of doctrine to interpose between himself and the reality of his own maladjusted life. And as such it always remained. In short, instead of experiencing a Christian conversion and then in the light of that conversion examining the Church's dogmas to see if they truly represented it, he merely accepted orthodox dogma, because its fixity comforted his fluid nature and wove about it a thin but voluminous fabric of philosophical ideas.

Much of the Church's dogma is true because it defines and summarizes characteristic religious experiences; some of it is false because man has outgrown in knowledge and experience the data upon which it was based. The task of the free mind is to discriminate between these two types, before attempting to translate either into terms of its own thought and to renew them with its own faith.

But that task Coleridge never attempted. He was not strenuous enough either to believe or disbelieve vitally; he was too bewildered in a world of fact, to wish to sacrifice one stone in an edifice which appealed to him just because it seemed firm, final, and touchingly mellowed with age. And so the foundations of his religious thought were generally formulas and its superstructure edifying abstractions.

He could write for example at this time of the Bible – 'without . . . stopping to contend on what all dispassionate men must deem undebatable ground, I may assume inspiration as admitted; and equally so, that it would be an insult to man's understanding to suppose any other revelation from God than the Christian scriptures. . . . If therefore these scriptures, "impregnable in their strength" . . . *do* inculcate the doctrine of the *Trinity*; however surpassing human comprehension; then I say, we are bound to admit it on the strength of *moral demonstration*.'

Such 'moral demonstration' as this surely surpassed any of the sophistries of which he accused the Socinians. It does indeed far less than justice to his ultimate conceptions. In the last years of his life, for example, he could write that he considered the Bible most inspired because in it 'there is more that *finds* me than I have experienced in all other books put together . . . and at greater depths of my being.' Nevertheless it is well to quote these pulpit platitudes, since they reveal in a crude form the lack of real meaning which was always to characterize his religious writing.

As will later be shown, Coleridge sought to justify a nebulous faith and idealism by a specious use of Kant's metaphysical distinction between 'Reason' and 'Understanding,' claiming on these grounds not only that religion is an act of faith' or of 'reason' in the Kantian sense, which it is, but that also the dogmas of a church and the scriptural 'evidences' upon which it based its authority could not be affected by any criticism, however destructive, of the mere 'understanding.'

The following quotation from the letter already cited will serve to show how conveniently vague and high-sounding the distinction could become when interpreted by a devout Trinitarian: – 'All should remember that some truths from their nature, surpass the scope of man's limited powers, and stand as the criteria of *faith*, determining by their rejection or admission, who among the sons of men can confide in the veracity of heaven. Those more ethereal truths, of which the Trinity is conspicuously the chief, without being circumstantially explained, may be faintly illustrated by material objects. . . . The Trinity is a subject on which analogical reasoning may advantageously be admitted, as furnishing at least a glimpse of light, and with this, for the present, we must be satisfied. Infinite wisdom deemed clearer manifestations inexpedient; and is man to dictate to his Maker?'

Unction such as this is the inevitable result of sacrificing a mundane critical conscience to 'the veracity of heaven,' and of forming an illicit relationship between free metaphysical inquiry and a tied theology.

§ 3

Naturally therefore conversion to orthodoxy did not affect Coleridge's practical ways of life. Religion was a speculative retreat full of verbal avenues and intricate bypaths, in any one of which he faintly hoped by some incredible 'saving grace' to be suddenly made a new man, as he had hoped to renew the miracle of 'The Ancient Mariner.' Meanwhile opium continued as pervasive, and fact and fiction as confused. He still described himself too as 'penniless' and 'resourceless' and as wasting in remorse (and it might be added in Trinitarian metaphysics) 'the energy which should be better employed in reformation.'

From Stowey he returned to Bristol, and after Sara and the children had left for home, attended by De Quincey, who most conveniently wished to visit Wordsworth and Southey, he retired to the house of a Mr. Morgan and there fell ill. Coleridge showed great discretion in his choice of households in which to fall ill. For here, as at Dove Cottage, there were two ladies who tended him with 'sister's and mother's love,' Mrs. Morgan herself and her sister Charlotte; and 'choked up with heavy lumber' as the entrance passage to his heart may by now have been, it ever remained exceedingly susceptible to comforting bedside manners.

On this occasion he expressed his gratitude (the gratitude, as he wrote, which 'suspends the heart's despair') in a set of typically 'soft and pamby' verses, comparing his two new comforters to the

'Two dear, dear Sisters, prized all price above,
    Sisters, like you, with more than sisters' love,'

whom Mrs. Coleridge, when she read the verses on their appearance in the *Courier*, had little difficulty or satisfaction in identifying as Dorothy and Sarah Hutchinson. 'Dear and honoured Mary and Charlotte' were in fact very shortly to take the place of these 'other selves,' as he called them, when a tragic misunderstanding divided him from the Wordsworth family.

Meanwhile late in November, still suffering from a 'low bilious fever,' and with only two locks of hair and two profiles to remind him of his new benefactors, he arrived in London and took up his residence once again at the top of the *Courier* building in the Strand. Here, depressed by 'the comfortlessness of seeing no face, hearing no voice, feeling no hand that is dear,' he sank more than ever under the dominance of opium. Nevertheless he arranged at last to give his lectures on the English Poets, 'in illustration of the general principles of poetry.' Since, during the next ten years, he was to deliver a succession of these lectures, varying in detail, but essentially the same, it will be better to examine their quality later as a whole.

Here it will suffice to say that they dealt generally with the subjects of taste, imagination, fancy, and passion, as the sources of pleasure in the fine arts and with the connection of such pleasure with moral excellence; that Coleridge imported into them many of the principles of German criticism, but that he did so in no real sense as a plagiarist, but because such principles did fit his own experience. For example, when he spoke of the 'naïve' as an essential quality of poetic genius, it was his own essential *naïveté* which dictated the statement, although Kant expressed a similar view. Similarly when he contrasted, like Schiller, the pure moral feeling which underlay even gross passages in Shakespeare with the vicious prudery of Richardson, or with Lessing condemned the artificiality of French tragedy and dubbed Voltaire 'a petty scribbler,' it was his own essential naturalism which he was voicing. In addition he had a sense of humour unknown to German criticism.

For these lectures, like his conversation, satisfied a persistent need of self-expression. 'My thoughts,' he wrote, 'crowd each other to death'; in lecturing he eased the pressure and he also achieved something of that 'joy without consciousness' which he read into Bacchus, as the symbol of 'the organic energies of the Universe' still untroubled by the criticizing intellect. The essence of poetry as also of moral excellence was to him this universality, a fusion of all opposites in creative ecstasy, an organic communication of life, and to discourse upon it spontaneously, to empty his mind of the accumulated ponderings and yearnings of years, was at least a tolerable substitute for realizing it. To have written or even prepared his lectures would have destroyed the mood of melting fluency which he so much appreciated and by which alone he could escape a congested self-consciousness and that perpetual sense of the inexpressible which convinced him that 'processes of thought might be carried on independent and apart from spoken or written language.'

The result was that he ranged amazingly wide, was often disappointingly discursive, and indulged in constant digressions. But when his mind was held by an object and his whole being concentrated itself in an act of immediate apprehension, his criticism was of that creative order which blends synthesis with analysis, and estimates a work of art by an absolute as well as by a relative standard. This co-ordination between abstract principles and their concrete application depended too much upon an animated mood. Often, when depressed, he lost himself in abstractions: but when he achieved it he stood and still stands in the front rank of English critics.

On this first occasion, however, he could not even be relied upon to appear in the lecture-room, and when he did, it was in a state either of coma or exhaustion, 'his lips . . . baked with feverish heat, and often black in colour' and labouring 'under an almost paralytic inability to raise the upper jaw from the lower.'

So he dragged on until late in June 1808, when the course was completed; and shortly afterwards he fled from his own loneliness and the narcotic excuses it involved to Allan Bank, the Wordsworths' new house at Grasmere.

§ 4

The change in his health and spirits was immediate and phenomenal. Love was indeed 'the genial sun of human nature,' and though 'he divided his rays in acting on me and my beloved,' they still remained vitalizing enough. It was 'a duty, nay . . . a religion to that power to show' . . . that 'for itself can it produce all efforts, even if only to secure its name from scoffs as the child and parent of slothfulness.'

Such was the result of renewed intercourse with the Wordsworths, and above all with Sarah Hutchinson. He even claimed to have mastered the opium habit. 'I am hard at work,' he wrote, 'and feel a pleasure in it which I have not known for years; a consequence and reward of my courage in at length overcoming the fear of dying suddenly in my sleep, which, Heaven knows, alone seduced me into the fatal habit.' He was submitting his case 'carefully and faithfully, to some physician': already he felt 'the blessedness of walking altogether in light,' and should he entirely recover, he deemed it 'a sacred duty to publish my cure, tho' without my name, for the practise of taking opium is dreadfully spread.'

' A good conscience,' he noted, 'and hope combined are like fine weather that reconciles travel with delight,' and although he had no intention of returning to his wife, he was sufficiently in love with life to meet her on the friendliest terms at Allan Bank. Throughout the autumn his letters continued in this key, telling of an improvement beyond his boldest hopes, of 'a painful effort of moral courage remunerated by tranquility – by ease from the sting of self-disapprobation.' 'Judge me,' he wrote glee-fully, 'from the 1st January, 1809.'

And behind it all lay the comfort of Sarah Hutchin-son's appreciatory regard. His pulse was quickened by it, he breathed a new and genial air, and in a reaction from baffled inertia he plunged headlong into a journalistic venture, which was 'to make or mar' him. The perfidy of subscribers to the *Watchman* was forgotten; he cherished an 'honourable Ambition to be useful, aided by the wish to be generally acknowledged to have been so'; he would prove himself a practical idealist, a worthy object of sis-terly affection; while collaboration with Wordsworth suggested a pleasant parallel in prose with the enchanted days of the first *Lyrical Ballads*.

The weekly paper, of which he issued a prospectus in December, was in fact planned as an outlet for his new religious views. It was 'to aid in the formation of fixed principles in politics, morals, and religion.' Leading articles, reviews or news were to have no place in it, and should passing events be chronicled, it was in the light of that 'true philosophy' of which Christianity was the perfect expression.

He called it *The Friend*, and possibly if his Quaker subscribers had not shown what he considered a particular meanness in their mode and discontinuance of payment, the fact that 'in the essentials of their faith,' in 'unwearied beneficence and unfeigned listening and obedience to the Voice within,' he believed as they did, might have tempted him from the securer haven of the Establishment.

The first number was provisionally announced to appear on January 7, 1809, but 'vexations, hindrances, scoundrelism, disappointments, and pros and cons,' without, he was convinced, 'the least fault on my own part,' delayed publication for six months. His greatest difficulty was to discover a printer. Southey had been cheated by his printer, and Coleridge, in his anxiety to avoid a similar fate, was led into an act of unpractical folly.

Instead of arranging to have the paper published in London, where it would have had some chance of a reasonable and efficient circulation, he preferred to depend on local efforts. His first choice was a Kendal bookseller, named Pennington, whose chief claim to consideration was that he was 'a *genius* and mightily indifferent about the affairs of this life'; but in February he discovered a really 'clever young man,' a Mr. John Brown, of Penrith, who only required £38 worth of type to set him going. Penrith was separated from Grasmere by twenty-eight miles of rough road which included the Kirkstone Pass. The postal system between the two places was primitive and in rough weather quite uncertain. Nevertheless Mr. Brown's impressive cleverness won the day.

March however came and still the public had no opportunity of forming fixed principles. Coleridge's spirits, too, were beginning to suffer, and an attack of the 'mumps' and the death of Dr. Beddoes, who had undertaken to cure him of his laudanum habit, took, as he wrote, a large slice of hope out of his life. In other words, it offered him an excuse for drugging his anxieties by renewed indulgence. And one so sensitive must have been conscious of Wordsworth's distrust. He was convinced, he told Poole, that Coleridge would never now achieve anything, that everything was 'frustrated by a derangement in his intellectual and moral constitution,' that he had 'no voluntary power of mind whatsoever' and was incapable of 'acting under any *constraint* of duty or moral obligation.' Even if *The Friend* should appear, he was certain that it could not continue for any length of time, and he begged Poole to prevail on Coleridge to abandon the venture before it was begun.

But no one could have persuaded Coleridge to do that now. Had he not staked all his credit as an effective being on this cast? Was not his attachment to Sarah Hutchinson poignantly involved in its success or failure? And so on June 1, after friends had advanced money for the stamped paper, the first number at last appeared.

Meanwhile he had received nothing but lists of hypothetical subscribers, and the manner of payment, 'the ugliest part of the business,' as he wrote with a laudable but unfortunate contempt for money, had not even been decided upon. Possibly, judging others by himself, he thought that the best way to sell his goods was not to demand it until people had thoughtlessly incurred the debt, but the only way of honouring it ever suggested was a vague announcement in the second number that payment should be made at the close of each twentieth week.

After despatching the second number on June 8 he returned from Penrith to Grasmere. He was in a mood of genial optimism, claiming fictitiously that the material for the next two numbers was ready 'in a very superior style of polish and easy intelligibility,' and that henceforth regularity was secured. But although Allan Bank was more homely than Penrith lodgings, although he could lie in bed and dictate to Sarah Hutchinson, while Dorothy stifled her feelings as best she could in cookery and the housework, his distance from the publishing centre was the final fatality of this ill-starred scheme. A printer thirty miles away was not only inconveniently, but conveniently remote. He did not trouble the conscience save by fits and starts, and so weeks would pass without a line being written, and then in a frenzy of remembrance he would compose a whole number in two days, only to be provoked and disheartened by a delay in its delivery.

By the New Year, failure, though he would not admit it, was already stamped upon the venture. Of the small number of subscribers, two-thirds nearly had discontinued, or, what was worse, continued to receive the paper without payment, while even the faithful complained of its dullness and fretted at its transcendentalism.

And indeed there was some justice in their complaints. It was not merely that Coleridge preached – for, as Lamb jestingly remarked, he never did anything else, and yet his audiences were generally captivated – but the style of his preaching was not suited to weekly journalism.

The journalist, if he is not a pure impressionist, must at least concentrate his thought within narrow limits; he must aim at point, variety and brevity. His style, as Hazlitt wrote, must be 'bright and quick as the first feelings of truth': it must have a concentrated flavour. That is why the best journalism is generally prejudiced. It gains in force in proportion to its prejudice. But Coleridge always wanted to say everything about anything, and he could seldom keep his eye fiercely focussed upon an object for the vapours that rose from his sense of underlying profundities and wreathed about his mind.

Again, true as it might be that 'no two things that are yet different, can be in closer harmony than the deductions of a profound philosophy and the dictates of plain common sense,' the plain man wanted common sense in concrete terms and not in those of abstract ratiocination. Coleridge however credited him with his own extended metaphysical reading and his own relish for thought as thought, and continually indulged in abstruse meditations upon first principles. Necessarily such meditations could not be treated popularly, as he at one time hoped, 'and with that lightness and variety of illustration which formed the charm of *The Spectator.*' Addison provided 'reading made easy' because he skimmed the cream off the surface of life, and Coleridge wrote truly enough – 'Of parentheses I may be too fond, and will be on my guard in this respect. But I am certain that no work of impassioned and eloquent reasoning ever did or could subsist without them. They are the *drama* of reason and present the thought growing instead of a mere *Hortus siccus.*'

Nevertheless the fact remained that weekly journalism was no place for so extended a drama of reason. The ordinary reader became lost in its involved periods, and doubtless in simpler and crueller terms would have confirmed Coleridge's own strictures when he wrote that 'there is often an *entortillage* in the sentences and even the thoughts (which nothing can justify), and always almost, a stately piling up of story on story in one architectural period, which is not suited to a periodical essay . . . least of all suited to the present illogical age, which has, in imitation of the French, rejected all the *cements* of language.'

And even those who survived the style found the substance unsatisfying. They felt dimly that the compromise which Coleridge had adopted in religion and sought to apply to political affairs was not a vital one. It was the compromise of a man who looked back instead of forward, who was occupied in steering a middle and abstract course between 'the ague of Hobbes' and 'the fever of Rousseau,' who was 'upholding the principles both of Taste and Philosophy, adopted by the great men of Europe from the middle of the fifteenth till towards the close of the seventeenth century' because of his inability to live in his own century and relate his ideals to its problems. To add a 'sanctifying spirit' to the views of Hampden, Milton and Sidney, to review 'the fair humanities of old religion,' was a poor substitute for studying contemporary events in the light of really personal and constructive values.

Yet remote as much of Coleridge's idealism was from actual experience, his attempt to apply ideal principles to the consideration alike of art and religion and national and social life was right in intention and significant in its issue.

The Romantic poets of whom Coleridge and Wordsworth were the forerunners did not discover ideal values; at most they rediscovered them; but they were unique in attempting, often imperfectly, to humanize them, to bring them into vital relation with ordinary life. Just as Coleridge tried to read poetry in the light of human experience and not as a detached literary display, so he wished to connect human conduct with æsthetic values. His expression of these values was often tainted by a conventionally religious standpoint, but in a true sense such values are religious.

Modern idealism originated in the Christ of the Gospels,

in one sense perhaps the first Romantic, as a writer has recently called him, and it grew up with the Christian era and the sensitive individualism which Christianity expressed. But for centuries it remained a retreat to which men, jarred by the conflict of the world, resorted. Its religious expression was other worldly or entangled in theological abstractions. Its literary and artistic expression was equally abstract, save in some of the plays of Shakespeare; and even he, if the evidence of the 'Tempest' is to be believed, ended in abandoning his attempt to reconcile the discord of man with the perfect harmony which his imagination conceived. Chaucer frankly dismissed such a harmony to regions of clerical discourse, and such poets as Spenser conceived of it and worshipped it only in subliminal and generally fanciful terms. The mystical poets of the seventeenth century read it uncritically into the phenomenal beauty of nature, but pondered little on the ideal potentialities of man, treating him at best as a sinner to be saved by the sacraments of the Church. The eighteenth century went further and tried to forget the need of ideal values in correctness and in uninspired common sense.

But with the new century they began to be reasserted, not as an abstract but as a practical necessity. For the first time it was claimed that a Christian humanism should affect every department of life. The poets who made this claim were generally too ecstatically conscious of the harmony they desired to bring it into true relation with practical concerns; but from their day Romanticism ceased to be a merely private or æsthetic or academic concern. Its values became indeed gradually a directing force in the life and thought of the West. Modern man, not only as a seeker after an inward harmony but as a responsible citizen, was more and more compelled to accept or reject its moral values, to choose between its creative faith in the potential reasonableness and humanity of man and a realistic and self-interested view of him as a creature fore-doomed to lust and selfishness and lethargy. And if he accepted the former view, he was more and more bound to apply his faith constructively to every department of life.

In this effort to link up a religious consciousness with everyday things, to treat art, not merely as a luxury or an activity governed by values of its own, but as imaging creative principles, applicable to life as a whole, Coleridge was a pioneer. In his literary criticism he related art intimately to human experience; in *The Friend* he attempt-ed to estimate even political action by the creative prin-ciples which he saw working in great poetry and which he translated imperfectly into philosophic and religious terms. It was a forlorn and confused experiment, but it deserved at least the commendation of one of his acquaint-ances: — 'Of Coleridge . . . I think the better for his *Friendly* productions; there is writing of a high order thickly interspersed, and . . . it must be owned that he often develops sentiments which few have elevation enough to cogitate.' Doubtless few had such elevation, but *The Friend* was an early venture in that process of education, by which men were led to apply truly human standards not only to art and religion, but also to life.

§ 5

Coleridge, however, could derive little consolation from a solitary admirer. Only Wordsworth's wish prevailed on him to continue his 'march through the wilderness,' and by January 1810 he had ceased to make even sporadic efforts and had fallen back on some old letters from Ger-many and 'Sketches and Fragments of the Life and Char-acter of the late Sir Alexander Ball.' Worthy man as the late Governor of Malta undoubtedly was, pleasing as the panegyric must have proved to Sir Alexander's family –

surprising too, since its author and his subject were rumoured to have parted 'on a mutual notorious hatred of
each other' – it was scarcely calculated to help in the 'formation of fixed principles' or the retention of wavering
subscribers.

But early in March the blow fell. Sarah Hutchinson's
long visit was to end in a fortnight. 'Coleridge,' wrote
Dorothy, 'most of all will miss her, as she has transcribed
almost every paper of *The Friend* for the press.' He missed
her so much that the paper, 'an enormous title page,' as
Hazlitt a little unfairly called it, 'an endless preface to an
imaginary work,' ended on March 15 with her departure.

For in Mrs. Wordsworth's 'amiable sister' Coleridge
lost not only an industrious amanuensis, but the last spur
to a dormant conscience. 'There is a sense of the word,
Love,' he was to write in even sadder days to Wordsworth, 'in which I never felt it, but to you and one of
your household,' and the same letter contained the significant crescendo, 'Dear Mary! Dear Dorothy! Dearest
Sara!' And in his note-book he had confessed all the
subtly sad, vague luxury of his emotion.

' "I fear to speak, I fear to hear you speak, so deeply
do I now enjoy your presence, so totally possess you in
myself, myself in you. The very sound would break the
union and separate you–me into you and me. We both,
and this sweet room, its books, its furniture, and the
shadows on the wall slumbering with the low, quiet fire,
are all *our* thought, one harmonious imagery of forms
distinct on the still substance of one deep feeling, love
and joy – a lake, or, if a stream, yet flowing so softly, so
unwrinkled, that its flow is life, not change – that state in
which all the invidious nature, the distinction without
division of a vivid thought, is united with the sense and
substance of intensest reality."

'And what if joy pass quick away? Long is the track

of Hope before – long too the track of recollection after
. . . so Nature, with Hope and Recollection, pieces out
our short summer.'

But she was gone, and soon enough there was to be no
track of Hope before. Dorothy had served his poetry,
Sarah Hutchinson his prose, but both ventures had ended
in failure. Yet from this failure he derived a certain contentment, the peace of resignation. It seemed to him
more a material than an ideal failure. He had made an
effort to help mankind and mankind had rejected him.
As for his effort to save himself, it had been always a
delusion, always beyond his powers. He had passed beyond self-disgust into the quiet of self-acceptance. His
nature, he realized, could not be conquered or directed.
Its very virtues were the quality of its defects. He had
energies and could exert them, but 'not in anything which
the duty of the day demanded.' Even his wife ceased to
irritate him. He addressed her once again as 'my dear
Love' and humbly asked if she could put him up, and he
passed the next four or five months at Greta Hall, spilling
his usual snuff over the carpets, and bewildering her by
his gentle equanimity.

She could not fathom the change, knew not 'what to
think or what to do,' so uniformly kind was his disposition.
He seemed actually happier than for years. For he could
indulge in abstractions to his heart's content, without
attempting to relate them to actual life. He could be dutiful in apothegms, such as, 'To perform duties absolutely
from the sense of duty, is the *ideal*,' and then he would
go on to prove by argument and analogy the impossibility
of its realization. Happiness to him was 'the state of that
person who, in order to enjoy his nature in its highest
manifestations of conscious feeling, has no need of doing
wrong, and who in order to do right is under no necessity
of abstaining from enjoyment.'

In a negative sense he had achieved this innocent Epicureanism for which he always hungered. He had ceased to consider whether he was doing wrong. He was simply enjoying his nature, jotting down an occasional hint of an idea for a 'Christabel' which he knew would never be continued, or sardonically recommending Lloyd's *State Worthies* as a manual for every man who would rise in the world.

Truly 'Repose after agitation' was 'like the pool under a waterfall, which the waterfall has made.' The last number of *The Friend* lay on his desk, and though the sight of it filled Mrs. Coleridge's heart 'with grief' and her eyes 'with tears,' it filled her husband's heart with a secret serenity. It had taught him the folly and futility of conscientious effort. With a conscience for the time unteased by remorse he could sun himself in the admiration that his conversation provoked, read Italian to his family and 'be perfectly content to be doing nothing else.' In material things he might be shipwrecked, but over the immaterial world of his own thoughts he floated as over a wan, autumnal sea.

CHAPTER SEVEN

ADRIFT

§ 1

LIFE, however, Coleridge was to discover, could still wound, and from the most unexpected and most desolating quarter. In October 1810 Basil Montagu and his family stopped at Greta Hall on their way south from Scotland, and Coleridge accepted an offer of a vacant place in their chaise and hospitality on their arrival in London. Meanwhile Wordsworth, upon whom they called, had taken the opportunity of confiding to Montagu that some of Coleridge's habits made him a difficult guest in a well-ordered household, hoping in this way, as he later explained, to prevent any embarrassments which might arise. Doubtless his intentions were kindly, although his manner of expressing them was probably too sententious to be happy. But the consequences were dire.

Coleridge had only been three days in Montagu's house when his host, with extreme tactlessness, informed him that he had been commissioned to say that owing to certain of his habits he had proved an intolerable guest at Allan Bank and that Wordsworth had no hope for him.

In a sense this was probably not as gross a libel upon Wordsworth's sentiments as has generally been claimed. He had confessed to Poole that he had ceased to hope for Coleridge as an effective being, and his subjection to opium and its rather sordid consequences were as likely to prove 'a nuisance' to Mrs. Wordsworth – even though she struck Moore as 'a comfortable sort of person enough' – as to Mrs. Coleridge or any other orderly housewife.

But Wordsworth's unhappy comments were significant of more than this. That hardening of his arteries as a creative being, which was to substitute moralizing in his poetry for vital, human sympathy, had already begun. The great decade of his life was over, and all that was prosaic and self-centred in his nature was in the ascendant. Coleridge's weak-willed benevolence therefore appealed to him less and less as the moralist superseded the poet. He saw all his faults with open eyes, and he had ceased to derive encouragement from his unworldly virtues.

But no more cruel way of informing Coleridge of a difference preordained in their respective natures could have been devised. That the friend in whom he placed such absolute confidence should have spoken of him in private in such a way was a terrible disillusionment, but that he should have actually, as he supposed, asked Montagu to inform him of his opinions was, as he gasped, not only 'cruel' – it was 'base.' It could only be interpreted as a method intentionally adopted of closing the doors of Allan Bank against him.

The cold callousness of it burst upon him 'like a thunderstorm out of a blue sky after fifteen years of such religious, almost superstitious idolatry and self-sacrifice.' Inevitably he expressed his feelings hysterically and with that element of cant which had now become constitutional. But he scarcely exaggerated when he wrote that 'all former afflictions of my life come less than flea-bites' compared to this. For he had truly given himself to Wordsworth, invested him with the faith which he had lost himself, and crowned him with an idolatrous halo. His friendship was in this sense 'enthusiastic and self-sacrificing,' even though it entailed no such material gifts as Wordsworth on his side had advanced.

'I call God Almighty to be my witness,' he wrote, 'as I have thought it no more than my duty, so did I feel a readiness to prefer him to myself, yea, even if life and outward reputation itself had been the pledge required'; and in confiding the facts to Mary Lamb his feelings so overpowered him that in a fit of weeping he could only stutter convulsively – 'Wordsworth, Wordsworth has given me up. *He* has no hope of me – I have been an absolute nuisance in his family.'

He was theatrical of course, but not consciously so. It was simply that he did not suffer as much as he claimed and felt he ought to suffer, because he was as incapable of facing pain starkly as he was of a keen thrill of joy. But one who leant upon an understanding sympathy as he did, who had known friends fail him, until Wordsworth as it seemed only remained, could not gather himself together to meet the blow. He was too amiable, and too conscious of dependence to cherish resentment. As with moral obligations the blow that should have roused him, stunned. It produced only a fermentation, not a reaction.

And there was a deeper cause of anguish even than Wordsworth's apostasy. Sarah Hutchinson, too, was ruled out of his life. Gone was 'the track of Hope before' which had sanctified his resignation, while 'the track of recollection after' was seared with the 'griping and grasping sorrows of life.' A score of times he began to write to her in Wales a detailed account of what had occurred, but gave it up from 'excess of agitation' until finally he learnt, from what source he did not state, that *all* of the Wordsworth family had decided against him unheard and that Wordsworth begged that he would no longer talk about it.

This was of course as distorted a version of the facts as Montagu's original narrative, but knowing how readily Coleridge confused fact and fiction, Wordsworth might surely have offered an explanation unasked.

The truth was that Coleridge's hysterical conduct in the matter only aggravated the half-contemptuous disgust which Wordsworth had begun to feel for the 'capacious soul' of other days. He heard that the breach between them was the common property of London literary circles and he conjectured, somewhat incorrectly, that Coleridge had confided the facts to anyone who would listen. He knew exactly with what a luxury of self-depreciation, with what histrionic epithets Coleridge would heighten the tale in his appeal for sympathy, and his pride revolted, his heart was hardened against such sentimentalism.

Did not Lamb also report that his supposedly stricken friend had powdered his head and looked 'like Bacchus, Bacchus ever sleek and young'? that he was 'going to turn sober, but his clock has not struck yet; meantime he pours down goblet after goblet, the second to see where the first is gone, the third to see no harm happens to the second, a fourth to say there is another coming, and a fifth to say he is not sure he is the last.' Inevitably Wordsworth doubted the sincerity of the feelings of such a man and justified his own silence. And yet so generous and essentially lovable a man as Coleridge deserved a more sensitive and tolerant reading of his character from one to whom he had given, spiritually, so much; and it was Wordsworth's failure to preserve his affection against a loss of conventional respect that wounded worst of all.

Quoting Jean Paul, Coleridge wrote in his note-book: 'I find all things upon earth, even truth and joy, rather than friendship'; although it would have been more correct to say that he had lost each in their fullness for the same reason. And he admitted his last loss with the same candid finality as those which had preceded it. 'There may be wrongs,' he noted, 'for which with our best efforts for the most perfect suppression, with the absence, nay, the impossibility of anger or hate, yet, longer, deeper sleep is required for the heart's oblivion, and thence renewal – even the long total sleep of death.'

And indeed so it was to be. Two years later a reconciliation was effected, 'but,' as he wrote – 'aye there remains an ineradicable But.' The following year confirmed the truth of this qualification.

Wordsworth lost his little son Thomas, and immediately on hearing of it Coleridge, abandoning all restraint, poured out a letter of unqualified sympathy. 'Write? My dear Friend! Oh, that it were in my power to be with you myself instead of my letter. The Lectures I could give up; but the rehearsal of my Play commences this week, and upon this depends my best hopes of leaving town after Christmas, and living among you as long as I live. Strange, strange are the coincidences of things! Yesterday Martha Fricker dined here, and after tea I had asked question after question respecting your children, first one, then the other; . . . And not two hours ago . . . I was asked what was the matter with my eyes? I told the fact, that I had awoke three times during the night and morning, and at each time found my face and part of the pillow wet with tears. "Were you dreaming of the Wordsworths?" she (Mrs. Morgan) asked — "Of the children?" I said, "No! not so much of them, but of Mrs. W. and Miss Hutchinson, and yourself and sister."

'Mrs. Morgan and her sister are come in, and I have been relieved by tears. The sharp, sharp pang at the heart needed it, when they reminded me of my words the very yester night: "It is not possible that I should do otherwise than love Wordsworth's children, all of them; but Tom is nearest my heart." . . .

'O dearest friend! what comfort can I afford you? What comfort ought I not to afford, who have given you so much pain? Sympathy deep, of my whole being. . . . In grief, and in joy, in the anguish of perplexity, and in the fulness and overflow of confidence, it has been ever what it is! There is a sense of the word, Love, in which I never felt it but to you and one of your household! I am distant from you some hundred miles, but glad I am that I am no longer distant in spirit, and have faith, that as it has happened but once, so it never can happen again. An

awful truth it seems to me, and prophetic of our future, as
well as declarative of our present *real* nature, that one mere
thought, one feeling of suspicion, jealousy, or resentment
can remove two human beings farther from each other
than winds or seas can separate their bodies.'

His words were indeed prophetic enough. Admittedly
the tone of the letter is excessive. Coleridge, when he
was moved, could not write otherwise. He never outgrew
an adolescent emotionalism. Yet his obvious sympathy,
however fulsome and fanciful its expression, should have
provoked a generous response. Certainly the conclusion
of the letter was exasperating. Coleridge expatiated in
typical vein on 'religious fortitude,' and added, 'more
cheering illustrations of our survival I have never received,
than from the recent study of the instincts of animals,
their clear heterogeneity from the reason and moral
essence of man and yet the beautiful analogy.' But the last
sentence was pitifully sincere. 'Dear Mary! dear Dorothy!
dearest Sara! Oh, be assured, no thought relative to
myself has half the influence in inspiring the wish and
effort to *appear* and to *act* what I always in my will and
heart have been, as the knowledge that few things could
more console you than to see me healthy and worthy of
myself.'

Wordsworth's reception of this letter finally removed
any doubts as to what his attitude towards Coleridge was.
He had ceased, as earlier Southey had, to credit Coleridge
with any sincerity. The sentimental idealism which had
once in Stowey days given life to his own poetic genius
now jarred upon him, since experience had proved time
after time that it never issued in action. Even such a letter
of sympathy as this rang intolerably false in his dour
Northern ears, while the confession of particular fondness
for Sarah Hutchinson may have displeased the rigid and
self-assured moralist that he was becoming.

Coleridge at such a time was not likely to take offence easily, but he was bitterly wounded by Wordsworth's reply. It proved to him that the reconciliation, which for a moment he had believed this new bond of sympathy might transform into a reality, was impossible. He had offered himself with all the sincerity of which he was capable and had been rebuffed. And surely what he was in 'will and heart,' even if its realization were a myth as Wordsworth believed, should have counted for something. A few months later indeed Wordsworth, in a mood of possible contrition, tried to heal the wound he had inflicted.

But with all his faults Coleridge had the genius of reading men's hearts. He understood that the difference between them was irremediable. Wordsworth's nature had narrowed, and his had remained as expansive as ever. Between the two there would never be real sympathy again, because on one side there was a latent intolerance amounting to contempt. 'O worse than all,' he wrote,

'O pang all pangs above,
Is kindness counterfeiting absent love!'

Possibly his hopes of reformation were as delusive as ever. Yet circumstances, as will be shown, favoured their realization as perhaps they had never done before, and it is at least possible that while Coleridge helped Wordsworth to realize his genius, Wordsworth at this time prevented Coleridge from recovering the remnants of his.

Yet it was typical of him not to harbour bitterness. Certainly in his last years he complained in confidence to a friend of Wordsworth's reception of his criticism in the book in which he at last enunciated the grounds of his disagreement with certain elements in Wordsworth's theory and practice as a poet. But no book testifies more surely to the magnanimity in which he was Wordsworth's superior than the *Biographia Literaria*. To Wordsworth himself the praise in that book seemed 'extravagant, and the censure inconsiderate'; but although the searching criticism was perhaps unduly extended, it is well to remember the years during which Coleridge had suffered for his supposed complicity with the confused thought he there analysed in masterly fashion. And the spirit behind the whole performance was tenderly considerate, in a time too when criticism presumed on its right to fight ruthlessly and unscrupulously for its opinions, and had so presumed in the person of Hazlitt and others in assaults on Coleridge himself.

But never for a moment did Coleridge exploit his vast superiority as a critic at Wordsworth's expense. Despite the gulf of eighteen disillusioned years he was still at heart the generous, self-abasing friend of Nether Stowey days, impulsive in his praise, chivalrous in his attack and delicately anxious not to hurt in the necessary process of defining and illustrating the just grounds of his criticism.

In these qualities at least Wordsworth had something to learn from his friend whose effusiveness, improvidence and weakly self-delusion not unnaturally provoked a frown of conscious superiority.

§ 2

No fruitful purpose would be secured by tracing in detail the events of the last twenty-four years of Coleridge's life. There were still fluctuations in it, still alternations of hope and despair which like the waves of an ebbing sea grew less and less noticeable. For he had ceased to try and conquer himself: his only aim was to limit the amount of his opium consumption without intensifying 'the gnawing recollection behind the curtain of my outward being.' The same motive underlay his perpetual talk, 'a counteracting principle,' as he wrote, 'to the intensity of my feelings, and

a means of escaping from a part of the pressure.' But
although doubtless it was this in origin, it became with
every year more a loose habit of eloquence than either
an outlet for or antidote to any intensity of feeling of
which indeed he ceased gradually to be capable. At best
it was a mild and desultory intoxication which less and
less frequently advanced to full and brilliant inebria-
tion, his mind being merely carried forward by its own
momentum.

Certainly he was absorbed in the process, so absorbed
that anyone who had the daring to intrude upon his
declamation was passed over unnoticed like a pebble by
a wide stream. But if the intruder persisted, Coleridge
was, to change the metaphor for one adopted by one of
his audience, easily unsaddled, despite the wonderful skill
with which he rode his hobby. A disputant recalled him
to consciousness, his audience ceased to be sympathetic
ghosts and himself a ghost among them; he noticed the
snuff of which maybe for an hour or more he had been
taking pinches, rubbing between his fingers, and deposit-
ing on the carpet, and the spell of almost involuntary
association by which ideas poured from his mind or whole
paragraphs from his memory in intricate logical or sometimes merely grammatical connection was broken. Inevitably so unconscious an activity entailed a tendency to pass
loosely from subject to subject, in an indifferent sense of
the inter-relationship of all things, entailed, too, much
repetition, particularly when, as so frequently, his theme
was metaphysical; but he had read so widely and reten-
tively, that though the essence might be the same, the
permutations and combinations of its expression were
infinite.

And always at the heart of his talk, however dimly seen
through the voluminous folds of his verbosity, was himself, the 'Mariner' of his great poem grown portly and

middle-aged, but still haunted by remembrance of 'a woeful agony'

> 'Which forced me to begin my tale;
> And then it left me free . . .'

It was this that magnetized his audience apart from the verbal display. Whether in literary criticism or religious ideology he was for ever seeking a spiritual harmony, hailing it as achieved in this poet or that thinker, and condemning others for their inability to grasp its principles or to appreciate its necessity. Or again he was trying to forget his own failure to achieve it in poetry or thought or reciprocated love by philosophizing its elements.

How completely he could lose himself in the rush of such philosophizing, such a revolving, invertebrate sentence as the following from his note-book will show: 'The lover worships in his beloved that final consummation of itself which is produced in his own soul by the action of the soul of the beloved upon it, and that final perception of the soul of the beloved which is in part the consequence of the reaction of his (so ameliorated and regenerated) soul upon the soul of his beloved, till each contemplates the soul of the other as involving his own, both in its givings and its receivings, and thus, still keeping alive its *outness*, its *self-oblivion* united with self-warmth, still approximates to God.'

Into such subtle sophistries had his feelings for Sarah Hutchinson disintegrated.

Thus for the last twenty-four years of his life, save for one last delusive spurt of hope and animation, Coleridge pursued a more and more posthumous existence, his figure with each year more portly, his shuffle more pronounced, his mental control over his tongue less and less purposeful. Dying imperceptibly he continued to analyse the constituents of a creative life which he had once intensely, but never healthily, experienced. And to kind friends, to edifying thought, and to Nature he turned for the comfort, the homeliness which might protect him against the fear of himself and his inadequacy to cope with life or face the fact of death. For 'even when all men have seemed to desert us and the friend of our heart has passed on, with one glance from his "cold disliking eye" – yet even then the blue heaven spreads itself out and bends over us, and the little tree still shelters us under its plumage as a second cope, a domestic firmament, and the low creeping gale will sigh in the heath-plant and soothe us by sound of sympathy till the lulled grief lose itself in fixed gaze on the purple heath-blossom, till the present beauty becomes a vision of memory.'

More and more he cultivated this 'fixed gaze,' which did not generate feeling but, like the fixed gaze imposed by the mesmerist, submerged the conscious in the subconscious. The record of such moments in his note-book became increasingly frequent, and gradually everything positive in his nature was subdued to a mood of wistful charity. Life lost the little definition which it had ever possessed for him, as his figure thickened and his face assumed a look of worried benignity. A pietistic mysticism, blended of subjective dreaming and conventional dogma, trenched more and more upon the vital analysis and exposition of imaginative experience which his literary criticism represented.

§ 3

From 1810 to 1816, save for a brief period of escape due, as he explained, to 'bitter consciousness of my own infirmities and increasing irregularity of temper,' he made his home in London with the Morgans. They treated him with unfailing tact and kindness, and the anxiety which he reasonably entertained lest they too would find him a 'nuisance' was ungrounded. Their attempts, however, to break him of his subjection to opium proved doubtless in his weaker moments a nuisance to him, unsuccessful as they were.

For some time, however, he strove to justify their efforts. He was really fearful lest he should alienate even 'dear, dear' Mary's and 'dearest' Charlotte's esteem or chill their affection. He was continually about to consult a Dr. Abernethy and contemplating taking lodgings and entering on 'my dread ordeal.' But as he grew more secure in his friends' affections the project was abandoned.

Nevertheless despite a visit to Greta Hall with all its painful associations aggravated by a violent cold and intermittent fever attributed to the dampness of the house and weather; despite, too, financial worries aggravated by a loss of £50 with which that 'clever young man,' Mr. Brown of Penrith, absconded, his health by 1812 had greatly improved and his indulgence decreased. Previous to the Morgans' efforts his ordinary consumption of laudanum was from two quarts a week to a pint a day, but although 'he suffered dreadfully during the first abstinence, so much as to say that it was better to die than to endure his present sufferings,' Mrs. Morgan's reply that it was indeed better that he should die than that he should continue to live on as he had been living proved effective. Consequently he could write on April 21 to his wife, with whom he actually talked of settling once again in London: 'My health, spirits, and disposition to activity have continued such since my arrival in town, that every one has been struck with the change, and the Morgans say they have never before seen me *myself*. I feel myself an altered man, and dare promise you that you shall never have to complain of, or to apprehend, my not opening and reading your letters. Ever since I have been in town, I have never taken any stimulus of any kind, till the moment of my getting into bed, except a glass of British white wine after dinner, and from three to four glasses of port when I have dined out. Secondly, my lectures have been taken up most warmly and zealously. . . . Thirdly, Gale and Curtis are in high spirits and confident respecting the sale of *The Friend* (he was proposing to republish the periodical as a complete work). . . . 'Nothing intervenes to overgloom my mind, but the sad state of health of Mr. Morgan, a more faithful and zealous friend than whom no man ever possessed. Thank God! my safe arrival, the improvement of my health and spirits, and my smiling prospects have already exerted a favourable influence on him.'

Three days later he proclaimed himself 'alive, well, and in full fleece,' and in May, still further to secure himself from being 'overtaken and hurried back by the surges just as I had begun to feel the firm ground under my feet,' he completed, outwardly at least, his reconciliation with Wordsworth.

This happy convalescence, 'a resurrection, a palingenesy of our youth,' as he too optimistically described it, was largely due to the success of the two courses of lectures which he delivered at the rooms of the London Philosophical Society off Fleet Street and at Willis's Rooms in King Street. The Morgans guaranteed his regular attendance, and although the lectures varied according to his mood, from the level of inspired clairvoyance to that of diffuse digression, they made a great impression. On Byron's testimony, who with Rogers attended more than one of them, Coleridge became 'a sort of rage,' and the first course concluded with much applause from a crowded room.

The third course, delivered in the autumn, was not quite such a success, although it improved towards the end, but again on appearing for his last lecture he was 'received with three rounds of applause and very loudly acclaimed at the close.'

His elation over his success was increased by the production early in 1813 at Drury Lane of his play *Osorio*, now named *Remorse*. The critics were not very kind, but it ran for twenty nights; he was applauded by the pit on being recognized in a box, and, quite apart from the printed edition of the play, which quickly ran into three editions, it brought him £400. This financial success occurred at a happy moment, since it coincided with Josiah Wedgwood's withdrawal of his share of the annuity. The grant had been made unconditionally, and Coleridge might well have been hurt as well as depressed by its withdrawal. But he was too cheerful. A letter of congratulation from Poole on the success of his play heartened him like 'an unexpected strain of sweetest music,' and in replying to it he paid a tribute to Wedgwood's 'beautifully balanced' character, reiterated his affection towards him, and wrote in reference to his withdrawal of the grant: "Tis well . . . because it has given me the strongest impulse, the most imperious motives I have experienced, to *prove* to him that his past munificence has not been *wasted*!' For the time at least he had forgotten 'the folly of all motive-mongering, while the individual self remains.'

And then like a blight upon the new summer of his hopes descended the conviction of Wordsworth's antipathy, of which the circumstances have already been related. Immediately he lost all the ground which he had gained. 'Alas,' as he had said of Macbeth's end – 'Now all is inward with him; he has no more prudential prospective reasonings . . . he puts on despondency, the final heart-armour of the wretched, and would fain think everything shadowy and unsubstantial.' He renewed and continually increased his indulgence in opium, he spun a

web of metaphysical fancies about his mind and conscience, and he entered again that dreary hell of introspection and passivity from which he was only to be
partially rescued, when he drifted three years later, an
irreparable derelict, into the muffled harbourage of Highgate.

§ 4

Meanwhile in this last paroxysm of hope Coleridge
had achieved something of permanent creative value. At
first as a lecturer he surpassed himself, to quote Crabb
Robinson, 'in the art of talking in a very interesting way,
without speaking at all on the subject announced.' When
advertised, for example, on December 5, 1811, to lecture
on *Romeo and Juliet*, he began with a defence of school-
flogging, went on to remark 'on the character of Elizabeth
and James I as compared with that of Charles I; distinguished not very clearly between wit and fancy; referred
to the different languages of Europe; attacked the
fashionable notion concerning poetic diction . . . and
warmly defended Shakespeare against the charge of im-
purity.' At another time, in delivering a rhapsody on
brotherly and sisterly love, he was 'seduced into a dissertation on incest.'

Nevertheless many of such effusions, when he avoided
'the indefinities and the infinities,' were exceedingly fine
in themselves. They were 'beyond the reach of the
analytic faculty,' but a keen analysis underlay their synthesis; and when he fastened his mind upon Shakespeare,
he discovered a kinship of poetic experience in which
self-confession, a hunger for the universal, and a fine
critical sense were almost perfectly harmonized.

In order to understand Shakespeare, he remarked in
one of his lectures, 'it is essential that we should reflect on
the constitution of our own minds. Man is distinguished

from the brute animals in proportion as thought prevails over sense; but in the healthy processes of the mind, a balance is constantly maintained between the impressions from outward objects and the inward operations of the intellect; for if there be an overbalance in the contemplative faculty, man thereby becomes the creature of a mere meditation, and loses his natural power of action. Now one of Shakespeare's modes of creating characters is to conceive any one intellectual or moral faculty in morbid excess, and then to place himself, Shakespeare, thus mutilated or diseased, under given circumstances.'

In studying Shakespeare's characters, therefore, Coleridge studied himself; he was the first critic, with the exception of Lamb, to pass inside them, because he was the victim of the Romantic consciousness in its most disintegrating form. In Hamlet he read, with more self-apology, it may be admitted, than justice, an exact portrait of what he conceived himself to be. In this character, he said, Shakespeare 'seems to have wished to exemplify the moral necessity of a due balance between our attention to the objects of our senses, and our meditation on the workings of our minds – an equilibrium between the real and the imaginary world. In Hamlet this balance is disturbed: his thoughts and the images of his fancy, are far more vivid than his actual perceptions, and his very perceptions, instantly passing through the *medium* of his contemplations, acquire, as they pass, a form and a colour not naturally their own. Hence we see a great, an almost enormous, intellectual activity, and a proportionate aversion to real action consequent upon it, with all its symptoms and accompanying qualities . . . he vacillates from sensibility, and procrastinates from thought, and loses the power of action in the energy of resolve. . . . The effect of this overbalance of the imaginative power is beautifully illustrated in the everlasting broodings and superfluous activities of Hamlet's mind, which, unseated from its healthy relation, is constantly occupied with the world within, and abstracted from the world without, giving substance to shadows, and throwing a mist over all commonplace actualities. It is the nature of thought to be indefinite – definiteness belongs to external imagery alone. . . . Hamlet's senses are in a state of trance, and he looks upon external things as hieroglyphics. His soliloquy:

"O! that this too too solid flesh would melt," etc.,

springs from that craving after the indefinite – for that which is not – which most easily besets men of genius; and the self-delusion common to this temper of mind is finely exemplified in the character which Hamlet gives of himself. . . . He mistakes the seeing of his chains for the breaking them, delays action till action is no use, and dies the victim of mere circumstance and accident. . . . Where there is a just coincidence of external and internal action, pleasure is always the result; but where the former is deficient, and the mind's appetency of the ideal is unchecked, realities will seem cold and unmoving.' 'Action,' he concluded, 'is the great end of all; no intellect however grand, is valuable, if it draws us away from action and leads us to think and think till the time of action is passed by, and we can do nothing.' 'A satire of yourself,' said some one to him. 'No,' he replied, 'it is an elegy.'

And such in fact it was. The bias is too personal to make it a just piece of creative criticism; Hamlet was not so eaten away by idealism as himself; but as critical self-portraiture it is perfect. Coleridge could not cure himself, but he understood his disease, even if such knowledge did not prevent him from disseminating a comforting religious idealism in his last years which was false in exact proportion to that lack of objectivity which he traced here to its sources in his own temperament.

But although the impulse behind his lectures on Shakespeare was, little less than his later mysticism, a desire to comfort himself by self-confession, they embodied by contrast so much of vital truth because the Shakespearean characters expressed under diverse forms and relations the dualism that haunts the Romantic consciousness between imagination and fact, the dynamic and the static, the infinite and the finite, fixity and flux, freedom and necessity, Life and Death. Coleridge's genius had been worn away by the friction of these opposites, and so although he was inclined to impose himself upon his subject, he was generally in profound harmony with it. Here at last circumstances enabled him to reconcile the subjective with the objective in the very act of reducing to their elements characters whose chief poetic significance lay in their struggle to do so for themselves.

And for this reason, in his literary criticism as distinct from his religious idealism, his consciousness of what was ill in himself served a creative purpose. In interpreting himself through other characters he had the strength to face reality, while self-knowledge enabled him to substitute a psychological for an ethical judgment of human nature, and thereby to forecast the modern attitude to 'vice' as the distortion of normal vital functions. Of such an attitude his analysis of Iago's resentment and revenge as 'the motive-hunting of a motiveless malignity' is a typical example, or his explanation of Hamlet's wild recoil from the shock of the Ghost's appearance as a sort of defence-reaction.

He brought a similar science of mental philosophy to his analysis of what æsthetic experience represented both for the artist himself and for his audience, illustrating for instance the quality of artistic illusion by reference 'to

our mental state, when dreaming.' And such appreci-
ations as the following of dramatic genius penctrated to a
new level of understanding. Of the storm and shipwreck
with which the *Tempest* opens, he said:

'It prepares and initiates the excitement required for
the entire piece, and yet does not demand anything from
the speĉtators which their previous habits had not fitted
them to understand.' And of Miranda, that she 'is never
direĉtly brought into comparison with Ariel, lest the
natural and human of the one and the supernatural of the
other should tend to neutralize each other.' Again of
Shakespearc's interweaving of the lyrical and the dramatic
he noted, 'You experience the sensation of a pause without the sense of a stop.' Of Oliver in *As You Like It* he
remarked, 'In such charaĉters there is sometimes a gloomy
self-gratification in making the absoluteness of the will
. . . evident to themselves by setting the reason and the
conscience in full array against it'; and of Viola's speech
in *Twelfth Night* beginning:

'A blank, my lord: she never told her love! –
But let conccalment,' etc.,

that 'after the first line (of which the last five words
should be spoken with, and drop down in, a deep sigh),
the aĉtress ought to make a pause; and then start afresh,
from the aĉtivity of thought, born of suppressed feelings,
and which thought had accumulated during the brief
interval, as vital heat under the skin during a dip in cold
watcr.'

Such physical analogies were as illuminating in his
criticism as they were irrelcvant in his religious metaphysics, because he had really felt himself into the natures
which he was discussing.

And it was his minute knowledge of human nature
and how it aĉts under given circumstances, derived from

an intensive study of himself, which distinguished his analysis from that of many modern psychologists. Life was for him a stage and not a laboratory; a stage peopled with dynamic figures who were to be apprehended in all their fluctuations of feeling and action by a creative insight, not dissected like corpses. Indeed he opposed the mechanistic conception of life in his critical practice far better than in his metaphysical arguments. For because his insight was creative, it was metaphysical as well as psychological. In studying Shakespeare he sensed the universal elements of Nature as well as her particular manifestations.

Doubtless many modern critics, who would banish metaphysics from criticism, suspect such a double vision; and at times when Coleridge's grasp of abstract elements trespassed upon his sense of the concrete in character, or when he was discussing the principles of poetry, their suspicion is justified. Yet for the true appreciation of all art into which romantic or metaphysical consciousness enters (and no art is truly great which lacks it) such a double vision is essential.

Coleridge at his best perfectly combined a sense of the universal and the particular. He read the surface with subtlety but always in relation to elemental forces underneath. He possessed negatively the three powers which he attributed positively to Shakespeare – 'wit, which discovers partial likeness hidden in general diversity; subtlety, which discovers the diversity concealed in general apparent sameness; and profundity, which discovers an essential unity under all the semblances of difference.'

And it was this sense of a unity of feeling in a great poet underlying all its diverse manifestations in character and action, which enabled him to effect a revolution in men's attitude to Shakespeare. He realized that a play and its characters are but projections of a dramatist's consciousness. To judge a play merely externally as a form of art obeying certain fixed laws was to miss its essential significance. 'For art,' as he wrote, 'cannot exist without, or apart from nature; and what has man of his own to give to his fellow-man, but his own thoughts and feelings, and his observations so far as they are modified by his own thoughts or feelings?'

To say this is not of course to deny the importance of technique. An artist has to communicate his feelings effectively, and for that he must study and perfect his medium, but the success of the means which he adopts, as Coleridge was never tired of insisting, can only be fairly judged by those who are capable of understanding the end he has in view. No-poets cannot comment on the greatest of poets. Shakespeare's thoughts and feelings were rooted in a consciousness of life superlatively rich and profound. In his drama 'there is a vitality which grows and evolves itself from within – a key-note which guides and controls the harmonies throughout.' He was a force of nature subtly keyed up to intelligence. To apply to such a poet the conventions of correctness or the dogmas of formal unities, or to condemn him, as eighteenth-century critics had done, as an anomalous, wild and irregular genius, was as irrelevant as to condemn Helvellyn because it lacked the lines of a neo-classic garden.

It was because Coleridge had experienced the elemental in Nature and based all his criticism on a personal intuition of Shakespeare himself that he could justly appraise the exquisite appropriateness of Shakespeare's technique, could show in detail how instinctively organized the body of his art was, and could prove that his judgment, far from being submerged in imagination, was implicit in its expression. He showed therefore that a poet was great, not by any mere sleight of hand, but in proportion to the wealth and complexity of experience which he succeeded in harmonizing. How essential this organic harmony was and how far it surpassed any symmetry imposed upon experience from without he knew from his own sad experience, and it was the same experience which led him to associate it with the truly moral.

The moral in art as in life he knew to be the perfect humanizing of the natural, the harmonizing of instinct and intelligence, of the unconscious and the conscious. In this sense his own failure as a poet was a moral failure. His roots in nature were diseased. But in Shakespeare it was always the natural which was keyed up to the imaginative: his head and his heart and his senses too were in perfect accord, and so he could create life with a 'happy valiancy,' which contrasted poignantly with Coleridge's own neurotic state. But Coleridge could appreciate what he could not emulate: when he spoke of 'the close and reciprocal connection of just taste with pure morality,' he implied that absolute disinterested morality, which is one with a perfect exercise of the imagination.

And so he could champion Shakespeare's morality on the grounds of its essential vitality and truth against the correct writers of the succeeding age. Shakespeare did not preserve decency of manners at the expense of morality of heart. 'If he occasionally disgusts a keen sense of delicacy, he never injures the mind; he neither excites, nor flatters, passion, in order to degrade the subject of it; he does not use the faulty thing for a faulty purpose, nor carries on warfare against virtue by causing wickedness to appear as no wickedness, through the medium of a morbid sympathy with the unfortunate. In Shakespeare, vice never walks as in twilight: nothing is purposely out of its place; he inverts not the order of nature and propriety, does not make every magistrate a drunkard or glutton, nor every poor man meek, humane,

and temperate; he has no benevolent butchers, nor any
sentimental rat-catchers.'

In short the moral, as he conceived it through Shakespeare, was the vital in all its chaotic, originating force
subdued to perfect justice, relevance and coherence. It
was the complete and harmonious expression of the
human in its farthest reach and the natural at its greatest
depth. It was the ideal which he could not achieve either
as a poet or a man himself.

And as in Hamlet he read his own morbidity, so in
Mercutio he recalled his own most animated moments —
'O! how shall I describe that exquisite ebullience and
overflow of youthful life, wafted on over the laughing
waves of pleasure and prosperity. . . . Wit ever wakeful,
fancy busy and procreative as an insect, courage, an easy
mind that, without cares of its own, is at once disposed to
laugh away those of others, and yet to be interested in
them — these and all congenial qualities, melting into the
common *copula* of them all.' And in *Richard II*, 'that
sweet lovely rose,' he read his own sweetness of temper,
his own languid, lyrical bent, the bloom of an inherent
weakness — 'an intellectual feminineness which feels a
necessity of ever leaning on the breast of others . . . we
see in him that sophistry which is common to man, by
which we can deceive our own hearts, and at one and the
same time apologize for, and yet commit, the error . . .
his faults are not positive vices, but spring entirely from
defect of character.' Or in *Lear* he recalled the ingratitude, which had dogged his own 'intense desire of being
intensely beloved, selfish, and yet characteristic of the
selfishness of a loving and kindly nature alone; the self-
supportless leanings for all pleasure on another's breast;
the cravings after sympathy with a prodigal disinterested-
ness, frustrated by its own ostentations, and the mode
and nature of its claims.'

Doubtless in such interpretations Coleridge was apt to intrude himself too much upon his subject. The interpretative critic is an artist, faced with the same problem as other artists – the problem of adjusting himself truly to his subject. Without personal emotion, without a kindred reach of experience, he cannot project himself into the subject and so realize it from within; but without also a fine critical sense he cannot justly subordinate his egotism to the claims of his subject. In great interpretative criticism creative sympathy and critical judgment are perfectly balanced. It is so sensitively personal as to be impersonal. Feeling and analysis combine in a disinterested divination.

Coleridge in his criticism as in all his other activities showed a subjective bias, but he showed it least in his study of romantic poetry because he had explored in himself all the wild and weakly fluctuations of the romantic consciousness. It is only in such occasional generalizations as the following that he obviously obtruded his own predispositions upon Shakespeare: 'He is always the philosopher and the moralist, but at the same time with a profound veneration for all the established institutions of society, and for those classes which form the permanent elements of the state – especially never introducing a professional character, as such, otherwise than as respectable. If he must have any name, he should be styled a philosophical aristocrat, delighting in those hereditary institutions which have a tendency to bind one age to another, and in that distinction of ranks, of which, although few may be in possession, all enjoy the advantages.' Conservative as Shakespeare may have been in some superficial aspects, he was never such a sententious Tory as this.

And the same lapse from precise contact with his subject may be seen in Coleridge's occasional tendency to indulge in superstitious worship, in his claim for example that Shakespeare's genius was 'superhuman' – a claim which was as likely to encourage a false estimate as the conception of his genius as 'frantic' which he so justly disproved. The same tendency to a vague idolatry blinded him to technical imperfections. He did not of course possess our modern analytical knowledge of sources, and he was interested in the dramatic truth of character rather than perfection of stagecraft. That the dramatic purpose in *Hamlet*, for example, is confused, as has recently been argued, because Shakespeare's own conception is imperfectly grafted on to the groundwork of an old melodrama, was a kind of criticism which he never attempted. And illuminating as his deductive insight was, it would have profited by more inductive research.

But in these lectures it was chiefly in his exposition of the abstract principle of poetry that he indulged his discursive tendency. As a poet his imagery had tended to evaporate into hazy day-dreaming; as a metaphysical critic his ideas tended to evaporate into hazy word-spinning. But if he could not define with sufficient objectivity, he could describe the essence of creative ecstasy more luminously than it had ever been described before; how it had the 'sweetness and easy movement of nature,' how it gave an illusion of 'energy without effort' and balanced and reconciled 'opposite or discordant qualities,' how harmoniously it melted down and fused 'the sensual into the spiritual,' how in it alone 'are all things at once different and the same; there alone, as the principle of all things, does distinction exist unaided by division; there are will and reason, succession of time and unmoving eternity, infinite change and ineffable rest.'

In such descriptions of that in which ideal experience consists, of the 'exquisite harmony of all the parts of the moral being, constituting one living total of head and heart,' he escaped from discursiveness into pure intuition because he was describing the ideal which he had wasted his life in trying to realize. It was this co-ordination of all the faculties in a creative act which he saw to be the essential characteristic of Shakespeare's genius. And while the greatness of his tragedies lay in the conflict between the ideal and the real, a conflict which Coleridge poignantly understood, Shakespeare's final gesture in the *Tempest*, in which he turned from the strife which harrowed and which nothing, it seemed, might heal, and conceived the ideal miraculously achieved, was particularly calculated to appeal, since it was his own lifelong gesture purged of all its elements of weakly and wistful surrender, and fresh with all knowledge transmuted into a second innocence.

In short, Shakespeare revealed the romantic consciousness in all its positive power to one who had suffered from its negative disabilities. And in association with such a commanding genius, with one who mastered the sensibility which made him 'a superior spirit, more intuitive, more intimately conscious' than his fellows, Coleridge himself became positive. He ceased to be merely meditative and waxed creative. As little could the flux and reflux of so subtle a mind and heart as Shakespeare's 'be brooded on by mean and indistinct emotion, as the low, lazy mist can creep upon the surface of a lake, while a strong gale is driving it onward in waves and billows.'

In Shakespeare he discovered a world more real than the actual, and yet one in which the actual rose by some dynamic force within itself to the ideal, and in which the ideal was never attenuated or querulous, but heroic even in its defeat: a world in which evil itself, even 'to the last faintings of moral death,' was tensely vital, in which the natural and the supernatural were but progressions of each other, or, like joy and pain, the alternations of one rhythm; in which man, in the fine flower of his humanity, had not forgotten his kinship with the elements but felt amid the very pomp and violence of regal activity the swirl of darkness beneath his feet and a morning radiance in the air he breathed; a world in which womanhood was holy 'with a purity unassailable by sophistry,' so perfect was the conjunction of mind and sense and spirit; and in which love combined passion with affection, and vivacity with the calm depth derived from 'a will stronger than desire.'

In this world, so buoyant in its strength and candour and organic diversity, Coleridge moved like a renovated being. He was 'enlarged by the collective sympathies of nature,' by a live sap that set his declining faculties functioning so vitally that at times he was compelled to pass beyond the vocabulary of ideas and crystallize his interpretation in imagery.

'What is *Lear*? It is storm and tempest! – the thunder at first grumbling on the far horizon, then gathering around us, and at length bursting in fury over our heads – succeeded by a breaking of the clouds for a while, a last flash of lightning, the closing in of night and the single hope of darkness! And *Romeo and Juliet*? – It is a spring day, with the song of the nightingale; whilst *Macbeth* is deep and earthy, composed to the subterranean music of a troubled conscience, which converts everything into the wild and fearful!'

§ 5

From 1813, however, Coleridge's life resembled more and more a morass of ignoble indulgence smothered in vapours of thought. In the autumn of this year he undertook, on Cottle's suggestion, to give a course of lectures in Bristol, but although, after two failures to appear at the time announced, habit and memory enabled him to deliver them, many of his friends remarked 'with great pain, that there was something unusual and strange in his look and deportment.' At one of them indeed he grasped Cottle's hand with great solemnity and assured him that 'this day week I shall not be alive'; and after another he called him on one side and borrowed £10 from him on the ground that 'a dirty fellow' had threatened to arrest him for that amount; while on a visit to Hannah More who lived in the neighbourhood his hands shook to such an alarming degree that he could not take a glass of wine without spilling it, though one hand supported the other.

He had reached that stage of opium indulgence when only by continually increasing his consumption he could prevent the dream state it induced from lapsing into a physical nightmare in which he really did fear for his life.

At last even Cottle discovered the cause of these disquieting symptoms, and 'influenced,' as he wrote, 'by the purest motives' called him to repentance. He addressed a sententious and theatrical letter to Coleridge, bidding him recall his image in past years and compare it with 'the wild eye! the sallow countenance! the tottering step! the trembling hand! the disordered frame!' 'Will you not,' he concluded, 'be awakened to a sense of your danger, and I must add, your guilt?'

But Coleridge needed no awakening. 'O for a sleep, for sleep itself to rest in!' was his perpetual prayer. What use was it, he pathetically replied, to pour 'oil of vitriol . . . into the raw and festering wound of an old friend's conscience?' Was it not his tormenting consciousness of guilt which sent him, despite the danger and the degradation involved, to the laudanum bottle? His only defence was the casuistical one that he was 'seduced into the Accursed habit ignorantly . . . not by any temptation of pleasure, or expectation, or desire of exciting pleasurable sensations.'

Certainly he was passive even in his vices, but his 'utter impotence of the volition' was a fact which no appeals to conscience could affect. In a second letter Cottle counselled prayer. But although this, like incessant talk, like opium itself, might comfort at the moment, it could not cure. 'I feel,' he wrote, 'with an intensity unfathomable by words, my utter nothingness, impotence, and worthlessness, in and for myself. I have learned what a sin is, against an infinite imperishable being, such as is the soul of man! I have had more than one glimpse of what is meant by death and outer darkness, and the worm that dieth not. . . . But the consolations, at least, the sensible sweetness of hope, I do not possess. On the contrary, the temptation which I have constantly to fight up against is a fear, that if *annihilation* and the *possibility* of *heaven* were offered to my choice, I should choose the former. . . . No spiritual effort appears to benefit me so much as the one, earnest, importunate, and often for hours, momently repeated prayers: "I believe, Lord, help my unbelief! Give me faith but as a mustard seed and I shall remove this mountain! Faith! faith! faith! I believe. Oh, give me faith! Oh, for my Redeemer's sake, give me faith in my Redeemer."'

Alas! Coleridge was still too free a spirit, was at once too volatile and too self-conscious to be really affected by such religious auto-suggestion, while he was too weak and damaged a one to conquer by personal effort a conviction of his own fatality. He was a case now, not for the moral, but the medical man. Yet when he suggested putting himself under the control of a Dr. Fox, if enough money could be procured, the moral Cottle made no response.

Southey's suggestion was equally useless. He begged

Poole to urge Coleridge to return to Greta Hall and defeat the foe by regular work. He assured him that his children would receive him with joy, his wife 'certainly not with reproaches,' and himself with encouragement. It was all well meant, and since Southey had for some time most generously fathered Coleridge's family, since he saw Mrs. Coleridge's spirits and health 'beginning to sink under her misfortunes,' and the problem of supporting Hartley at College had yet to be solved, it was more than reasonable.

Yet how could Coleridge return to such a household? Nothing could be more humiliating than the consciousness that people were making a special effort to be indecently decent, cheerful and helpful towards one whom they regarded as something far other even than 'an archangel somewhat damaged' (for Lamb, who coined the phrase, never forgot the seraph in the wasted man); as in fact a being at best to be pitied and at worst deplored for his culpable weakness. All his life Coleridge had suffered from moralists: Southey, Sara, Wordsworth, even Poole had aggravated his disease by frowning upon it. He had ceased to hope for the unreserved sympathy which once at least might have enabled him to conquer it himself: only science remained to temper its malignity and religious sophistry to soothe his conscience into forgetfulness.

And so when Southey wrote to consult him about his children's future, he did not answer. What indeed could he reply to one who apprehended, as he had every right to apprehend, 'some shameful and dreadful end to this deplorable course'? It was only to simple, unaccusing folk, like his landlady, that he could talk fondly and forgetfully of his children and of their prospects. But there were times when he could not forget; even Cottle's epic, *Messiah*, which he corrected for a fee of £10, and the same

writer's ascription of all his ills to satanic possession, provoked a hollow ridicule. He might strike the chance
spectator as a 'most amusing man,' but his humour was
the defence-reaction of an effeminate Hamlet.

And on quitting Josiah Wade's house in Bristol to
return to the Morgans, he confessed to his host with an
unusual sincerity the passive finality of his despair.

'Dear Sir,' he wrote:

'For I am unworthy to call any good man friend –
much less you, whose hospitality and love I have abused;
accept, however, my intreaties for your forgiveness, and
for your prayers.

'Conceive a poor miserable wretch, who for many
years has been attempting to break off pain, by a constant
recurrence to the vice that reproduces it. Conceive a
spirit in hell employed in tracing out for others the road
to that heaven from which his crimes exclude him. In
short, conceive whatever is most wretched, helpless, and
hopeless, and you will form as tolerable a notion of my
state as it is possible for a good man to have.

'I used to think the text in St. James that "he who
offended in one point offends in all," very harsh; but I
now feel the awful, the tremendous truth of it. In the
one crime of opium, what crime have I not made myself
guilty of! – Ingratitude to my Maker! and to my benefactors – injustice! and *unnatural cruelty to my poor children*! – self-contempt for my repeated promise – breach,
nay, too often, actual falsehood!

'After my death, I earnestly entreat that a full and
unqualified narrative of my wretchedness and of its guilty
cause, may be made public, that at least some little good
may be effected by the direful example.'

Thus in his mind opium had become the prime, instead of the contributory, cause of all his failure. The
prime cause, as has been sufficiently shown and as he

knew in his calmer moments, lay deeper. It lay in his nature, which had been indulging in narcotics, less physically but no less spiritually demoralizing, ever since childhood, and was to continue to indulge to the end.

For the rest of his life he was to expend what energy remained to him in tracing out for others a road to heaven. But 'a spirit in hell' is no competent guide in such matters. He is too feverish to be disinterested. And so the great work which Coleridge now engaged himself to write, which was to contain all knowledge and proclaim all philosophy, and which he never ceased boasting his ability to complete, if circumstances did but allow him, was to prove the same vain dream of his fading mental powers as 'Christabel' had proved of his poetical.

Its title was: 'Christianity, the one true Philosophy; or Five Treatises on the Logos, or Communicative Intelligence, natural, human and divine.' Despite the impressive sub-titles attached to each treatise, the whole conception was misty, and, to quote his own description of a political letter, 'like most misty compositions, *laborious*.'

That in itself was enough to prevent its realization. But Wordsworth's failure in his 'Excursion' to prove, as he had hoped, a modern Lucretius and reconcile poetry and philosophy, increased his attachment to the project. Wordsworth seemed to him at best to have only placed 'commonplace truths in an interesting point of view.' Dimly perhaps he connected his disillusionment of the man with his inability to produce the great philosophic poem for which in his idolatry he had looked. There was doubtless something narrow and sectarian about Wordsworth. It had shown itself in the poetical theory with which he himself had been so unjustifiably associated in the public mind, and the fact was a further inducement to effort. His *Magnum Opus* should be the very opposite of sectarian. It should embrace everything in the wide sweep

of its sympathetic logic. And behind this mist of con-
jectural universality he sank lower and lower in the scale
of material degradation. Neither at Ashley, where he
shared a cottage with them, nor at Calne in Wiltshire,
could the Morgans exercise any restraint over his indulgence. More and more his letters betrayed the sordid
shifts of the inebriate.

In the summer of 1815, however, he rallied. A long
visit from his son Hartley and a successful performance
of *Remorse* by a travelling company cheered him; Cottle
too had agreed to publish his scattered poems, and although he wrote that they must wait for a series of Odes on
the sentences of the Lord's Prayer, a series which, like
the *Magnum Opus* itself, reported already as nearly fin-
ished, 'has never been seen by any,' he was led to contemplate, as a preliminary, a preface to the poems.

Since the *Magnum Opus* was 'planned to be illustrated
by fragments of Autobiography,' it was natural that this
preface should pass imperceptibly into the same category.
For Coleridge now had two avenues of escape from the
present – the past and the metaphysical. In the book, or
rather the disconnected scrap-book of criticism, speculation and reminiscence, so often expressed before in
letters and talk, into which this preface grew, Coleridge
wandered, now dilatory and discursive, now brilliantly
absorbed, down both avenues. 'I have a great, a gigantic
effort to make,' he wrote, 'and I will go through with it
or die.'

And for once he kept his vow, because an instinct of
self-defence and self-realization in the face of self-disgust
sustained him, and because in fact the effort required was
little greater than that of his daily conversation. The
hours from eleven to four and from six to ten which he
spent regularly in his study dictating to the admirable
Morgan were periods of happy release. The hopeless

present faded into the past with its fond aspirations and its pathetic memories. It was a tale of failure, no doubt, but it had become an image in his mind which no longer hurt but even provoked at times a wistful humour.

And even if inclination had not led him into autobiography, he could not have discussed his poetry or poetry in general without self-confession. Poetry inevitably took him in thought to Wordsworth and to the controversy concerning Wordsworth's Poems and Theory, in which his name had been so constantly included. At last he was free to speak without 'the dread of giving pain, or exciting suspicions of alteration and dyspathy,' which had restrained him before, free to deny that he was a 'mere symbol of Wordsworth and Southey.'

And doubtless, incapable as he was of any vindictive feeling, this act of abstract self-justification gave him peculiar satisfaction. In practical things he was at a hopeless disadvantage: there he had no justification to offer, but in theory, in the knowledge of what genius was and how it worked, was he not the moralists' superior? Had he not through his very want of all prudential values come nearer to the heart of creation?

Wordsworth therefore was the central point about which the whole inconsequent narrative, with its digressions and circumlocutions, turned. For he was the central point of Coleridge's life. It was in his reactions to Wordsworth that he had both discovered and lost himself, and could the genius of the two men have been combined, literature might have had another Shakespeare. Coleridge knew Wordsworth's virtues as a poet by comparison with his own defects, and he knew Wordsworth's defects in comparison with his own virtues. The result was that the chapters which he devoted to Wordsworth's critical theory and to the defects and beauties of his poetry are among the finest pieces of sustained and penetrating criticism which exist.

Here there was no wandering from the point into vague abstractions. His differences with Wordsworth were not mere matters of theory: they had been bitterly tested in the conduct of life, and so 'in completely subverting Wordsworth's theory,' and in proving that the poet himself had 'never acted on it except in particular stanzas, which are the blots of his composition,' he was subconsciously attacking the elements in Wordsworth's nature which had ultimately divided them. At the same time his knowledge of the constitutional defect in himself which had caused that division, his fatal want of finite power and objectivity, enabled him to define and illustrate Wordsworth's unique excellencies with sensitive precision – the 'perfect appropriateness of the words to the meaning,' the 'correspondent weight and sanity of the Thoughts and Sentiments,' 'the sinewy strength and originality of simple lines and paragraphs,' 'the perfect truth of nature in his images,' and 'the gift of Imagination in the highest and strictest sense of the word.'

And even in his analysis of Wordsworth's theory of Poetic Diction he was careful to separate truth from matter-of-factness, acting in this so differently from many later critics, who have disproved to their own satisfaction Tolstoy's somewhat analogous theory of Art by separating statements from their context and demonstrating their absurdity, while making no attempt to appraise his general principles.

Coleridge by contrast did full justice to the truth of Wordsworth's underlying idea, his preference for language dictated by impassioned feeling over the mere artifices of connection or ornament, which characterized a false, because superficial, poetic style, while at the same time demonstrating, both on the ground of first principles and by searching illustration, the literal-mindedness with which he had applied and so falsified the idea.

In doing so he was merely amplifying a theme which he had often developed in private conversation, and it involved him, after his usual involuntary fashion, in other collateral themes of his talk, in a discussion of the law of Association from Aristotle to Hartley, of the nature of poetry in the light of German criticism, of Shakespeare as the perfectly co-ordinated poet of his lectures, and of the distinction between Fancy and Imagination.

But apart from such irrelevances as 'remarks on the present mode of conducting critical journals' and 'an affectionate exhortation to those who in early life feel themselves disposed to become authors,' an essential unity of purpose did underlie all these themes, grew naturally, if diffusely, out of the autobiography with which the book began, and was intimately connected with the conjunction of Wordsworth and himself.

For poetry for Coleridge was not a special activity to be studied within recognized limits. It was a symbol of life functioning ideally; the creative processes which he traced in it were for him a replica of the divine process of creation, and in the nature of the great poet he read also the nature of God. 'The poet,' he wrote, 'described in ideal perfection, brings the whole soul of man into activity, with the subordination of its faculties to each other according to their relative worth and dignity. He diffuses a tone and spirit of unity that blends, and (as it were) *fuses*, each into each, by that synthetic and magical power, to which I would exclusively appropriate the name of Imagination. This power, first put in action by the will and understanding, and retained under their irremissive, though gentle and unnoticed control, *laxis effertur habenis*, reveals itself in the balance or reconcilement of opposite or discordant qualities: of sameness, with difference; of the general with the concrete; the idea with the image; the individual with the representation; the sense of novelty and freshness with old and familiar objects; a more than usual state of emotion with more than usual order; judgment ever awake and steady self-possession with enthusiasm and feeling profound or vehement; and while it blends and harmonizes the natural and the artificial, still subordinates art to nature; the manner to the matter; and our admiration of the poet to our sympathy with the poetry.'

To him, therefore, æsthetical criticism was intimately connected, as it was to Kant, with ethical values. The climax of his argument on the nature of poetry – the distinction between Fancy and Imagination – was only a special application to poetry of the mystical theory of experience in general which he opposed to a mechanistic in the chapters on the law of Association.

And that theory was based necessarily on an examination of his own experience. Few knew better than he how much of a fact the law of Association was. Did not his conversation and his poetry constantly illustrate its workings? But he knew too how inadequate it was to explain all that was real in either. How frequently, for example, for want of some guiding and originating idea his own talk revealed only a logical or verbal connection! It needed but one step further for it to degenerate into the pure hysteria over which nothing but the accidental law of Association presided. His experience as a poet taught him the same thing. If the materialist claim was really valid, the poet had only to be set going like a clock and one image evolved from another with the same mechanical sequence as one minute from that which preceded it.

The apparently involuntary workings of imagination which begot 'The Ancient Mariner' were something far other than this. Doubtless there was material continuity and interconnection, as there was between the cells of a body or between moments in time or points in space, but behind the physical conditions, behind the mechanism of fact, there was an originating impulse, a shaping idea which alone gave to the body of poetry, as it gave to the human body, an organic reality. In short, the idea preceded and begot the image, the subject the object, and 'I am,' 'It is.'

It was because Spinoza reversed the process that he considered his philosophy false. 'Does lust,' he wrote in a letter, 'call forth or occasion love? Just as much as the reek of the marsh calls up the sun. The sun calls up the vapour – attenuates, lifts it – it becomes a cloud – and now it is the veil of divinity.'

The extent to which Coleridge overstressed the part of the subjective in the creative process may be considered later. He overstressed it because his own temperament was excessively subjective; and this in what he called his Natural Theology led him to disregard the facts of Nature as insignificant and so impute to the God of his own idea the absolute authority, benevolence and omniscience to which the facts of the physical universe lend no support.

But in his æsthetic criticism the subjective bias was less apparent. Briefly, he distinguished between Imagination and Fancy as between an originating and a merely organizing faculty. Imagination was 'the living power and prime agent of all human perception, and as a repetition in the finite mind of the eternal act of creation in the infinite I AM.' It was an exceptionally vital, individual force which, working on multitudinous experience, passively absorbed and assimilated, subdued it to the unity of a single consciousness in an act of recreation.

Fancy on the contrary was incapable of assimilating the objects of experience. It knew them only externally, as 'fixities and definites,' and these dead forms, as Coleridge considered them, it arranged with conscious choice or elegant cunning. In short, the imaginative poet was an idealist, the fanciful poet a materialist.

The difference between the two was overdrawn by Coleridge. Imagination and Fancy were surely better considered as kindred than as antithetical faculties. They differ only in degree, Fancy revealing the same organizing and even originating powers as imagination but on a shallower basis of experience. Certainly its roots in reality do not lie so deep, but no art could exist in which a creative as well as an organizing power was not implicit. The best lyrics of a Waller or a Lovelace, for example, are not more than charming and fanciful; they do not penetrate passionately into life, but they are distinguished from the merely artificial versifying in which these poets also indulged by the creative and so ideal purpose which rendered them organic. Life does not burn intensely in them, but it burns enough to sustain each part in a necessary relation.

Coleridge overstressed the distinction because it was a projection into metaphysical terms of his own baffled experience. It was because for him there was an absolute gulf between the two, because he had little sense of the 'fixities and definites,' of which imagination as well as fancy must take notice, that he had failed to grow to imaginative maturity. In his dejection he forgot how wonderfully imagination had been blended with fancy in 'The Ancient Mariner' and 'Christabel.' He remembered only that his most ecstatic moments as a poet had been purely subjective, that the objective world had passed at such times into a dream of which his poetry was a melodious incantation; and so he failed to do justice to the vital principle at work in poetry more concretely defined or less elementally inspired.

And yet in his application, as distinct from his definition, of his theory he was never the dogmatist. He was unerring in his sense of what was original in poetry and what mechanical, what was alive and what dead, as also in estimating the degree of its vitality. And the fact that he himself was to so great an extent an *'automaton* of genius,' a 'passive vehicle of inspiration,' made him bitterly aware of the conflict which must underlie art's ultimate harmony, the wrestling of the creative power with the intellectual energy, and of the positive imagination with the material of negative sensibility. Each faculty, as he knew, in the great poet threatens 'the extinction of the other.' Perfect intuition and expression lay in the energetic equilibrium of opposites, the equilibrium which he had sought in vain.

Wordsworth at his best had achieved it; he lacked Shakespeare's degree of passion and power, but like him he had 'studied patiently, meditated deeply, understood minutely till knowledge, become habitual and intuitive, wedded itself to his habitual feelings' and gave birth to a poetry at once personal and universal. At his worst he had failed to subdue the objective to a subjective purpose, failed to assimilate the matter of thought and observance and recreate it in his own image.

And so the *Biographia Literaria* was not only a book in which poetical experience was philosophically analysed as it had never in English been analysed before: it was also a final summary of the relation in which, ever since Nether Stowey days, Coleridge had stood as a poet to Wordsworth.

For ten fruitful years Wordsworth had generally succeeded in combining the subjective and the objective, and then the materialist in the guise of the literalist and the moralist, had submerged the originating idealist.

Meanwhile Coleridge, save for a few brilliant pre-

carious months, had never succeeded in reconciling the
ideal and the real, but he had learnt in anguish the nature
of the harmony which he could not achieve. He was a
victim of the friction, growing ever more acute with
each century of the Christian era, the friction between
instinct and intelligence.

In this sense the problem of modern poetry is, as Coleridge realized, interwoven with religious values. Christianity destroyed the unity of the Pagan consciousness.
The individual drew apart from Nature. He opposed his
moral values to Nature's physical processes. He did not
merely reflect life, he criticized it. And gradually the gulf
widened. Art, philosophy and human life, therefore,
became more and more a problem of adjustment between
the world within and the world without, an attempt to
capture reality by reconciling the individual and the
ideal with the generic and the real.

In Coleridge the problem was beyond solution; the
world within was all-powerful. And the *Biographia Literaria* was essentially in its anecdote and its criticism an
explanation of this dualism, and of how in the greatest
poetry, as, so Coleridge claimed, in the creative processes
of the Universe, it was resolved.

§ 6

The industry and concentration expended upon the
Biographia Literaria was inevitably followed in 1816 by a
relapse. Certainly Byron's advice that he should repeat
the dramatic success of *Remorse* kept him working in a
desultory manner at a play, and the same poet had persuaded Murray to publish 'Christabel,' to which Coleridge also added 'Kubla Khan' and 'The Pains of Sleep.'
The addition was a mistake, since the extremely narcotic
flavour of the two shorter poems was certain to affect the
reader's judgment of the longer, and the very hostile

reception of the volume as a whole by the critics may be, to some extent at least, attributed to this conjunction.

But the opium question had now become so serious that some practical step seemed imperative. He had tried on a doctor's advice to cut himself down to the smallest dose that would keep him tranquil and capable of literary labour, but always he had failed for two reasons: the one mental, and the other physical.

Either, with more moderation, he became more conscious of the pitiable indulgence of which he was the slave and so fell back into his old habits to drug his conscience; or, if he resisted this temptation, there always came a point when his physical agony was unendurable. For a time his spirits mounted and, like a convalescent, he felt a keener relish for life, 'till the moment, the direful moment, arrived when my pulse began to fluctuate, my heart to palpitate, and such a dreadful falling abroad, as it were, of my whole frame, such intolerable restlessness, and incipient bewilderment,' that he felt his whole being to be in danger of imminent dissolution.

He realized at last that without a doctor in close and authoritative attendance he would never pass this point, and fear as much as remorse compelled him to put himself at least for six months under medical control. With this end in view he went up to London in March, and there, lodging significantly enough at a chemist's laboratory in Norfolk Street, renewed for a week his old intercourse with Lamb.

Much indeed had passed over his head since he had drowned his thoughts of Mary Evans at the 'Salutation and Cat' in 'egg-hot' and 'smoking Oronooko.' Yet Lamb, who could look behind a heavy body and a flabby face, found 'his essentials not touched. He is very bad,' he wrote, 'but then he wonderfully picks up another day, and his face, when he repeats his verses, hath its ancient

glory . . . ; the neighbourhood of such a man is as exciting as the presence of fifty ordinary persons. 'Tis enough
to be within the whiff and wind of his genius for us not to
possess our souls in quiet.'

It was doubtless in one such mood of drug-dazzled
glory that he had written the song by Glycine, which was
the only moment of creative ecstasy in the play entitled
Zapolya – a laboured melodrama modelled upon the
Winter's Tale – which he brought with him to London
and which Covent Garden rejected. For the last time in
this lyric, artificial as it is, he recaptured something of the
liquid, dancing glitter which had proclaimed him in his
youth a veritable child of light:

'A sunny shaft did I behold,
    From sky to earth it slanted:
And poised therein a bird so bold –
    Sweet bird, thou wert enchanted!

'He sunk, he rose, he twinkled, he trolled
    Within that shaft of sunny mist;
His eyes of fire, his beak of gold,
    All else of amethyst!

'And thus he sang: "Adieu! adieu!
Love's dreams prove seldom true.
The blossoms, they make no delay:
The sparkling dew-drops will not stay.
    Sweet month of May,
        We must away;
            Far, far away!
            To-day! to-day!"'

But he was leaving now for good the world of enchantment and excess. Henceforth he was to live regularly,
but in a cloud of numbness through which life, if it played
at all, played to him on muted strings.

On April 9 he consulted a Dr. Adams, and after candidly stating his case asked him if he knew 'a physician who will be not only firm but severe in his regimen,' and who, if possible, could offer him a place of retirement and a garden. Dr. Adams applied to Mr. Gillman, a very kindly man and with interests other than medical. Mr. Gillman had not contemplated an addition to his household, but when Coleridge visited him on April 11, he was completely captivated. It was thus that Coleridge later described his host's attitude in calling down blessings on his head: 'Your love to me from first to last has begun in, and been caused by, what appeared to *you* a translucence of the love of the good, the true, and the beautiful from within me – as a relic of glory, gleaming through the turbid shine of my mortal imperfections and infirmities, as a Light of Life seen within "the body of this Death." '

Coleridge promised to return the next day, a Saturday. He gave himself one more week-end of freedom and indulgence; but on Monday evening he arrived to accept that voluntary confinement, which, except for a few fugitive days, was to last until the end.

¶CHAPTER EIGHT

IN PORT

§ I

FOR eighteen years Coleridge 'sat on the brow of Highgate Hill . . . like a sage escaped from the inanity of
life's battle.' More accurately, he was a voluble Romantic
bankrupt seeking forgetfulness of his failure in the kingdom of Earth by instructing the elect in the principles
which ensured their entrance into the kingdom of
Heaven. Long before his death he had become, like
so much of his oracular idealism, almost a myth, certainly a memorial.

Nor can he be said to have profited altogether by the
respectability and security which he had at last accepted,
and which encouraged sometimes a rather pompous
priggishness, a tendency to interpret the very qualities
which, before the Gillmans supervened to preserve him
from their consequences, were a source of continual contrition, as actually justifying the pose of a complacent
sage. In short, apologetic self-deception inclined to harden
into a solid and satisfied hypocrisy, so that even Lamb
after a morning call was constrained to write that he found
something 'in him or his apothecary . . . so unattrac-
tively — repulsing, — from any temptation to call again
that I stay away as naturally as a lover visits.'

Yet even when his person had grown rotund and
relaxed, his mouth watery and his nose snuffy, he preserved about him an air of voluptuous repose, an air too
of docile benignity, of affectionate childishness, which
made his visitors forget the shapeless body, the shuffling
walk, and all the signs of impotent senility. He was the
best proof of his theory that reality transcends the physical. Within the slack, shambling bulk of the man there
lurked still a bright, mellifluous spirit, often submerged,
but always liable to peep out from the vaguely luminous

eyes, and with any encouragement to slide off into a continuous flow of converse.

He would begin to discourse on some high theme in a sweet low tone, would seem 'to dally with the shallows of the subject and with fantastic images which bordered it: but gradually the thought grew deeper, and the voice deepened with the thought; the stream gathering strength seemed to bear along with it all things which opposed its progress and blended them with its current; and stretching away among regions tinted with ethereal colours, was lost at airy distance in the horizon of fancy.'

These were his best hours, the hours when in a temple of talk he became indeed 'the priest of invisible rites behind the veil of the senses,' when he made even the unintelligible appear plain by a strange power of hypnotic and hierophantic suggestion.

But they became less and less frequent as the years passed. More often he was 'credulous and talkative from indolence': the pulse of thought beat faint in the vast body of his speech; a tedious preaching tone, very different from his once liturgical chant, crept into his voice, and neither truth nor ethereal fancy gave wings to the endless files of words which he conducted through ingenious manœuvres, marshalled in perplexing periods or allowed to trail across his auditors' hearing, like a lagging rearguard on a route-march.

Doubtless the deterioration in his talk was connected with the opium restriction to which he submitted. He never ceased to take it, but he was never allowed to take enough for exhilaration. He was in this way cured of the terror which previously had haunted him in the periods of reaction, but this terror had acted as the particular stimulus of his conversation. He had been so ecstatic a talker because he was in flight from a fiend, and when the fiend ceased to pursue him he tended to lapse into a sententious amble.

And as opium consumption decreased, another narcotic took its place — 'a department of knowledge . . . the study of which, rightly and *liberally* pursued, is beyond any other *entertaining*, beyond all others tends at once to tranquillize and enliven, to keep the mind elevated and steadfast, the heart humbler and tender: it is *Biblical theology* — the philosophy of religion, the religion of philosophy.'

The religious thought to which Coleridge devoted all his last years was not wholly void of contemporary value. Indeed he proved a rallying point for many who wanted their minds propped against the invasion of new doubts, much as Tennyson did thirty years later; for many earnest Christians, too, who were equally dissatisfied with the dry and superficial religion of conventional ecclesiastics and the crudities of evangelical zealots. Coleridge seemed to supply a philosophical basis for theological dogmas, and so to renew them. He claimed that Christianity, rightly understood, was identical with the highest philosophy, and that its essential doctrines were 'necessary and eternal truths of reason — truths which man, by the vouchsafed light of Nature and without aid from documents or tradition, may always and anywhere discover for himself.'

In private he could even go further and aver that 'he should have been a Christian had Christ never lived; that all that was good in the teaching of Christ was to be found in Plato, in Zoroaster, Confucius and the Gymnosophists; that the miracles had no force as affirming truths, were of no more weight than so many conjuring tricks.'

Certainly such a statement showed an insensitiveness to the personal reality of Christ and his distinctive genius. But if Coleridge had honestly acted upon this opinion

and disentangled Christian values from the accretion of
stereotyped dogma and flimsy historical evidence in
which ecclesiastical minds had encased them, the writings of his later years might have had a real significance
today.

But that of course he did not do. Kant had translated
Christianity into terms of rationalistic philosophy, and
whether his idealistic hypothesis be accepted or not, it is
at least disinterestedly and searchingly developed. Coleridge claimed to do the same, but he was far too easy and
accommodating an idealist to purge religious thought of
dead dogma. No thinker can achieve reality without
accepting limitations, but they must be limitations imposed by himself over his own discursiveness, and not
by an external authority on his own freedom of thought.
It was because Coleridge lacked the power to do the
former that his acceptance of the latter was without value.
It had become, he confessed, as much his nature to evolve
the fact from the law as that of the practical man to deduce
the law from the fact, and the law as he conceived it was
so generously latitudinarian that he had little difficulty in
reconciling with it any facts and any dogmas he wished.

So fearful was he lest 'true philosophy' should unsettle
the '*principles* of faith, that may and ought to be common
to all men,' that he glossed over Anglican dogmas with the
same eloquent facility as he glossed over the facts of nature,
and his so-called Natural Theology was an agreeable but
quite arbitrary attachment of his own philosophic pre-
conceptions to the Church of England's creed.

The result of such a compromised union, dictated as it
was by his own need of the fixity and assurance of insti-
tutional religion, was that the real elements in his idealism
were progressively sacrificed to sanctimoniousness, the
pure religious instinct of the poet to the religiosity of the
sectarian, to whom Christ was not the divinest 'Son of

Man,' the poet of new values and of a new world, but an
abstraction dressed in ecclesiastical dialect, an incarnation
'in Trinity or tri-unity.'

The philosopher who drew upon his instincts as a poet
could not fail to mingle truth with fiction: to adopt his
own metaphor, 'though Etna smoked above, there were
electrical flashes from the crater and sometimes a bright
eruption'; but the philosopher who came to terms with
the cleric was as devoid of real value as the poet of Grasmere who had come to terms with the country gentleman.

§ 2

The chief writings in which Coleridge embodied his
religious and moral thoughts during these declining years
were *The Friend*, *Aids to Reflection* and two *Lay Sermons*
addressed to the Higher and Middle Classes. The first
was almost 'a complete rifacimento' of the Grasmere
Journal, the second rose out of a proposed selection of
'Beauties' from the writings of that 'wonderful man'
Archbishop Leighton, writings which, in Coleridge's
opinion, renewed the inspiration of the Apostolic epistles,
and even provoked a preposterous analogy with the
thought and style of Shakespeare. The *Lay Sermons*
were more specifically tracts for the times, and offered
various edifying suggestions for the cure of 'existing Dis-
tresses and Discontents' – among them a plea that statesmen should content themselves with the Bible as 'the
best guide to political skill and foresight,' and as an actual
foreteller, to those who could read it allegorically, of
coming events.

Of these publications *The Friend* contained the most
reality. Coleridge's attempt in the original version to
relate his idealism to the practical concerns of life has
already been remarked, and something of the creative
sincerity which belonged to the original survived its

reconstruction. The style too, if often a style in deliquescence, was often also supple and caressing, as if blending the manners of Hooker and of Jeremy Taylor, which he so much admired; it was rich too in picturesque illustration; and to read many passages aloud is to understand the spell which his conversation cast. In places too he did commune with that 'very and permanent self' which he informed his readers was the first step to knowledge.

But as a whole *The Friend* reflected, little less than his other writings of the period, the false compromise which was the condition of a limp idealism. The youthful reader, whom in his avuncular mind's eye he saw standing beside him like his own youth, 'fresh and keen as the morning Hunter in the pursuit of Truth, glad and restless in the feeling of mental growth,' was bidden to learn early 'that if the Head be the Light of the Heart, the Heart is the Life of the Head,' and that 'Consciousness, of which all reasoning is the varied modification, is but the Reflex of the Conscience when most luminous.'

In short, there was no truth but moral truth. The 'Understanding' which observed phenomena and based its judgment on the appearance of things was worthless: the 'Reason' only, by a sort of moral intuition, could perceive things as they really were, and grasp truth independently of the senses.

Such a theory of course accorded exactly with Coleridge's nature. But his creed like his experience was disorganic. As he had said of Macbeth: 'He has by guilt torn himself live-asunder from nature, and is, therefore, himself in a preternatural state: no wonder, then, that he is inclined to superstition, and faith in the unknown of signs and tokens, and super-human agencies.'

All religions are myths, and all philosophies systems, in which experience is materialized, but the degree of their reality corresponds with the degree of their truth to nature, the depth, proportion and amplitude of the experience which underlies them. The child and the savage are natural mythologists, but they lack the experience to make their mythology conform with truth, to inform their innocence with knowledge. It is this basis of knowledge implicit in innocence which distinguishes revelation from superstition and mysticism from mystification. But since details to Coleridge were of little value except so far as they illustrated and proved a principle, they could be shelved when they failed to do so; and since the evidence of the senses was worthless, the moral 'Reason' was free to claim anything as truth which pleased it.

Hence arose often enough 'a fatuous vapour, a warmthless bewildering mockery of Light, exhaled from its corruption or stagnation,' and there was nothing to prevent, as inertia crept over him, a mere repetition of myths which he found edifying as a 'Liberal' Churchman and a 'progressive' Tory. The miracles, for example, might be 'really or only seemingly supernatural,' but he was soon 'content for sake of its divine truths to receive as articles of faith or . . . leave undisputed the miracles of the New Testament, taken in their literal sense.' They were so valuable, it seemed to him, in generating 'that predisposing warmth' of which Faith was born.

The Friend was riddled with such plausible casuistry, and it was as a brother conjurer that he penned an absurd eulogy of the quack educator, Dr. Andrew Bell, and, deploring the foundation of new secular, Universities, urged that the education of the future should be entrusted to a permanent nationalized learned order of clergymen.

A like pious unreality falsified his moral teaching. He professed indeed the most liberal views, desired to remove ignorance rather than to make the ignorant religious, and claimed that 'all effective faith presupposes knowledge and individual conviction,' that it was 'no mere acquiescence in truth, uncomprehended and unfathomed.'

But the individual conviction was to tally with his own. If not, it was shocking 'speculative infidelity'; and there was something at once pathetic and ridiculous in one who had failed so utterly to direct his own life, solemnly preaching that the preventive, remedy and counteraction of all evil, social and personal, was 'the habituation of the intellect to clear, distinct and adequate conceptions concerning all things that are the possible objects of clear conception,' after ruling out the whole objective world from such a category. His own failure was entirely due to a lack of clear conception and to a morbid absorption in those feelings 'which,' so he comfortably claimed, 'belong, as by a natural right, to those obscure ideas that are necessary to the moral perfection of the human being notwithstanding, yea, even in consequence of, their obscurity.'

The generation which, a century after Coleridge's day, has learnt by bitter experience how necessary, if humanity is to survive, is the application of Christian values to the political and economic, equally with the personal, concerns of human life, is not likely to quarrel with his intention; but it has learnt too how worse than useless is a religion of edification or a morality divorced from fact. Such merely delude, as they deluded Coleridge himself, with a sense of peace and security, by drawing a cloudy curtain over the discord. The failure of the Church, upon whose doctrine Coleridge grafted his bodiless idealism, to represent disinterestedly the values of Christ, is in itself a sufficient warning against a faith that sacrifices science to 'heart-dilating sentiments,' dogmas, or metaphysical abstractions.

To admit for truth 'a higher and deeper ground than

the intellect itself can supply' should not mean that 'only
those who have the will to believe *against* the evidence of
the senses can believe.' The mind must take the senses
with it in its search for truth if it is not to fall into the conventional or the inane. Certainly the subjective and the
objective, which are but antithetical aspects of the time-
order, are transcended in every pure act of spiritual
experience. But the experience must contain them both,
if it is truly to surpass them.

In his interpretation of Shakespeare's genius Coleridge
had recognized an intuition which represented a perfectly
co-ordinated activity of the whole being, an identification
of that which *knows* with that which *is*, and at times even
in *The Friend* he could translate such a consciousness into
religious terms without debasing it, as for example when
he wrote: 'This elevation of the spirit above the semblances of custom and the senses to a world of spirit, this
life in the idea, even in the supreme and godlike, which
alone merits the name of life, and without which our
organic life is but a state of somnambulism; this it is
which affords the sole sure anchorage in the storm, and
at the same time the substantiating principle of all true
wisdom, the satisfactory solution of all the contradictions
of human nature, of the whole riddle of the world. . . .
But let it not be supposed that it is a sort of knowledge:
no! it is a form of BEING, or indeed it is the only knowledge that truly *is*, and all other science is real only as far
as it is symbolical of this. The material universe, saith a
Greek philosopher, is but one vast complex *mythus*, that
is, symbolical representation, and mythology the apex and
complement of all genuine physiology.'

But it was because Coleridge's mythology was not the
complement of a genuine physiology that he imposed a
fanciful allegory upon the material universe instead of
deriving from it a true symbolism.

As a moralist he wished to bring his idealism into effective relation with the practical concerns of life, but through inability to face and analyse the practical, he could only graft it on to a conventional Toryism. As a 'Natural Theologian' he wished to relate his faith to Nature, but through inability to study the facts of Nature he only succeeded in grafting a philosophical Ethic on to the theological paraphernalia of his time.

His excuse was that the 'Reason, being one with the ultimate end, of which it is *the* manifestation,' had no concern with 'things (the impermanent flux of particulars).' In this he showed the familiar presumption of the idealistic egotist who, rather than face a universe at least as cruel in its governing conditions as benign, attributes to the world at large his own self-conceived values and his own morality. He composes a picture of what the world ought to be, and in defiance of the evidence claims that so it is. He is inspired with benevolence himself and hungers after moral perfection, and he imports into all reality, under the name of God, the same high sentiments. Since Coleridge's day men have increasingly devoted themselves to an objective study of Nature and have discovered how ignorant she is of what she is going to produce, and how careless of perfection when she has produced it. They have learnt how complete is her unconcern for the moral values of man, that she reveals no more than a blindly disinterested vitality, and that purpose in the universe, if it exists, is a matter of hesitating evolution based on a method of trial and error. Such a discovery in no way renders an idealistic standpoint untenable. Einstein indeed, by proving that experience cannot be interpreted in terms of space and time, has confirmed idealism physically. But it is an idealism disencumbered of mythology and moral assumptions, distinctively human though its roots are in nature, and tested at every point by a reference to fact.

As a modern writer has put it: 'Unless we hold in mind the analysis of the world towards which the physical is bringing us, we shall not understand the synthesis of the world towards which the philosopher is bringing us.' In short, the physical and the metaphysical, science and imagination, are recognized to be mutually dependent, and the only idealism which is not prejudiced to be that which is grounded in matter itself. Consequently man has generally assumed far more responsibility for conquering and controlling his experience. He no longer believes in the protection of a blandly benevolent God in whom everything brutal and everything inexplicable can be comfortably forgotten. He has adapted his conception of God to a view of Life rather as an evolutionary process, to be interpreted not statically as of old, or as an image of eternally fixed principles, but dynamically, or like a stream of consciousness moving towards some end yet dimly realized, charged with vast possibilities of development and altered direction, to which he himself can effectively contribute.

In such a conception man seeks to-day to harmonize his new scientific experience, and it would of course be unfair to charge Coleridge with mental dishonesty because his conception of God lacked the material basis which the science of a later day supplied. But it lacked more than this. 'The starry heavens above' and 'the moral law within' should fill anyone, as they did Kant, 'with awe,' but the problem, which Kant as a philosopher and Wordsworth as a poet faced, was to bridge the space between them.

Coleridge made no attempt to solve that problem. He took an easy leap into the dark, and however ecstatic such a leap may be, it can only result in a false conviction of the

fall of man from an imaginary perfection, and paralyse
his efforts to rise from an actual savagery. And as excess
of pain brings indifference, so excess of sensibility brings
senselessness, or what Mr. Santayana has called 'a sub-
sidence into the primordial life of undifferentiated feeling.' A too expansive love of everything, whether associated with 'the starry heavens above' or 'the moral law
within,' approximates to a love of nothing. Coleridge
himself half-admitted the fact in a lecture on the Gothic,
when he said: 'But the Gothic art is sublime. On entering a cathedral I am filled with devotion and with awe; I
am lost to the actualities that surround me, and my whole
being expands into the infinite, earth and air, nature and
art, all swell up into eternity, and the only sensible impression left, is, that I am nothing!'

Doubtless such 'free unresisted action, the going forth
of the soul, life, without consciousness, is, properly, infinite, that is unlimited,' but the essential problem of the
artist and thinker is to impose limit upon it, and so com-
pel it into the sphere of the conscious and intelligible.
This is not to deny that all dynamic writing is charged
with far more than a conscious meaning, suggests an
infinite background and timelessness overbrimming the
banks of time. But just as the infinite cannot be communicated save as the overtones of the finite, so the idealist
cannot achieve true freedom unless he faces necessity.
If his idealism is to be honest and real, he must relate his
absolute convictions to the actual and relative. He must
accept that 'reality-loving limitation behind which the
Absolute can lie concealed,' of which Goethe wrote, and
his thought must not flow over Nature, but finely penetrate to her texture.

Coleridge failed as thinker because his thought was
neither static nor dynamic, but fluid. As a Church apologist he would have done well to lay to heart his own

aphorism – 'He who begins by loving Christianity better than truth, will proceed by loving his own sect or church better than Christianity.'

For the half-truth embodied in the more typical statement that 'to become a believer one must love the doctrine, and feel in harmony with it, and not sit down coolly to inquire whether he should believe or not,' removed, as he wished to do, the only means by which truth could be distinguished from fiction.

Certainly, as Pascal wrote, it is necessary to love to understand; to this extent all true perception is moral; and Coleridge had brilliantly exemplified the truth in his analysis of Shakespeare. But while love supplies the creative sympathy necessary to all true insight, it will degenerate into mere sentimentalism if not sustained by a keen critical sense. Coleridge could not be critical of conventional religion because he needed its peace and security too much – needed, as he wrote in *Aids to Reflection*, a God 'with a merciful consideration of our infirmities, a gracious acceptance of our sincere though imperfect strivings, a forgiveness of our defects.' His theology was no more disinterested than his morality, and his idealism, so weak in its reference to fact, played the inevitable pander to both.

And so in his religious teaching he degraded Kant's philosophy of absolutes to serve the uses of a merely local and Conservative piety, and deluded himself into believing that the discords in human nature could be healed by rapt contemplation of those meaningless 'spiritual objects, the universal, the eternal and the necessary,' in which a permanent nationalized learned order of clergy was to instruct the coming generations.

He had ceased to be either a God-tormented or a God-illuminated man. He was for the most part a God-befuddled one.

While therefore he was as right in intention in opposing the materialistic school which derived from Condillac
in philosophy, as he was in opposing that which derived
from Boileau in poetry, his achievement in both spheres
was prejudiced by his temperament. Such lyrical poetry
as 'Kubla Khan' may possibly give 'most pleasure when
only generally and not perfectly understood,' but a fantastic metaphysic is worthless.

Truth was to be 'educed by the mind out of its own
essence,' and his mind's essence was decayed. He was
never in full and wholesome harmony with Nature because his nature was not in harmony with itself. In his
last years the disintegration had become so advanced, and
the vital impulse so dimmed, that he was at the most capable only of a sort of moral mortification, of 'a sinking
inward into ourselves from thought to thought, a steady
remonstrance, and a high resolve.' That he should seriously address himself in *Aids to Reflection* to those 'desirous
of building up a manly character' only reveals how
moribund he had become. He had ceased even to know
himself.

Certainly *The Friend* has a value which survives its
transcendental falsifications and its muffled moralizing.
Even a sickly spirit, if it seek after deeper harmonies and
finer perceptions, is always apt to flower in beauty and
self-revelation at a happy impulse of emotion. Coleridge's language was always subtly woven; it breathed
too a pious sympathy, and at moments there descended
upon it the radiance of a miraculous insight. All these
qualities may be found in *The Friend*, and it has also
passages of tender and dissolving eloquence, as well as of
mere metaphorical emptiness, typical of one who was
engaged in solacing his sad heart rather than thinking
constructively, to whom wisdom was not prudential, and
so could flow into words like a soft caressing current,

unimpeded by, or gently overtopping the boulders of fact.

Such a passage is the following:

'There never perhaps existed a schoolboy, who, having, when he retired to rest, carelessly blown out his candle, and having chanced to notice, as he lay upon his bed in the ensuing darkness, the sullen light which had survived the extinguished flame, did not, at some time or other, watch that light as if his mind were bound to it by a spell. It fades and revives, gathers to a point, seems as if it would go out in a moment, again recovers its strength, nay, becomes brighter than before: it continues to shine with an endurance, which in its apparent weakness is a mystery; it protracts its existence so long, clinging to the power which supports it, that the observer, who had lain down in his bed so easy-minded, becomes sad and melancholy; his sympathies are touched; it is to him an intimation and an image of departing human life; the thought comes nearer to him; it is the life of a venerated parent, of a beloved brother or sister, or of an aged domestic, who are gone to the grave, or whose destiny it soon may be thus to linger, thus to hang upon the last point of mortal existence, thus finally to depart and be seen no more.'

Such indeed was the destiny of Coleridge's genius through these last years at Highgate.

§ 3

But if the resting-place which Coleridge made for himself in religion was largely a delusion, Mr. and Mrs. Gillman were 'amiable and respectable' facts. Not that Coleridge could even accept his kindly hostess as a fact. She too was a Trinitarian formula, was 'of all women I ever knew . . . the woman who seems to have been framed by Nature for a heroine in that rare species of love which subsists in a triunity of the heart, the moral sense, and the faculty, corresponding to what Spurzheim calls the organ of ideality'; but her *a fortiori* virtues and her kinship with 'the Spanish Santa Teresa' did not prevent her, whom in a less metaphysical moment he called his 'very dear Sister and Friend,' from tending him with maternal solicitude.

Only when her 'restless and interrogating anxieties and her careworn countenance' accused him of exceeding the prescribed quantity of opium did he feel any inclination to run away. He indulged the inclination once, in 1824, for ten days, but he was glad to be recovered. Possibly it would have been nicer if Mrs. Gillman had contented herself with being only the 'tender sister' and not the 'anxious friend.' But he felt at last at home, and whether driving in Mr. Gillman's gig or shuffling along on foot among the 'delicious groves and alleys' of Caen Wood, his worst suffering, the sense of awful isolation, was at an end.

Melancholy still alternated with cheerfulness, but he felt neither keenly. The poor Morgans might go bankrupt, and so might his publisher Fenner; he himself might be driven by poverty into lecturing and journalism; Hazlitt and Jeffrey might attack his personal character so caustically in the *Edinburgh* that he even contemplated bringing a libel action; he might be taunted with having declined into 'torpid uneasy repose, tantalized by useless resources, haunted by vain imaginings, his lips idly moving, but his heart for ever still'; yet torpor was at least a non-conductor. He felt such things like echoes from a world whence he had withdrawn.

Only one event indeed really awoke him to a sense of past horrors, or imported him once again into 'the howling wilderness of sleep that I dread' – Hartley's deprivation of his fellowship in 1820 on the grounds of intemperance. Even the Bible could bring him no comfort

there. Truly the father 'had eaten sour grapes' and the
son's teeth were 'set on edge;' and could anything 'be
more dreadful than the thought that an innocent child
has inherited from you a disease or weakness, the penalty
in yourself of sin, or want of caution?'

Once again in a letter to a friend he rehearsed and tried
to excuse his own weakness. Surely no human being
was more indifferent to the pleasures of the table than
himself, or less needed any stimulation to his spirits. He
was *seduced* into the use of narcotics and saw not the
truth till his body had contracted a habit and a necessity.
His responsibility was for cowardice: not for the least
craving after gratification, but for yielding to pain, terror,
and haunting bewilderment.

Dreadful, however, though the parallel was between
himself and his son, even here the casuist discovered a
reason for shelving some of the responsibility. Doubtless
Hartley's weakness had been fostered by the culpable
indulgence, at least non-interference, of himself, but also
'in a different quarter, contempt of the self-*interest* he
saw seduced him unconsciously into selfishness.' So
dire, it was convenient to think, was the effect of Southey's
or of Sara's common prudence on a tender sensibility!

But even so sudden and heavy an affliction as this
passed as rapidly as a peal of thunder over Highgate.
More and more he felt that he could 'be well off nowhere
away from' his host and hostess. They interposed a solid
affectionate humanity between himself and the world and
memory. He had drifted at last into a region of security,
though it was the security of the padded cell, and when
the monotony of Highgate palled or his spirits were at a
low ebb, he was allowed a change of air at Muddiford or
Littlehampton or Ramsgate. The sea was never too cold
for his liking and he was very fortunate at each of these
places in striking up friendships with congenial fellow-

visitors, pacing the sands at Muddiford with Stewart Rose, the friend of Scott, 'while ebbing seas have hummed a rolling bass'; or at Littlehampton with Charles Augustus Tulk, the eminent Swedenborgian, who introduced him to Blake's poetry; or with H. F. Cary, whose translation of Dante he popularized by recommending it in one of his lectures.

And at home gradually the Thursday evenings became a conversational institution. Rumour of his extraordinary performance spread; how, as Carlyle said, after accumulating 'formidable apparatus, logical swim-bladders, transcendental life-preservers, and other precautionary and vehiculatory gear,' he would at last get under way, only to be 'turned aside by the flame of some radiant new game on this hand or on that into new courses, and ever into new; and before long into all the universe, where it was uncertain what game you would catch or whether any.' But how, after talking 'with eager musical energy two stricken hours, his face radiant and moist,' and communicating 'no meaning whatsoever to any individual of his hearers,' suddenly 'glorious islets' would 'rise out of the haze . . . balmy sunny islets of the blest and the intelligible,' or, to quote another writer, far horizons of thought flashing 'with the beauty of a sunrise at sea.' It was expectation of these moments that drew his audience and made them tolerant of 'the moaning sing-song' of 'theosophico-metaphysical monotony.'

And apart from Lamb, who, despite his gentle scepticism, loved Coleridge as only one who had 'more of the essentials of Christianity than ninety-nine out of a hundred professing Christians' could, and who was constant in his half-humorous, half-reverential attention, Coleridge attracted two new friends. One of these was a young business man named Allsop, who introduced himself after a lecture, and from the beginning behaved towards him 'more like a dutiful and anxious son than an acquaintance.' Judging by the account which Allsop later gave of their relations for the edification of his children, he was drawn to Coleridge as much by a native sympathy with his grandiloquent piety as by pity and astonishment.

And doubtless a young man with a tendency to moralize and to fail in business would find in Coleridge a comforting affinity, while equally comforting to Coleridge was his ignorance of the desolated past, behind which all the friends of his own youth, save Lamb, had withdrawn with varying glances of moral disapprobation. His relations with Allsop were unembarrassed by the past. He could offer sententious advice to his 'dear young friend' without fearing to provoke a veiled derision; and gradually between 1819 and 1826 their intimacy increased, fostered by a long series of exceedingly confidential letters, in which as of old he tended to flatter his self-esteem by self-apology. In one of these, for example, described truly by Allsop as 'a letter which no one but my lamented friend could have written,' he prefaced a request for a loan of money, 'provided it could be accepted without moral degradation,' with a diffuse lament over his circumstances, which in its sentimental cant was easily the equal of any of those that had sickened the heart of Southey and of Wordsworth.

Fortunately, however, Allsop was not a young poet, but a young moralist. Unlike Keats, who, meeting Coleridge on a walk, found his eloquence a curious but not a significant phenomenon, Allsop accepted all he said at its face value, and his affection must indeed have been clearly demonstrated to provoke the remark that 'as a mother would talk of the soothing attentions, the sacrifices and devotion of a son, eager to supply every want and anticipate every wish, so I talk to myself concerning you.' 'Oh,' he added, with a girlish rapture typical of

his younger days, 'we will exchange souls;' and with the
self-pitying infidelity of the romancer, though the reference was doubtless in the main to Wordsworth, he wrote:
'Would to Heaven I had had many with feelings like
yours, "accustomed to express themselves warmly and
(as far as the word is applicable to you, even) enthusiastically." But alas! during the prime manhood of my intellect I had nothing but cold water thrown on my efforts
. . . I have loved with enthusiastic self-oblivion those
who have been so well pleased that I should, year after
year, flow with a hundred nameless rills into *their* main
stream, that they could find nothing but cold praise and
effective discouragement of every attempt of mine to roll
onward in a distinct current of my own.'

At first indeed such a 'hope, promise and impulse' was
this new friendship to him that the ghost of a completed
'Christabel' once more appeared. Allsop, however, could
scarcely succeed where the forgotten Dorothy had failed.
The expected 'genial recurrence of the ray divine' did not
of course occur; but at least he had found a confidant.
His mind with its best faculties was no longer 'locked
up in one ungenial frost,' and in his letters he expressed
his opinions with more candour than in his printed works.
The fact that Allsop was a Radical may have had something to do with it, for Coleridge's sensibility always led
him to temper his opinion to that of his correspondent.
He expressed, for example, his desire to do away with
'the servile superstition which makes *Bibliolators*, and yet
holds from them the proper excellencies, the one continued revelation of the Bible documents, which they
idolize,' scorned 'the false reasonings and absurdities of
the rogues and fools with which all establishments, and all
creeds seeking to become established, abound,' and the
selfishness of statesmen who opposed the education of the
lower orders 'in the belief that the closer a nation shuts its

eyes, the wider it will open its hands'; and remarked of an attempt to suppress free opinion under the blasphemy laws, 'I hold the assertion, that Christianity is part and parcel of the law of the land, to be an absurdity . . . Carlile *may be wrong*; *his persecutors undoubtedly are so.*'

Of the petty elements in Wordsworth's character he had much to say, and of his poetry he wrote: 'I will not conceal from *you* that this inferred dependency of the human soul on accidents of birth-place and abode, together with the vague, misty, rather than mystic, confusion of God with the world, and the accompanying nature-worship, . . . is the trait in Wordsworth's poetic works that I most dislike as unhealthful, and denounce as contagious.'

Possibly the provincialism to which Wordsworth finally succumbed justified such a criticism, but Wordsworth might well have answered Coleridge in his own words that 'as there is a worldliness or the *too-much* of this life, so there is *another-worldliness*, equally hateful and selfish with *this worldliness.*'

Throughout all his letters to Allsop, however, Coleridge constantly bewailed in familiar strain the circumstances, particularly the lectures on literature and philosophy that he was compelled to give, like 'a retail dealer in instruction and pastime,' which prevented the completion of his *Magnum Opus*. It hovered like a dream of enormous dimensions over his consciousness of blasted powers; and the other new friend of these years helped to delude him into believing that one day it would materialize.

He became acquainted with Joseph Henry Green, a young surgeon and writer on medical subjects, in 1817. Like Coleridge he had been to Germany, studied philosophy there, and despite the 'horrid materialism' of a medical training he was convinced of 'a spiritual first

cause and a presiding free will.' He became Coleridge's
first disciple and offered himself for two afternoons of the
week as amanuensis and collaborator in laying the foundations of what was to be such a system of philosophy as
should 'virtually include the law and explanation of all
being, conscious and unconscious, and of all correlativity
and duty, and be applicable directly or by deduction to
whatsoever the human mind can contemplate – sensuous
or supersensuous – of experience, purpose, or imagination.'

The whole system, to which Green devoted not only
much of his time during the last seventeen years of
Coleridge's life, but also the last twenty-eight of his own,
was a chimera, a vast web of unfounded deductions, a
juggling with inconceivable entities. It is worth, however, mentioning one aspect, and that the central one, of
this fantastic system, as Green later reported it, since
here, as in all the literary activities of his life, Coleridge
projected into the universe the problem of his own personality and strove by a sort of algebraical formula to solve
in theory what he could not solve in practice.

Just as he had described the poet in ideal perfection as
reconciling opposites or discordant qualities, so he defined
the Deity as reconciling in Himself the opposition of
subject and object. God to him was the poet of the Universe, perpetually affirming Himself self-consciously by
an act of will, and the three persons of the Trinity were
the three elements in his consciousness: God the Father
being the 'I' or thinking subject, God the Son the 'Me' or
the subject regarded as object, and God the Holy Ghost
the reconciler of object and subject in a perfect unity of
experience.

The idea of 'persuading mankind of the truths of
Christianity' by such remote deductions from orthodox
dogma was of course ludicrous. And such a conception

is of interest merely because it represented once again his idea of a truly creative consciousness. He felt that it was impotence of will which had prevented him from experiencing and expressing life truly as a poet. He had failed because he could not reconcile the subject and the object. And so in his idea of God he merely perfected his own personality. Unfortunately, however, for the significance of his philosophy, the same disability which had frustrated him as a poet clung to him as a metaphysician, and an age intolerant of airy hypotheses can only refuse to attribute the objective reality which he claimed to so purely subjective a conception.

God is something more than a sublimation of mental philosophy, and to reduce Him to three elements of consciousness was merely to cling to anthropomorphism while pretending to believe in His 'absolute impersonality.' If God exists, all life, and not merely the private aspirations of the individual, must be a representation of Him, and it is useless to dismiss a theory of life which recognizes this necessity as 'pernicious,' since, in Coleridge's words, 'it excludes all our deep and awful ideas of the holiness of God, His justice and mercy. . . . "If you will be good, you will be happy," it says: that may be, but my will is weak; I sink in the struggle.'

God's perfect holiness, justice, and divine humanity therefore were proved, according to Coleridge, in defiance of many facts of life by his own moral weakness. He at once exaggerated and disregarded what he called the 'pravity' of Nature. Nature is neither depraved nor benevolent, but only neutral. If man will accept her as such and aim himself at reflecting her disinterested vitality, while wedding it to human values, he will cease to plead a mythical damnation of mankind as an excuse for cowardly and uncreative living.

So far as man fell, he fell only away from the unmoral

state of primitive Nature that he might climb by way of knowledge to a higher condition of consciousness, and so of life. But Coleridge lacked the courage to climb thus, and he excused his weakness by sentimentalizing his origins. For him it was a God of the past from whom he had fallen, and not a God of the future towards whom he aspired.

'I believe,' he wrote, 'and hold it as the fundamental article of Christianity that I am a fallen creature; that I am of myself capable of moral evil, but not of myself capable of moral good. . . . I am born a child of wrath. This fearful mystery I pretend not to understand . . . my conscience, the sole fountain of certainty, commands me to believe it.'

Thus a mediæval conscience can make cowards and casuists of us all. All his life Coleridge had been conscience-stricken. In other words, he had known that he was not living in true harmony with life. But instead of studying life to learn how he had transgressed its laws, he merely condoned his morbid conscience in the person of an ideally moral 'legislator,' and invoked a conventional redemptive power. In this way, and by attacking as infidels those who saw no such moral scruples in the working of the life-force, but who stressed man's responsibility to outgrow his savage origins and humanize the Natural – as infidels who made it 'necessary for us to reject and declare utterly null, all the commands of conscience, and all that is implied in those commands' – he tried to forget his own life-long inability to act upon the commands of that conscience which he invested with universal sovereignty.

In short, Coleridge lacked the courage to scan the face of Life disinterestedly, to mark not merely its expressive beauty but its scowls and wrinkles, its leers and lightning flashes and clouds of gloomy violence. Hungering for the divine and beatific, he saw only a radiant mist, and upon it he painted his own transfigured countenance, and having painted it proceeded to reduce it, as he had so often reduced it in its marred actuality, to its constituent elements. Still further to veil the purely personal quality of the process, he borrowed the doctrines of the Church and concealed himself behind their venerable vestments.

Green, however, and the *Magnum Opus* served at least to give an illusion of methodical purpose to these last ineffective years, to help him to repeat what he described in a lecture as 'the perpetual promises of the imagination.' And gradually the one dutiful disciple was joined by others, and in 1822 Coleridge even contemplated forming a class, since he had reason to suppose that the three or four young men who had already attached themselves to him in an informal way, had by conversing, reading and corresponding, benefited in the 'improvement and accelerated growth of their faculties, and in the formation, or at least in the grounding, strengthening and *integration*, as it were, of their whole character.'

Strange it would have been if one so disintegrated as he had exercised such an influence as he claimed over the disciples, with whom in rapt attendance he might have been seen strolling over Hampstead Heath. And since poor, eloquent, effeminate Edward Irving, who was eventually to die of a theosophical decline, was chief among them, there is little doubt that Coleridge was deluded in this as in other things. That he did however attract young men of manly character and noble ideals is sufficiently attested in the person of John Sterling, although even to him, who outlived his early enthusiasm, and passed on to the sterner creed of Carlyle, the association was scarcely beneficial.

The explanation of the attraction was that Coleridge

did seem to stand for values which were being submerged in a rising tide of brute materialism. The industrial age was beginning, and none could see then what new and more firmly grounded values might issue from it. They saw only that all the old stable principles, intellectual and moral, to which men had clung for centuries, were being disregarded, and in a world that was for long to divide its allegiance between utility and *laissez-faire*, a world that was spawning ugliness as automatically as its multiplying machines, Coleridge seemed like a forlorn lamp of ancient esoteric wisdom beaming through a gathering cloud of smoke rather than a will-o'-the-wisp dancing over its own morass.

He was the precursor of the Disraeli of *Coningsby* when he argued that 'Commerce has enriched thousands, it has been the cause of the spread of knowledge and of science, but has it added one particle of happiness or of moral improvement? Has it given us a truer insight into our duties, or tended to revive and sustain in us the better feelings of our nature? No!! when I consider that whole districts of men, who would otherwise have slumbered on in comparatively happy ignorance are now little less than brutes in their lives and something worse than brutes in their instincts, I could almost wish that the manufacturing districts were swallowed up as Sodom and Gomorrah.'

But although it was to his credit that, long before Shaftesbury, Coleridge printed and had distributed circulars advocating a Bill to regulate the employment of children in cotton factories, his social like his religious idealism was essentially ineffective. It was typical of him that in applauding the distribution of relief to the poor he should remark that 'it would, on the other hand, be wilful to blindness not to see that the lower orders become more and more improvident in consequence, more and more exchange the sentiments of Englishmen for the feelings of Lazzaroni.'

The possibility of hungry men indulging in the vice of improvidence has always haunted the minds of conventional and comfortable Conservatives, but such tenderness for the moral welfare of the victims of a predatory social system was surely a sublime example of hypocrisy in a man who had depended on 'the distribution of relief' throughout his life.

The philanthropic Conservatism of Coleridge's later life was sentimental like his early Jacobinism. He was sincere enough to know that the Conservative Party was composed of half-truth men, but he resisted everything really progressive, every pronounced desire to order and direct circumstance rather than leave it to 'divine Providence,' as dangerous in itself, or as conflicting with his abstract principles. Radicals were sceptics; neither imagination nor love could have a place in minds so coldly calculating. Political economy he dubbed 'solemn humbug' and denounced as directly tending 'to denationalize, to make the love of our country a foolish superstition,' and he vehemently opposed the Reform Bill as 'that huge tapeworm *lie* of some three score and ten yards.'

He could not range himself with the forces of the future which alarmed him, could not bring his ideals into touch with contemporary fact. He could only lament over change and speak in horror of Atheism and Materialism. He saw as little in Science as Science now sees in his metaphysical needlework. Querulously eloquent, he judged the present by the standards of the past, and so at best he had only palliatives to offer for a situation which offended his sensibility, but to which it was philosophically useless to apply so superficial a faculty as the understanding.

Yet behind the compromise there still lurked the poet eloquently hungering after the divine, selfishly enamoured of an infinite harmony. And it was this, combined with benevolence, piety, and an insistence on principles in themselves estimable, which drew to him the young and ardent, and for a time persuaded them that even his finite judgments were significant, that a world which was sacrificing principle to mechanism might actually be saved, not by an alliance of humanity and science, but by a Church which infused a Coleridgean metaphysic into the skeletons of its dogma.

§ 4

But although 'the Patriot' and 'the Christian' were henceforth the idols of Coleridge's esteem, and 'the Atheist' and 'the Materialist' the objects of his opprobrium; although *The Beggar's Opera*, which twenty years before he had acclaimed as 'perfection,' now filled him with 'horror and disgust. . . . So grossly did it outrage all the best feelings' of his nature; the poet in him glanced occasionally and fearfully into the abyss over which he had constructed a bridge of piety and edification.

It was a Limbo from which not only all the glitter of life, which he loved like a blind man that feels the sun upon his face, was banished, but in which death and darkness were themselves dreadful positives.

"'Tis a strange place, this Limbo! – not a Place
Yet name it so; – where Time and weary Space
Fettered from flight, with night-mare sense of fleeing,
Strive for their last crepuscular half-being; –
Lank Space, and scytheless Time with brawny hands
Barren and soundless as the measuring sands,
Not mark'd by flit of Shades, – unmeaning they
As moonlight on the dial of the day! . . .

Wall'd round, and made a spirit-jail secure
By the mere horror of blank Naught-at-all,
Whose circumambience doth these ghosts enthral.
A lurid thought is growthless, dull Privation,
Yet that is but a Purgatory curse;
Hell knows a fear far worse,
A fear – a future state; – 'tis positive Negation.'

Such was the Limbo which gaped beneath his moralizing,
and it was his fear of this

'Sole Positive of Night!
Antipathist of Light!'

of all the sagging weight of negation in himself, that had
forced him to surrender to conventional piety. As he
wrote:

'What hast thou, Man, that thou dar'st call thine own? –
What is there in thee, Man, that can be known? –
Dark fluxion, all unfixable by thought,
A phantom dim by past and future wrought,
Vain sister of the worm, – life, death, soul, clod –
Ignore thyself, and strive to know thy God!'

He had fed upon himself until naught remained but to
sit and cower 'o'er my own vacancy' – a vacancy which,
if it was not peopled with the ghosts of past failure, seemed
to forecast some such Hell as Dante had allotted to the
apathetic. It was no use turning to Nature: for in her
face too he could only read himself, unless he were
observing detail dispassionately; and that only diverted,
it did not fulfil and comfort.

There were moments indeed when still his senses
dreamily responded to the beauty of life, but they grew
less and less frequent. In one of them the nightingales

reminded him of his walks twenty years before in the woods about Alfoxden, so many were they and in such full song, 'particularly that giddy voluminous whirl of notes which you never hear but when the Birds feel the temperature of the air voluptuous.' In another, he wrote to Allsop: 'Hark yet again to that sweet strain! see how calm, how beauteous that prospect toward my garden! Would to God I could give out my being amidst flowers, and the sight of meadowy fields, and the chaunt of birds. Death without pain at such a time, in such a place as this, would be a reward for life. If I fear at all, I fear dying – I do not fear death.'

It was a state of dying, infinitely prolonged, that he feared, a continued consciousness of inability ever to give out his being. 'In vain,' he wrote,

> 'we supplicate the Powers above;
> There is no resurrection for the Love
> That, nursed in tenderest care, yet fades away
> In the chill'd heart by gradual self-decay.'

And so for the reality he substituted the convention, and was content to

> 'trace in leaves and flowers that round me lie
> Lessons of love and earnest piety.'

Yet there were times when his piety was more than conventional, when the elusive child in him peeped round the skirts of Archbishop Leighton, with a wistful wonder in eyes that never, like Polonius', became 'the watery eyes of superannuation.'

Never again could he run wild 'as the full moon in a fine breezy October night, driving on amid clouds of all shapes and hues, and kindling shifting colours, like an ostrich in its speed.' The sky above him was shrouded,

and it was 'a cruel sort of world,' but he could write
appealingly and without the whine of defeat, because
self-pity was sweetened by self-understanding, and resignation by an innocence at once childlike and benign. In
such moods his thoughts went back to 'dear, ever fondly
remembered Stowey' and happy Quantock times, to
'Love's first hope to gentle mind,' that was

> 'As Eve's first star thro' fleecy cloudlet peeping;
> And sweeter than the gentle south-west wind,
> O'er willowy meads, and shadow'd waters creeping,
> And Ceres' golden fields.'

And even when he wrote of age and joy's decline, it
was with a vernal charm – 'Winter assumes the character
of Spring, Spring the sadness of Winter' in 'Youth
and Age':

> 'Verse a breeze mid blossoms straying,
> Where Hope clung feeding, like a bee –
> Both were mine! Life went a-maying
>   With Nature, Hope, and Poesy,
>   When I was young!

> '*When* I was young? – Ah, woful When!
> Ah! for the change 'twixt Now and Then!
> This breathing house not built with hands,
> This body that does me grievous wrong,
> O'er aery cliffs and glittering sands,
> How lightly *then* it flashed along; –
> Like those trim skiffs, unknown of yore,
> On winding lakes and rivers wide,
> That ask no aid of sail or oar,
> That fear no spite of wind or tide!
> Naught cared this body for wind and weather
> When Youth and I lived in't together.

'Flowers are lovely; Love is flower-like;
Friendship is a sheltering tree;
O! the joys that came down shower-like,
Of Friendship, Love, and Liberty,
     Ere I was old!

'*Ere* I was old? Ah woful Ere,
Which tells me, Youth's no longer here!
O Youth! for years so many and sweet,
'Tis known that Thou and I were one,
I'll think it but a fond conceit –
It cannot be that thou art gone!
Thy vesper-bell hath not yet toll'd: –
And thou wert aye a masker bold!
What strange disguise hast now put on
To *make believe*, that thou art gone?
I see these locks in silvery slips,
This drooping gait, this altered size;
But Spring-tide blossoms on thy lips,
And tears take sunshine from thine eyes!
Life is but thought: so think I will
That youth and I are house-mates still.'

But the 'bird shattered and irremediably disorganized
in one wing' could only flutter a short way and then
come to earth again. The faint creative impulse sank back
on itself 'like a sigh heaved up from the tightened chest
of a sick man,' and gradually from 1826 he grew feebler.
Active as his mind still seemed, he was always 'an over-
tired man roused from insufficient sleep,' a guest who had

'outstay'd his welcome while,
And tells the jest without the smile.'

His very eloquence, now more intermittent, was the
symptom of an inward muteness, and the past like the
present became a faded picture on a wintry wall.

'For a while,' he wrote to Gillman, 'the mind seems to have the better in the contest, and makes of Nature what it likes . . . composes country dances on her moonshiny ripples, fandangos on her waves, and waltzes on her eddy-pools, transforms her summer gales into harps and harpers, lovers' sighs and sighing lovers, and her winter blasts into Pindaric Odes, Christabels, and Ancient Mariners set to music by Beethoven, and backs and chases the dodging stars in a sky-hunt! But alas! alas! that Nature is a wary wily long-breathed old witch. . . . She is sure to get the better of Lady Mind in the long run and to take her revenge too; transforms our to-day into a canvas dead-coloured to receive the dull, featureless portrait of yesterday: . . . she mocks the mind with its own metaphor . . .'

Thus does indifferent Nature treat the mind that would enjoy her without understanding, and snatch at truth and happiness without submitting to her law. And so for the poet, deserted by the forces of life, the poet for whom the amaranths no longer bloomed and work was without hope, there was nothing left but unction, unless it was a sudden verbal devotion to 'Duty' as 'the only sure friend of declining life.'

The more he came to look like a dissenting minister, the more his orthodoxy stiffened; the more verbal his faith became, the less real his experience. The grey eyes were at times still 'full of intelligent softness,' but more often they stared into space with a blank, sad gaze, and the face against the long white hair was strangely uncreased, strangely round and plump and childish. He had never allowed experience to strike deep into his being, and so the cheeks and eyes preserved their childlike appearance. But his roots were dead.

Spring called to him in 1827. 'What an interval!' he wrote in his note-book, 'Heard the singing birds this

morning in our garden for the first time this year, though
it rained and blew fiercely; but the long frost has broken
up, and the wind, though fierce, was warm and westerly.'

But no wind could unfetter his frost. He was a jelly
that had been poured into a mould and had stiffened.
'Morning and evening and in the watches of the night' he
earnestly besought the 'God who *seeketh* that which was
lost, who calleth back that which had gone astray' to
'shew him his sins and their sinfulness.' A few years
before he had written: 'It is requisite that the conviction
now become so self-evident, "that vice is the effect of
error, the offspring of surrounding circumstances, the
object of condolence and not of anger." ' But he had
ceased to be the psychologist as he had ceased to be the
poet. He was content to commit himself, in whom really
there was no darkness but only light faded through its
own unworldly excess to a neutral grey, but whom he
described as a 'poor dark creature,' to an 'Omniscient and
All-Merciful, in whom are the issues of Life and Death';
he still professed an 'earnest love of Truth for its own
sake,' but he held a steadfast conviction 'grounded on
faith, not fear, that the religion into which I was baptized
is the Truth, without which all other knowledge ceases to
merit the appellation.'

Certainly Coleridge did not fear death. He had too
slight a hold on physical life to shudder at its cessation.
As Lamb wrote: 'he long had been on the confines of the
next world . . . for he had a hunger for eternity.' But it
was a morbid hunger, never appeased; and behind his
conventional assertion of Christian conviction concerning
an after-life lay an agitated suspicion that in this as in so
many things he was deluding himself. It was easy to
boast like Tertullian, 'I believe, because it is impossible,'
or to argue that 'love is the proof of continuing, as it is
the cause and condition of existing consciousness. How

beautiful the harmony!' But love had failed him, and the strings of life were broken. Might not his belief also in an Omniscient Creator be but the 'dancing flames or luminous bubbles on the magic cauldron of my wishes?' Jeremy Taylor had written that 'it is possible for a man to bring himself to believe anything he hath a mind to.' But what was this belief? – 'Analyse it into its constituents – is it more than certain passions or feelings converging into the sensation of positiveness as their focus . . .?'

Hastily he put the inquiry aside. As he had said, when lecturing on *Romeo and Juliet*, 'the reverend character of the Friar is very delightful and tranquillizing.' His thought and his language became increasingly clerical. 'I shall be much gratified,' he wrote in accepting an invitation to be a godfather, 'by standing beside the baptismal font as one of the sponsors of the little pilgrim at his inauguration into the rights and duties of Immortality.'

In the summer of 1828 he actually joined Wordsworth and his daughter Dora in a tour of the Rhine district. He knew that he could never again feel or think in the same spirit with Wordsworth, but he had ceased to fear antipathies. 'Old friends burn dim,' he had written,

> 'like lamps in noisome air,
> Love them for what they *are*; nor love them less,
> Because to *thee* they are not what they *were*.'

But if any memories haunted him of other tours, of his first landing on German soil, not yet 'a sordid, solitary thing,' or of that dismal tramp through Scotland from which he escaped only into nightmares, – Dorothy was not there to reproach his recollection. Yet her absence was in itself, had he known, a reproach. A few months later she was to suffer the first attack of the mysterious nervous ailment from which she never really recovered and

which resulted in her reason being for the rest of her life
no longer in continuous command.

As late as 1831 he still believed that he was advancing
'regularly and steadily towards the completion of my
Opus Magnum on Revelation and Christianity.' But full
as the Reservoir might be of the reflections and reading
of twenty-five years, a system of pipes was never discovered to convey the living water to a thirsty public.
The same failure attended a last attempt to throw off
opium. At first God was reported to have 'worked almost
a miracle of grace in and for me by a sudden emancipation
from a thirty-three years' fearful slavery.' But however
admirable miracles might be in generating a predisposing
warmth for Faith, they could not work an effectual cure,
and nothing was left for the physical man but 'a weary
time of groaning and life-loathing.' Even the days of
orchestral remorse were over. Relapse, reprieve and convalescence followed each other 'with a little fluttering
distinctly felt at my heart, and a sort of cloud-shadow of
dejection flitting over me.' And gradually the flutter
grew less distinct and the shadow less regarded. Gradually 'the Ghosts of defunct hopes' ceased altogether to
chase 'the Jack-o'-lanterns of foolish expectation.' He
was no more than 'a shadow sleeping amid the wan yellow
light of the December morning . . . like wrecks and
scattered ruins of the long, long night.'

A visit from Emerson in 1833 provoked a last pathetic
outburst against Unitarianism from the 'short, thick old
man . . . who took snuff freely' and 'soiled his cravat and
neat black suit,' and whose vehemence was significant
only of senile sentiment arraigning its youthful counter-
part. Harriet Martineau, who visited him a few months
before, found him looking very old 'with his rounded
shoulders, and drooping head and excessively thin
limbs.' But he held her with his glittering eye and dreamy

involuntary voice. She forgot the flabby face in the weird light that seemed to possess it, like a huge crystal 'flashing back every impression of life and every possibility of thought,' to quote a later writer's comparison.

In May of the following year Poole saw him for the last time, and found his mind 'as strong as ever, seeming impatient to take leave of its encumbrance.' But long before this his mind had in fact taken leave of the body which it loathed. It moved airily about in a vacuum of its own, and this was why he could write that he was 'reconciled and harmonized.' He was not really harmonized: he had merely ceased to strike the bass notes in his nature which made a discord, and played only on the treble clef.

On July 13 he wrote to his godchild: 'I now on the eve of my departure, declare to you and earnestly pray that you may hereafter live and act on the conviction, that Health is a great blessing; and a great blessing it is to have kind, faithful, and loving friends and relatives; but that the greatest of all blessings, as it is the most ennobling of all principles, is to be indeed a Christian. But I have been likewise, through a large portion of my later life, a sufferer, sorely afflicted with bodily pains, languor, and manifold infirmities; and for the last three or four years have, with few and brief intervals, been confined to a sick-room, and at this moment, in great weakness and heaviness, write from a sick-bed, hopeless of recovery, yet without prospect of a speedy removal. And I thus, on the brink of the grave, solemnly bear witness to you, that the Almighty-Redeemer, most gracious in His promises to them that truly seek Him, is faithful to perform what He has promised; and has reserved, under all pains and infirmities, the peace that passeth understanding, with the supporting assurance of a reconciled God, who will not withdraw His spirit from me in the confli&t, and in His own time will deliver me from the evil one.'

How much more real value for him attached to these devotional dreams than to those generated in childhood by the *Arabian Nights* can only be conje&tured. At least they brought him serenity, and in the comfort of that serenity twelve days later he died.

§ 5

'Why was I made for love and love denied me?' Coleridge had written and denied his friends in the question; denied above all Lamb, who wrote of him shortly before his own death: 'His great and dear Spirit haunts me; never saw I his likeness, nor probably the world can see again. I seem to love the house he died in more passionately than when he lived.'

And yet essentially Coleridge was right. Love was denied to him as life and truth were in their fullness, constancy and strength. The chronicle which has now been brought to a conclusion sufficiently records the reason. Coleridge's life is among the saddest in literary history. A being splendidly endowed with genius, sensibility and intelle&t, large in comprehension, elemental in instin&t, generous, affe&tionate and enthusiastic, broke himself on the rocks of a world which he could not see.

This was the fatal defe&t of his nature, of which an impotent will was perhaps less the cause than the consequence. For treason to the material is visited with even direr penalties than treason to the ideal, and the more humanity refines itself, the harder it is to preserve that conta&t with the physical, that 'identity between the a&tual and the real,' which Coleridge himself described as essential to perfe&t reality and without which the spiritual life can only be a sickness and a sigh.

Ever since the Renaissance and the Reformation intellectual Man has tended to grow farther and farther away from his roots in physical as in social life, and his experience to become more and more personal and exclusive. And although great and necessary has been his consequent advance in self-knowledge, he has paid the penalty in an idealism which has had little organic necessity, in mere subjective dreaming or in an exploitation of perverted, subtle and languid moods. The vice of over-cultivation is evident in the artist who seeks self-indulgently after beauty, instead of creating beauty as a condition of true experience, as in the idealist who in escape from the facts of life loses himself in abstractions or clings to a morality which reflects only personal prejudice or contemporary utility.

Despite an elementalism which conditioned perhaps the most miraculous lyric in the English language, Coleridge suffered as artist, idealist and man from this subjective hysteria. Stricken with the loneliness inevitable to all who strive after an absolute beauty, he made spasmodic efforts to re-establish his sense of the reality of life by human attachments and concrete activities, and he sought forgetfulness of his failure in opium, metaphysics and religiosity. Even in his poetry he was the same fugitive, and so could seldom find there anything but transitory appeasement, and never perhaps but once, victorious fulfilment.

Speaking of Milton in one of his last lectures, he remarked: 'He was, as every truly great poet has ever been, a good man; but finding it impossible to realize his own aspirations, either in religion, or in politics, or society, he gave up his heart to the living spirit and light within him, and avenged himself on the world by enriching it with the record of his own transcendental ideal.'

In this passage Coleridge enunciated his own ideal, and the two poets are sufficiently near in type to emphasize,

by the contrast between their achievements, the truth
that it matters not how transcendent a poet's intention may be (indeed it cannot be too transcendent), or
how much he employs the methods of improbable illusion, provided always his experience is grounded in the
physical. There was a firm Pagan element in Milton, a
sensuousness exquisitely refined but never disintegrated
by humanistic or Christian thought. And so, however
metaphysical his thought might be, or however involved
in contemporary dogma and cosmology, its expression
remained individual and organic, while even in his
morality he transcended the conventional more often than
he echoed it and continued to the end essentially true
to the values of a creative imagination.

It was this physical basis which Coleridge lacked.
There was a gaping fissure in his nature between the
physical and the spiritual, and so between himself and the
natural world. Consequently his poetry died away for
want of a true morality, and he could only smother his
latter years in a conventional one.

It might have been of him that Meredith wrote in
A Reading of Earth:

> 'If we strain to the farther shore,
> We are catching at comfort near.
> Assurances, symbols, saws,
> Revelations in Legends, Light
> To eyes rolling darkness, these
> Desired of the flesh in affright,
> For the which it will swear to adore,
> She yields not for prayers at her knees;
> The woolly beast bleating will shear.
> These are our sensual dreams;
> Of the yearning to touch, to feel
> The dark Impalpable sure,

And have the unveiled appear; . . .
Yet we have but to see and hear,
Crave we her medical herb.
For the road to her soul is the Real:
The root of the growth of man:
And the senses must traverse it fresh
With a love that no scourge shall abate,
To reach the lone heights where we scan
In the mind's rarer vision this flesh:
In the charge of the Mother our fate;
Her law as the one common weal.'

From childhood Coleridge had little root in the real, and
so the organic life of nature never ran healthily through
him, like the sap through the stem and branches of a tree,
to be translated by the higher faculties into terms of vital
spiritual activity. Rather he was shut away from life in
the chamber of himself, and there his restless, ever-work-
ing fancy, his subtle logic-spinning mind, his fluent
emotion, stirred up a bewildering ferment. He longed to
communicate, to give himself to things and people, and
to take them into himself, but although he diffused
emotion, it could not bring him into vital contact with
objects, and without that contact the object could not be
truly transmuted into subject and feed a healthy consciousness. 'I fled in a Circle,' he wrote, 'still overtaken
by Feelings, from which I was ever more fleeing, with my
back turned towards them.' His flight from feeling was
but the consequence of his flight from things, since feeling only ceases to be a fever when it is wed by sensation to
things and only ceases to be a luxury or a languor when
both are wed to thought.

Generally Coleridge's emotion was not even explo-
sively dissipated: it was merely vapourishly diffused. His
spirit, uncentred in a world of fact, either streamed out

into the void where there was no certain foothold, or fed upon itself in a haunted solitude: while the world, which he could neither feel nor focus with a clear, impersonal vision, impressed and punished him unduly with its power to betray and hurt.

Yet terrible as was his shipwreck, and heart-rending in the light of a genius so seraphic, and a nature so credulously loving, it is to his defects, to his tainted temperament, that posterity owes his three or four inimitable poems. He wrote himself of Nelson that 'to the same enthusiastic sensibilities which made a fool of him with regard to his Emma, his country owed the victories of the Nile, Copenhagen, and Trafalgar.'

To the feverish sensibility which led Coleridge to the laudanum bottle and the piety of Archbishop Leighton, his country owes the miracles of 'The Ancient Mariner,' 'Christabel' and 'Kubla Khan.'